Gender and the Political Economy of Development

From Nationalism to Globalization

Shirin M. Rai

Polity

The right of Shirin M. Rai to be identified as author of this work has been asserted in accordance with the Copyright, Designs and Patents Act 1988.

First published in 2002 by Polity Press in association with Blackwell Publishers Ltd

Reprinted 2004

Editorial office:
Polity Press
65 Bridge Street
Cambridge CB2 1UR, UK

Marketing and production:
Blackwell Publishers Ltd
108 Cowley Road
Oxford OX4 1JF, UK

Published in the USA by
Blackwell Publishers Inc.
350 Main Street
Malden, MA 02148, USA

ISBN 0–7456–1490–6
ISBN 0–7456–1491–4 (pbk)

A catalogue record for this book is available from the British Library and has been applied for from the Library of Congress.

Typeset in Palatino on 10.5/12 pt
by Kolam Information Services Private Limited, Pondicherry, India
Printed and bound in Great Britain by Marston Book Services Limited, Oxford

This book is printed on acid-free paper.

Gender and the Political Economy of Development

For

Jeremy, Arjun and Sean

Contents

List of Tables

Acknowledgements

Many people have contributed to this book, in different ways, at different moments. All these contributions have made this book possible and better than what it might otherwise have been. I find the process of writing a painful one. To have critical minds and sympathetic eyes going over what I wrote has been extremely important to me. Also important have been friends who have tolerated my outpourings of angst, tried to make sense of my confusions and been supportive, regardless. Conversations – with students, with colleagues, with my family – have supported my work in a way that is unquantifiable, but critical. Making lists is never a very satisfactory way of marking recognition – especially of friendships and supports. However, it does allow me, selfishly, to acknowledge many debts. My thanks to the Department of Politics and International Studies at the University of Warwick, who provided me with critical time to revise the book. My thanks also to colleagues at Polity for their confidence, in the face of all evidence, that this book would be finished – Lynn Dunlop, Justin Dyer, Anthony Giddens, David Held, Louise Knight, and to the two anonymous referees whose comments have undoubtedly strengthened this text. Thanks to those who have read and commented on all or parts of this manuscript and who have been encouraging colleagues and indulgent friends – Molly Andrews, Stephanie Barrientos, Peter Burnham, Robin Cohen, Rebecca Earle, (again) Anthony Giddens, Catherine Hoskyns, Jane Parpart, Ruth Pearson, Jindy Pettman, Jan Aart Scholte, Hazel Smith, Matthew Smith, Kathleen Staudt and Caroline Wright. My thanks especially to my husband Jeremy Roche, who read everything I wrote, and commented with his usual incisiveness and compassion. Without his support this book would not have been finished. In addition to Jeremy, my thanks to those others who have sustained me at a very personal level, and made allowances for me when none should have been needed – my parents Satya and Lajpat Rai, and Arjun and Sean, my sons, whose delight at the completion of this project was expressed in a much treasured 'Well done Mummy!'

The shortcomings are, of course, mine alone.

Leamington Spa, June 2001

Table 2.1 is reproduced by kind permission of Jane L. Parpart, M. Patricia Connelly and V. Eudine-Barriteau. Table 4.3 is reproduced by kind permission of the publishers, Elsevier Science. Every effort has been made to trace copyright holders, but if any have been inadverterly overlooked, the publishers will be pleased to make the necessary arrangements at the first opportunity.

Introduction
Mapping Gender and the Political Economy of Development

This book explores the gendered nature of the political economy of development. As such, it is based upon certain assumptions about gender, and about political economy. My starting point, building upon the work of many feminist scholars, is that the arena of political economy is a gendered arena. This means that women and men are positioned differently upon it, have varied resources available to them, which allows them to articulate and mobilize in common interests as well as diverse ones, in different ways. A second concern of the book is to reflect upon the differences among women as much as between women and men. 'Difference', as a concept, has been much theorized within feminist scholarship, and my work builds on that literature. What does difference among women mean in practical political terms when issues of nationalism, class and caste, for example, threaten the edifice of unity among women? How, for example, do we analyse the consequences of structural adjustment policies (SAPs) for women without taking into account the different social and political positions they occupy in different geographical contexts? A balance sheet on SAPs would need to take these differences into account as much as it would the differences between women and men. Third, the book explores the relationship between structure and agency. Here again, I take a gendered approach to explore how structures of economic and political power frame women and men, and what are the consequences of these gendered positionings for the engagements of women and men as political actors. The shifts in the discursive and policy agendas in development need to be mapped onto the existing structural boundedness of the political economy. While I argue for the continued political engagements of women in changing political and economic contexts, I also reflect upon the structural constraints within which these engagements take shape, and am cautious about the reification of participation/engagement by women and men.

My work is greatly indebted to the work of many others in the field of gender and development, but also more broadly to feminist theorizing on women and politics. Perhaps one of the most enduring contributions of women's activism and feminist theorizing is the challenging of the boundaries between the public and the private as defining (and defining out) politics. By expanding the definition of politics to encompass both the public and the private spheres – indeed, by asserting that the two were mutually constitutive – feminists were able to show how women, far from being absent from the political sphere, were very much present as an 'absence' – that their exclusion from the public was necessary for the private and the public to be dominated by masculine interests and power. By insisting that 'experience' was an important starting point of knowledge, feminists have sought to contextualize the basis of politics itself (Scott, 1992). They have added to the analysis of politics their insights, which have involved stretching the boundaries as well as the definitions of terms and of organization. Feminists have insisted that gender, as social construction of sex, is reflected in the political roles women and men are able to perform, and indeed frames the very definition of politics and, by default, what does not constitute politics. Colonial and post-colonial understandings of politics provided further insights for the study of gender and politics. Nationalist movements' engagement with modernity took the form of a 'complex inter-relationship of contest and collusion between indigenous patriarchal norms and those held by [colonial] administrators [that] is visible in the colonial regulation of agrarian relations' (Sangari and Vaid, 1993: 7). Differences among women on grounds of class, race, ethnicity, religion, sexuality, disability and politics, among others, have prompted the question: how can a disparate group of women recognize themselves in the category of 'woman', whose interests can then be represented in the political arena? Does consciousness-raising about the patriarchal structures that frame politics also need to result in the construction of recognizable similarities among women? The understanding and working with/around this issue of difference remains a challenge for women's movements and scholars in developing strategies of change. I have built my understanding of a gendered politics through reviewing and participating in these debates.

The Personal as Political

This book has been written over a rather long period of time. It started out as an introductory text on gender and development, but as I started writing it has taken a different shape. Sometimes the words on the page seemed to have a will of their own, as they wove a pattern that I did not anticipate. Perhaps one of the reasons why this book has taken the shape it has is to do with my personal/ political history.

I was born in New Delhi, India, in what has been called the Golden Age of development – the 1960s (Hewitt, Johnson and Wield, 1992). Development and nationalism were the two intertwining themes that were present not only in the curriculum at school and university, but also in the everyday discussions about politics at home. Jawaharlal Nehru was Prime Minister of India when I was born. His was the defining influence on the developmental trajectory of India. Nehru quite naturally, and deliberately, aligned development with nationalism – the national struggle against the British Raj had also been a struggle against India's 'backwardness'; modernization of India had become the *raison d'être* of India's freedom. Those who supported his view of the world and those who opposed it had to respond to this vision.

I grew up in a family that was 'modernist', but not avowedly nationalist. This despite the fact that both my parents had participated in the national movement in the 1930s and 1940s. For them, as for many young people at that time, the nationalist struggle against the British Raj was the struggle of the 'people' against imperialism and critically against capitalism; a nationalism strongly mediated by socialism. Development then got defined through the lenses of Marxism. Thus, it was natural for me to begin to look at development from the starting point of nationalism – but also to be aware of the differences in the various approaches to nationalism and development from very early on. Perhaps this is why this book begins with an exploration of nationalism – how it shaped the discourses of development, and how it affected the materiality of women's lives through policy-making and through the institution of certain norms in the constitutions of the decolonizing nation-states.

My own history also influenced the particular route I have taken to the study of Gender and Development as a discipline. One of my early memories at school was reacting strongly against the place given to Sita in the Hindu classic *Ramayana*. Arguing with teachers about why Sita, and not her husband Ram, was made to prove her purity at the end of a terrible ordeal was not only a means of challenging the authority of the teacher at school, but also an instinctive reaction against visible social inequality between the sexes. Here again, home played an important role – I was brought up on a diet of the equality ethic that my parents so strongly espoused in a context of a general social bias against girls. What became clear to me was that (a) boys and girls are not, but should be treated as, equal, (b) education for girls matters, and (c) politics matters.

Growing up in the 1970s was perhaps not as exciting as growing up in the 1960s, but as a young woman it did provide an opportunity to view – if from the sidelines and sometimes, misguidedly, with certain disdain – the growing women's movement in India. Memories of college halls full of women protesting against dowry murders, against verbal abuse directed at women students on the streets, against police harassment of women when they went to report against violent husbands, became important nodes to tap into once I began to think about gender relations as reflective of systemic and structural inequalities between men and women. However, this came later. During my university years in Delhi, it was Development Studies that attracted me – and Ester Boserup was not part of my curriculum. My curriculum reflected the concerns of the mainstream academia in the field. Development Studies as a discipline is after all a product of post-war concerns about economic and political development in the decolonized Third World. And yet, as Naila Kabeer points out, 'liberal market-oriented models of economic growth have set the broad parameters for development planning and framed the fluctuating significance accorded to markets, states and non-governmental organizations as alternative agencies of resource allocation in the development process' (1994: 13) While this predominance of the economic realm followed a general hardening of the disciplinary boundaries of economics and political science and later sociology, and the marginalization of classical political economy perspectives, my curriculum in the Political Science department at Delhi University did retain the focus on the political. This focus on the domestic as well as the international has remained important to my thinking on development. This interweaving of the political with the economic/development studies perspective was further strengthened when I chose to specialize in Chinese politics for my doctoral studies.

It was when I was doing fieldwork in China in 1987 that it slowly began to dawn on me that gender matters were critically important in understanding the lives of those I was speaking to every day on university campuses. Marxism and nationalism combined here to create a powerful discourse of equality, on the one hand, and of systematic inequality, on the other. I was being constantly told by women students that the Party cadres responsible for allocating jobs routinely sent women students to be primary school teachers, nurses and support staff, while men went to the more challenging, higher-status professions. Listening to these complaints became the key to my engagement with issues of gender and development. Amartya Sen, following Marx, has emphasized that employment for women can hold the key to their empowerment (Drèze and Sen, 1990a; Sen, 1995). What I learnt from my Chinese women friends was that the terms of employment, however, are not simply reflective of gender biases in society but also constitutive of these. The importance of political systems was also evident here. As a student of Chinese politics, I knew the limited options that these students had for opposing what they clearly saw as a policy against their interests. It was at this time that I also became interested in post-structuralism; the intellectual map that I had started out with could not explain the complexity of the world in which I now found myself immersed.

If China triggered my interest in gender relations, colleagues at the Centre for the Study of Women and Gender at the University of Warwick helped me sustain and develop it. From this staging post, through various conferences and seminars, the world of feminist scholarship opened up for me. Teaching a Master's and then a Bachelor's course on Gender and Development allowed me the space to develop my ideas. Straddling two disciplines was – and is – not always easy, but it was – and continues to be – both challenging and rewarding. As I made my slow way through the labyrinth of 'Women's Studies' literature, discussed and read up on issues of 'difference', taught as I learnt, felt my insecurities being handled with care and respect, I became aware of the strength of the community of women – academic and activists, colleagues and students, within my immediate context, and globally.

However, as always, 'enlightenment' and 'despair' have gone together. While my explorations of feminist literature explained a great deal, they also left me with many important but unanswered questions. As I wrote this book, these questions became more and more important to me, and I think this is reflected in the unfolding of the book. At the heart of this confusion is the question of difference among women. Sojourner Truth's refrain 'ar'n't I a woman?' is about blackness; it is also about gender, but fundamentally it is also about slavery and the struggle against it. Structures and agents, systems and actors, are important, as is the relationship between them. As I have read and contributed to the debates on differences among women (Liddle and Rai, 1993, 1998), it has left me feeling uneasy – it seems that the focus of these debates remains firmly on the cultural and race differences, social and linguistic boundaries, bodies and sexualities. Despite a commitment to confronting differences, there is an underlying assumption that 'women' can be spoken of – carefully, sensitively, fracturedly even – as 'women'. Is this because the debates on differences among women, especially in the 1980s and the early 1990s, have focused on some structures of power and not others? As Anna Pollert asks, 'why it is that a "grand narrative" of "patriarchy" survives amid the fashion of post-structuralist fragmentation...?' (1996: 641). Is it because of this that feminists have been able to examine some relations of power so acutely and not others? And, importantly, where does this leave the transformative impulse of feminism(s)? Indeed, can we use words like 'transformative' any more? When examining the bundle of policies called SAPs, for example, and their consequences for women and men of Third World countries, how could relationships and indeed conflicts of interests between countries and between social classes not inform my understanding of gender relations? Does this mean that the insights provided by post-structuralism are invalid? I have found these extremely helpful, but perhaps most so when I have been able to hold them in tension with an understanding of structures of power that encompass our lives. Of course, I am not the only one asking these questions, but these were the questions that I was asking. Here, I was guided by Joan Scott's perceptive comment that while gender relations are a reflection of power relations, concepts of power are not always literally about gender (cited in Monteón, 1995: 45).

While dwelling on the personal/political, I also need to add a cautionary word: although I have used appropriate case studies and examples from across the world to illustrate my arguments, there remains a bias towards the 'Asian' perspective. This is as much to do with my personal roots in India as with my academic roots in Chinese studies. I can only apologize for this, but believe that the wider points of the arguments are not fundamentally affected by this focus.

Feminist Transformations

At the beginning of the twenty-first century no one can deny the strides women have made in practically every sphere of life, in almost all countries of the world. The UN World Survey on the Role of Women in Development (DAW, 1999) clearly demonstrates this.

In terms of women's paid employment the figures show a clear rise from about 54 per cent in the mid-1950s to just under 70 per cent in 2000. 'In fact, with the sole exception of Africa, women's employment has grown substantially faster than men's since 1980' (p. 8). Accompanying this positive indicator, however, there is also the downside of increased levels of occupational segregation by sex, which, in their variations, show that cultural and historical as well as political factors are important in determining the extent of such differentials (pp. 16–17). In rural areas, for example, the introduction of tradable cash-crops has resulted in a gendered shift in the management of household resources. Women are increasingly concentrated in food production and men in cash-crop production. While women are expected to contribute towards cash-crop production, especially in the labour-intensive areas, they are also organizing food production without men helping out as they did before.

Technology and globalization have resulted in the 'flexiblization' of the labour market, which has included a sharp increase in part-time work, as well as that of the informal sector. Both areas show a substantial female presence, as well as variations according to class and education – self-employed urban and rural poor, on the one hand, and highly educated and paid professionals providing cutting-edge service to business, on the other. Migration has been another important feature of women's employment under globalization. Women and men are migrating in almost equal numbers. However, 'most female migrant workers engage in traditionally female occupations in the service sector' (DAW, 1999: 31). The economic picture is therefore a mixed one.

If we look at the social indicators for women – health, education, training – the story gets even more complicated. National states have been under pressure from the global economy. Deflationary biases in macroeconomic policy have been considerably affecting the policies governments might adopt. Public spending cuts have been required of governments, and this has had an overall negative impact on the social indicators for the poor of both sexes. However, yet again, we see gendered differentials in the ways in which these policies are played out. Women's employment, while rising in areas of growth, is more vulnerable than men's when there is a downturn in the economy. The reduction on social spending has meant that women are carrying the burden of child-care and care of the elderly. Women are also suffering disproportionately when public funding for health and education is reduced (see DAW, 1999: xviii).

How have women responded to these challenges? The feminist movements have gained momentum across the world. There are several reasons for this, ranging from the new economic opportunities for women, the fall of the Soviet Union and the political mobilization of women in different arenas, to the promotion of feminist agendas by international organizations. The achievements of women can be charted not only in the sphere of the economy, as above, but also in the spheres of policy-making and institutional politics. While only 4.7 per cent of heads of states in the world are women, the figure for women members of the representative houses in democratic states now stands at 13.4 per cent (DAW, 2000b). Understandably, there is a long way to go, and the picture of progress is patchy. However, on the whole it is a hopeful picture. Having said that, the success of women in the political arena poses difficult questions about the discrepancy between this success and the more worrisome indicators of women's socio-economic well-being quoted above. Why is it possible for us to speak of gender mainstreaming, of quotas for women in political institutions, and point to the increasing civil society associational activity for and by women, while, at the same time, millions of women are finding their life-energies sapped by the struggle for survival?

The processes of decolonization were not the same in different countries – ideologies, cultural and social histories, imperialist systems and international contexts all influenced nationalisms, and conceptions of development. In chapter 1, therefore, I explore some of these tensions and the difference these made to the gendered post-colonial regimes. I reflect upon what questions were asked about development in the context in which they were asked, and how these fundamentally influenced the ways in which the processes of development unfolded. I argue that nationalism circumscribed development priorities in post-colonial contexts, gave them a hierarchy – of gender, class and ethnicity, among others – created some new spaces and closed off others. I conclude that the place of women within the discourse of development cannot be understood without reference to the economic and political agendas set by nationalist elites, and the negotiations around and challenges to these agendas by the various women's movements.

In chapter 2, I examine the trajectory of Development Studies as well as of debates on gender and development. Given my interest in nationalism and post-colonial development, I start by examining the growth of Development Studies and development discourses in the wider international political contexts. How could I explain the processes of decolonization in India and China, for example, without reference to the Soviet Union, the United States and the Cold War? Did the language of threat not influence the hierarchies of development policies? Did opposition to post-colonial states not get stifled in the name of unity against communism/imperialism/capit-alism? The maturing of Development Studies itself could not be explored without examining the struggles over meanings – of equal-ity, growth, development, modernization. And were these meanings not fashioned in the shadow of the Cold War? This conviction that international relations needed to be foregrounded in order to under-stand the politics of development became even more pronounced as I waded through the literature of globalization.

Debates on globalization form the substance of chapter 3. In dis-cussing these debates, especially those on the ways in which the (new/old) nation-state is being transformed, I see globalization more as a process than a product and much less an outcome of either late modernity or postmodernity. It is a political process, and an embedded one. It is embedded in relations of capital, and is therefore deeply contested. Technological advances have allowed an ever-deeper penetration of capitalist relations into national and local economies, while the discourse of globalization as actor has allowed for a 'naturalization' of the process that is highly problematic. I take issue with the imagery and arguments of globalization as the prod-uct of the invisible hand of the global market, as well as the depoliti-cized inevitability of globalization. However, the acknowledgement of the importance of technological change and its impact on our social and political life allows me to examine carefully and with respect the new forms of social protest, networking and contesta-tions that are shaping our gendered world.

Chapter 4 focuses on the various ways in which global restructur-ing is affecting people's lives and examines the changing nature of work and women's position within the new political economy. I examine the unfolding of regimes of global restructuring, and the impact this has had on the lives of women and men, and on the struggles that they are engaged in. I do this by, first, assessing SAPs and their gender-differentiated results. I reflect upon the challenges that feminist economists have posed, at a theoretical level, to neo-liberal economics in analysing the impact of SAPs, and raise tentative questions about this feminist critique. I conclude that global restruc-turing is also widening the gap among women along class lines, and among women of the North and South. Addressing this issue remains important for the legitimacy of feminist critiques of neo-liberal eco-nomics, which underlies the processes of global restructuring.

In chapter 5, I reflect upon the various responses to globalization's pressures on women's lives by undertaking a multi-level analysis of new forms of governance – global, national and local. I highlight the differences that are emerging among women as a result of these mobilizations, as well as the terms of solidarity among them. I briefly discuss how the politics of citizenship and deliberative democracy have been helpful in fashioning new arenas of feminist politics. I conclude by examining the discourse of empowerment, and suggest that without a focus on the concept of power – structural as well as discursive – this discourse remains partial. I argue that women's movements need to re-establish the connection between the recognition of difference and the redistribution of economic and social resources.

I conclude by reflecting upon gendered strategies deployed to cope with the pressures of globalization, as well as upon the challenges posed to it. I caution both against the celebration of the local space, and nostalgia for the centralized nation-state. Instead, I advocate a continued critical engagement by women's movements with economic and political institutions, which is self-reflective, and cognizant of the limits of such engagement. I argue that women's movements need to build upon their struggles and successes by constructing alliances with other emancipatory movements in order to strengthen the struggles for gender justice.

In Conclusion

Without wishing to use a terminology that is defeatist, or to suggest a trope of victimology, I argue that poor women across the South face very serious impediments in their lives under globalization, as do poor men. Though globalization is creating new opportunities for women – new paid jobs, for example, where none existed before – these are appearing in conjunction with deepening economic and social crises brought about by the logic of globalized capitalism. I argue that feminist movements – in contrast with women's groups of all descriptions – need to acknowledge that economic differences among women are increasing along the trajectories of class and North/South divides, at the same time as women as a whole are ostensibly able to bridge differences, network and mobilize across borders. I suggest that this is perhaps a good time to reflect upon the gains that have been made by women's movements across the world, especially under globalization, and to ask difficult questions about how feminist movements and debates can be moved beyond the politics of recognition to a politics that insists upon a redistribution of resources.

1 | Gender, Nationalism and 'Nation-Building'
Discourses of Development

... the relations between the people and the nation, the nation and the state, relations which nationalism claims to have resolved once and for all, are relations which continue to be contested and therefore open to negotiation all over again.

Partha Chatterjee, *The Nation and Its Fragments*

Introduction

Development[1] has historically been a nationalist project. The edifice of eighteenth-century anti-colonial nationalism, which is a gendered ideology of resistance as well as of power, has included 'development' as progress and civilization sustained by religion, culture and tradition as well as by science and technology, capital and markets. The creation of the nation-state, of 'its world of meanings' – in other words, nation-building – has been the starting point of what has been called 'the developmental state'. In this chapter I examine how nationalism and nationalist struggles have framed discourses and

---

1 This emerged as a popular term after the Second World War. It is often used interchangeably with 'modern', especially in an economic usage of the term, and therefore associated with industrialization, urbanization and, in the 1970s, with representative democratic political systems (see Huntington, 1968: chap. 2; Rostow, 1979). During the colonial period many of the ideas central to development were cast in terms of 'progress', which encompassed an understanding of modernity – both economic and socio-cultural.

strategies of development.[2] I argue that nationalist ideology framed the development agendas of elites in post-colonial contexts. Some agendas were prioritized and others were deemed of secondary importance, reflecting the gender, class and ethnic biases of post-colonial elites. Ideology, religion and imaging of the nation-state played a crucial part in setting the development agendas in post-colonial nations.[3] In the process of nation-building, the 'economic man' was the critical player in the development discourse, and his counterpart, the 'political man', was the citizen. 'The citizen's' interests were articulated in a universalist language, that allowed only certain issues of economic development to be addressed.[4] Both women and 'subaltern' men – of lower classes and castes and weaker ethnic groups – were co-opted into the elite nationalist programme despite the local struggles waged by them in their own interests (see Guha, 1982: 1–7). While nationalism provided new spaces for women to mobilize in – and even enabled them to use and endorse the universal construction of 'the citizen' in particular contexts – at the same time, it framed those spaces, landscaped them through rhetoric and language in particular ways. However, many women, themselves part of the national elites, participated in the construction of nationalist imaginings and programmes, even though the process itself led to their simultaneous co-optation within and/or exclusion from these constructions (see Bereswill and Wagner, 1998: 233). I argue, therefore, that the gendered nature of development discourses can be

---

2   It will be argued later in the book that nationalism continues to play an important role in the promotion of policies loosely defined as either liberalization or, more broadly, globalization. Indeed, some like Crafts (2000: 51) have argued that a nationalist backlash against globalization cannot be ruled out if liberalization does not (and there are many reasons why it might not) deliver high growth rates in Third World countries.

3   Here I argue with the grain of the quite different argument that O'Hanlon and Washbrook (1991) make in their study of approaches to Indian culture. They suggest that the 'political economy' approaches are important to the understanding of culture, whereas I am suggesting that the 'political economy' approach in development would benefit from extending into the field of cultural history to understand some of the important impulses and starting points of national development. Thus, a theoretical framework that is not too narrowly focused on one or the other is perhaps more able to demystify issues of culture and development.

4   It is fascinating to note, for example, that *The Nationalism Reader* (Dahbour and Ishay), first published in 1995, does not include a single feminist piece, not even under the section on 'The Contemporary Debate on Nationalism'. The only woman whose work is included is Rosa Luxemburg.

understood only if we take into consideration the processes of post-colonial state formation, the socio-economic trajectories set by nationalist elites and the struggles of women's movements against these, as well as their complicity in, them.

Gender and Nationalism

Feminist scholars have made an important contribution to the study of nationalism (Jayawardena, 1986; Anthias and Yuval-Davis, 1989; Enloe, 1989; Sangari and Vaid, 1993; Kandiyoti, 1991b; Hall, 1992; McClintock, 1993). They have suggested that women are central to the construction of nationalist discourses as biological reproducers of members of ethnic collectivities, as reproducers of the boundaries of ethnic/national groups, as central participants in the *ideological* reproduction of the collectivity and as transmitters of its culture.[5] They are also important to nationalism as signifiers of ethnic/national differences. Ideological discourses often highlight (symbolic) women to construct, reproduce and transmit ethnic/nationalist categories. Finally, women continue to be important as subjects – participants in national economic, political and military struggles. These different roles that women play means that '[l]iving as a nationalist feminist is one of the most difficult political projects in today's world' (Enloe, 1989: 46).

Gender relations are thus important as a frame for nationalist practices, and nationalism as an ideology is important for the configurations of gender relations within the national space. Biology and culture are key elements in the construction of new political spaces and of new discourses of empowerment. However, as Walby has commented, more work needs to be done on nationalism's *economic* consequences for women's lives such that the division of labour is not simply 'subsumed under biology or culture' but is made visible in the public domains of national development (1997: 182–3). Moving on from Walby, I argue that the gendered ideologies of nationalism framed the ways in which women's labour was configured, counted,

---

5 Hobsbawm points out that during the early period of theorizing the nation (1830–80) there were only three criteria that allowed a people to be recognized as a nation: its historic association with a current state or lengthy recent past; the existence of a long-established cultural elite, and a written literary and administrative vernacular; and a proven capacity for conquest (1991: 37). While the later theorizing may no longer see capacity for conquest as essential to the assertions to nationhood, cultural and historical capital remain necessary to the formulations of the yearning for selfhood of nations and peoples.

assessed and rewarded. Masculine pride and humiliation in the context of colonialism had fashioned '(colonized) woman' as a victim to be rescued – first by the colonizers and then by the colonized male elites – and as the centre of the household to be protected and cherished. Thus, she provided a node of self-awareness of a particular kind for men, and hence was made visible in the public arenas in particular ways. As I will make clear below, in decolonized nation-states, policy-making acknowledged some of these complexities only by denying them.

Women's labour and women's citizenship are markers of this confusion that we see repeatedly in liberal nationalist discourses as well as in Marxist ones. Whether it is population policies, human rights, conditions of employment or endorsing of monogamous family structures, nation-states have used the discourses of both nationalism and development to circumscribe women's lives. And because of the history of colonialism, the pain of struggling against the idea of the community, culture and family, women have found it at times hard to oppose the boundaries being drawn around them – sometimes in their own names – by others – largely nationalist, masculine elites. In this way, the power of discourse was systematically used to frame women's role in development[6] – whether as reproducers of the nation and markers of its cultural boundaries, or as participants in its economic life.

The Argument

Nationalism is a much theorized concept, as is development. While feminist scholarship provided a gendered critique of the concept of nationalism, interventions in the post-structuralist mode have opened up new spaces within Development Studies that allow us to examine the discursive power of nationalism in the economic agenda-setting of the nation-state (Crush, 1995; Escobar, 1995a; Marchand and Parpart, 1995; Sylvester, 1999). Building on both these sets of literature, I illustrate the importance of the language of nationalism for the construction of the agenda of development, and suggest that women's particular positionings within the family and society were central to both these projects. I argue that nationalism allowed conversations about development to take place between colonial and nationalist male elites. Women were largely excluded

---

6   As it has been used to frame women's role in the state since the birth of nationalism itself in the eighteenth century.

from these conversations, which themselves took place in very different contexts of power. However, I emphasize that these conversations, while exclusionary, were by no means discrete; on the contrary they were untidy, contradictory and allowed spaces for contestation that were utilized by women. The partiality of these conversations and exclusions was also reflected in the unfolding story of development in decolonized states. Nationalism and development, then, were 'Janus-faced' creatures (Nairn, 1981) at once mobilizing and excluding women from the project of 'nation-building'.

After examining the dominant yet unstable gender discourses of the colonial and nationalist elites, I explore the contributions of women activists to national movements and the articulated projects of nation-building, the spaces that women were able to create both within the nationalist movement and within the nationalist discourse, and also the dilemmas that they faced in participating in nationalist movements and discourses of nation-building. I suggest that the trajectory of women's participation within different types of nationalist movements and different political systems had a profound impact on the kinds of citizenships that they were offered, and their ability to be active in the public sphere. Here, it is important to keep in mind the evolving nature of nationalism, of the nation, and of its development. The particularity of political and economic contexts led to ' "rounds of restructuring" of the nation-state' (Walby, 1997: 190) and posed different issues of evolving social relations for women and for men.

I conclude from this discussion that nationalism and nation-states born of nationalist struggles posed particular challenges for women. While remaining central to the project of 'nation-building', women were made 'invisible' through universalized discourses of citizenship and economic development. Although the new citizenships allowed women to take their place within the political space of the nation as individuals, the ambivalence that surrounded these roles meant that this individuation remained fragile; the social symbolism of 'woman' continued to threaten the civic rights of women. Nation-states as products of nationalist struggles remain fractured and fraught terrains for women. Upon these terrains development was crafted – as means and goal of progressive society and economy, and as emblematic of legitimacy of the new nation-state. I argue that while women remained central to the continuing construction of national identity, they were marginalized in the new discourse of development.

The discourses of nationalism did not disappear with the decolonization of the 1940s to 1960s. They are again with us in complex and contemporaneous forms in the post-Cold War period – through the seeking of nationhood on the basis of race, ethnicity, religion and economy.[7] The processes of 'othering' communities, populations and groups continues to affect the drawing up of development agendas in Eastern and Central Europe, in parts of Africa and of Asia. Women have had to pay a high price for this new wave of nationalism, and have confronted issues that are very similar to those faced by women during anti-colonial struggles – rape, war, homelessness, insecurity, and being constructed without their consent as threats to, and symbols of, the new nations and national identities.

This chapter is divided into three sections: the first explores issues arising from the 'imaging of the nation' by political and economic elites: the second focuses on the ways in which this imaging was employed in the service of colonialism and nationalism; and the final section explores how feminist and women's groups interacted with nationalism, and with what results.

Imaging a Nation

Remembering and Forgetting

'All nationalisms are gendered, all are invented and all are dangerous...in the sense of representing relations to political power and the technologies of violence' (McClintock, 1993: 61; see also Hobsbawm, 1991). This quotation raises several important issues. In a substantial amount of literature on nationalism the gendered nature of the concept is neither acknowledged nor analysed. So for Ernest Gellner, 'Men are of the same nation if and only if they recognise each other as being from the same nation' (cited in McClintock, 1993: 62). By using 'men' to mean 'men and women' he eliminates the possibility of discussing gender, since he is eliding the very difference (between women and men) that gender-based analysis studies. The gendered nation thus remains unacknowledged while at the same time important to the constructions of nation. It is, for example, in the public space that men encounter each other and need recognizable markers for the nation to be imagined as home for them all (access to the public space is not automatic for women,

---

7   Indeed, some have pointed to this resurgent nationalism as evidence of the continued salience of the nation-state in the face of the forces of globalization (Anthony Giddens, lecture on 'The Third Way' at the University of Warwick, 9 October 2000).

and this fact affects the nature of nationalism itself). It is also the public space in which they encounter men who are not recognizable, or a threat to the recognizable self. This is because to the nation as an invention danger is an important motif – by naturalizing the nation as a recognizable togetherness, the threat to this togetherness can become central to the concept itself.

This threat can be either of physical violence against the national borders, or of psychological violence by challenging the normative values recognized by the dominant male elites of the nation as important to all, or of social and political violence against the institutions of the nation-state. The danger that lurks becomes the cement that binds men of a nation together in its defence. Danger is central also because it is often invented in order to raise national consciousness, which might be thought to be incipient and in need of mobilization. Political rhetoric becomes important in articulating this danger – to mores, customs, religion, which can find safety only within the political borders of a separate nation. Political rhetoric is at its most effective when it is able to harness the power of historical evidence. As the Greek historian Konstantinos Paparrigopoulos commented: 'History is not only a science. It is at once the Gospel of the present and the future of the fatherland' (cited in Ben-Amos, 1997: 129). As Gospel, history provides as well as legitimates accounts of 'the common possession of a rich legacy of memories' (Renan, cited in Ben-Amos, 1997: 129). Surendranath Banerjea, one of the founding members of the Indian National Congress in 1885, put it this way: 'The study of the history of our own country furnishes the strongest incentive to the loftiest patriotism... For ours was a most glorious past' (Kedourie, 1970: 235).

In this context, another/'s history can become a threat to the unity of the nation – 'forgetting, and even historical error are essential for the creation of a nation' (Renan, cited in Ben-Amos, 1997: 129). Memory and nationalism thus are intimately connected and history is crucial to the documentation and erasure of collective memory, to the remembering and forgetting of recognizable commonalties. It is through the writing in or editing out of history that the invention of the nation takes place, and is placed under threat. In the need for creating a commonly (male) accepted history are also the roots of patriarchal compromise between different male elites in order to determine the spaces occupied by women (see below). Political self-determination thus becomes important to the articulation of the self. The growth of republicanism in Latin America, for example, saw struggles over the meanings of the image of 'the Indian' – excavated from the past to provide legitimacy to the political aspirations of the nationalists. However, by 1850, once this purpose was served, Earle (2001) suggests, ' "the heroic Indian … had been converted into a wild beast lacking any capacity for civilisation" … virtually obliterating the brief period when all political factions had fought for the right to present the Indian as their own.' This gendered nationalist self, in its remembering and forgetting, in the articulations of danger and of nationalisms, remains tied to the notions of purity, of authenticity, which in turn are critically attached to the shadowy figure of the woman in the home. Nationalism in its psychological and political formulations thus posed significant problems for women.

Colonial, Nationalist and Feminist Tropes

There are three different discourses through which the figure of the national woman has been defined. The first was that of colonialism, the second of nationalism, and the third of feminism or the women's rights movement. In many ways these three were not discrete; they were overlain with the intellectual baggage and historical knowledges of the others. However, the context of power within which they took shape and were played out meant that the colonial discourse remained powerful even in the resistance to colonialism. This was because of the lack of confidence of nationalist elites in their own cultural histories, and in their desire to find acceptance within the dominant structures of power and ideologies (Fanon, 1990; Said, 1978; Nandy, 1983). The contexts of history, political economy and international politics were important to the development of these discourses, in all of which I find a selective engagement with the 'other'. In the process of drawing new parameters, challenging existing and emerging political forces, and creating visions of future development, nationalism emerges as the dominant discourse in the period of decolonization.

As Hoogvelt points out, 'Not only was the need for … colonies argued in economic terms, [increased trade leading to jobs at home], it was indeed often expressed as a vital national interest' (1997: 19). The competition among European colonial powers in the race for conquest was a competition among nations.[8] To lose this race was seen as a threat to national survival. As in any process of state legitimization of huge economic investment, the economic rationale was insufficient. The threat to the national integrity of Great Britain, for

---

8   Western European states had invested in colonial and semi-colonial states more than the entire wealth of Britain (Cairncross, 1975: 3).

example, was made the basis for ever-expanding colonial boundaries by political figures like Joseph Chamberlain and Cecil Rhodes: 'In their speeches and writings they argued that half the population of Britain would starve if...ever the British Empire narrowed down to a "mere" United Kingdom dimension' (Hoogvelt, 1997: 19). Another aspect of the colonial discourse concerned with threat was that of the barbarity of the colonized. As the English social philosopher Benjamin Kidd wrote at the turn of the eighteenth century: 'The task of governing from a distance the inferior races of mankind will be one of great difficulty.... But it is one that must be faced and over-come if the civilised world is not to abandon all hope of its continu-ing economic conquest of the natural resources of the globe' (in Hoogvelt, 1997: 20). Thus, the 'task of governing from a distance' the barbarian nations, though an economic necessity, was cast as 'the civilizing mission' of the Christian nations – a cultural trope of colo-nial expansion. Thus religion and nationalism converged in legitim-izing economic interests of the colonial states.

The nation-states of the Third World emerged out of their encoun-ter with imperialism. This encounter encompassed struggles over the cultural, economic and political resources of the state and was extremely bitterly fought. Nationalism was the mid-wife of new nations. There are three main nationalist tropes. The first is con-cerned with imperialist articulations of modernity[9] and the national-ist response to it. This was as much a consequence of political economy – that the insertion of new nations into the world economy required functioning within the international capitalist or (after the Second World War) socialist planning framework – as it was of modernization, of the new nations growing out of the chrysalis of 'traditional' culture to take their place in the modern world. Nation-building needs to be understood in this context: it was a consciously modernist political term that was employed widely during the period of decolonization. The nation – imagined as well as imaged, remembered as well as forgotten, traditional as well as modern – was to be built through the efforts of mobilized 'masses' led by national-ist elites imbued with a vision of the reclaiming of a glorious, if

---

9   Modernity, writes Dube, 'may be understood as the common behaviourial system historically associated with the urban, industrial, literate and participant societies of Western Europe and North America. The system is characterized by a rational and scientific world view, growth and ever-increasing application of science and technology, together with continuous adaptation of the institutions of society to the imperatives of the new world view and the emerging techno-logical ethos' (1988: 17).

vanished, past. This was the second trope of nationalism. Nation-building was thus a project that encompassed both the firming up of hegemonic cultural discourses through constitutional and legal arrangements, as well as economic and militaristic infrastructures that allowed the knitting together of disparate populations into one stable political entity – the independent nation-state. This was the third nationalist trope.

Feminist discourses were caught between two impulses, and fractured further as the nationalist movements progressed. One impulse was universalist – the recognition of global patriarchy, which can be witnessed in the writings of many western feminists writing during colonial times, such as Catherine Mayo and Eleanor Rathbone (see Ware, 1992; Liddle and Rai, 1998). Their particularistic, intimate narratives of the lives of women under traditional cultures were, however, often co-opted by imperialist media to reinforce the message of 'the civilizing mission' that was the 'white man's burden'. Women within nationalist movements largely disassociated themselves from these 'imperial maternalist' discourses (see Liddle and Rai, 1993). However, they too were caught between the attraction of a universalist language of citizenship rights, and the particular cultural and historical boundaries within which they knew women worked and lived (Agnihotri and Mazumdar, 1995; Geiger, 1997).

'Recasting history' (Sangari and Vaid, 1993) thus became a potent means of aggression and contestation within each of the three discourses. On both colonial and nationalist sides, the question of legitimacy was tied to that of civilization and civility, which, in turn, depended upon powerful constructions of gender and gender relations.

Colonial Ideologies and Constructions of Gender

Colonial attacks upon civilizations of the colonized countries took different forms to show how relations between men and women were symptomatic of the degeneration of the societies themselves. Colonized men of Aryan races, such as Afghans and Sikhs, for example, were routinely categorized as either 'martial' or boorish and aggressive. This was quite different from the depiction of the African male as 'in a state of barbarism and savagery which is preventing him from being an integral part of civilization' (Hegel, cited in Bayart, 1993: 3). Others, especially Chinese or East Asian men, were 'feminized' by emphasizing their (small) size, and eugenically 'weak' constitutions (Ling, 1997). 'Scientific' studies by colonial doctors abound in racialized descriptions of colonized men (Engels,

1989). All sets of men, however, were presented as brutal towards women, and therefore uncivil. For example, in his *History of India*, J.S. Mill wrote, 'The condition of women is one of the most remarkable circumstance in the manner of nations. Among rude people the women are generally degraded, among civilised people they are exalted' (cited in Kumar, 1989). The colonial project, then, encompassed the rescue of women in the colonies from the men of their own communities by an external authority that had both the force of state power and the legitimizing power of a modernist discourse. Men's relationship to women was used in colonial discourses as a 'means of mediating the West's relationship with the East' (Liddle and Rai, 1998). Women were central to this social construction of the 'civilized people'. The boundaries that were drawn around women constituted the markers of civility. Thus colonized women play a central role in the legitimization of colonialism.

For the colonial powers, ideas of civility were rationalized through tying these to the frame of modernity. Enlightenment formed the backdrop of nationalism in Europe, where capitalist development fuelled by the enterprise of the rational man was valorized. Modern social relations were spoken of in the same breath as capitalist norms of individuation. Capitalism, for its part, became synonymous with progress as it followed a series of stages of human activity – from hunting, to pastoral and settled agriculture, slavery and feudalism. It was the historical mission of colonialism to pass on the tools of progress to the colonized countries. This 'sharing of progress' was either brought about through the recognition of ancient civilizations' indigenous mores and then using these to craft new constitutions, as the Orientalists demanded for India, or through completely new arrangements. As Bayart points out, 'There are some links between the reluctance to recognise African societies as historical and political entities in their own right and their subjugation by the west from the period of the slave trade to colonization' (1993: 2). In the absence of recognition of pre-colonial civilization, for example in the Americas, it was emphasized that economic and social regeneration would be achieved only through the process of colonization itself (Cowen and Shenton, 1995: 42–59; also Earle, 2001). The crafting of modern economic relations thus had a profound impact upon not only the public relations of power between men at different levels but also the symbolic power relationship between the colonial and indigenous male elites. The dominant colonial male order was then able to humiliate the aspiring nationalist male elites in many different ways, perhaps one of the most potent being to recast the social relations among men and women of the colonies.

In the first stages of colonial conquest, humiliation was direct. As Stolcke writes in the context of Latin America, 'For the vast majority of indigenous women, the Conquest meant the loss of material, political and ritual privileges; exploitation of the labour, and sexual abuse by the invading soldiers and priests who crucified them in bed under the pretext of saving their souls' (1994: 8). In many countries and cultures, sexual abuse by the conquerors often meant the rejection of women by their male relatives in the name of 'honour' and 'purity' (Rai, 1996; Butalia, 1998). This was one way of dealing with the humiliation experienced by colonized men.[10] These rejected women were often made part of the political economy of colonial war against their own countries, by becoming the 'servicers' of soldiers' sexual needs. Prostitution, necessary for survival, placed them in a grey zone of society – vulnerable, forgotten and constantly abused; the responsibility of none. However, as the colonial power settled into 'administrative rationality', prostitutes became objects of regulation and confined exploitation, as can be witnessed in the making and implementation of the Contagious Diseases Acts by the British colonial state in 1864. While it is important to note that the prostitute women were also largely from the lower class/castes and therefore not necessarily of immediate concern to the nationalist male elites,[11] their concern about such women perhaps marks the process of formation of national sentiment.

The humiliation of the colonized male social order also took the form of selective refashioning of customary social and legal practices governing relations between men and women. These relations were both economic – regulation of property rights, de-legitimizing of certain forms of social organization of labour – and social – marriage and education. This refashioning emphasized the power relations between colonial and colonized male elites. As McClintock argues, 'All too often in male nationalisms *gender* difference between women and men serves to symbolically define the limits of *national* difference and power between *men*' (1993: 62). Gellner (1997) makes the same point, without the insight of feminist analysis, when he claims that it is the humiliation experienced by men of one national com-

---

10 In other cultures, such as Spanish America, this concern with purity was less evident. Indeed, the Catholic priests were continually dismayed by the lack of concepts of honour dependent upon sexual purity of women.

11 Indeed, in India, nationalist Congressmen tried to keep prostitute women and 'Congress ladies' apart from each other on political marches so as not to offend the sensibilities of upper-caste/class women and their male relatives (Desai, 1989).

munity in not being able to achieve communicative equality with men of the dominant national community that gives rise to nationalist passions.

It is important to note, however, that the colonial discourse on gender relations was not always challenged by nationalist movements. Some of it was also absorbed, rationalized and made the basis of the nationalist thinking on gender relations (see Metcalf, 1995: xi; Parpart and Staudt, 1990a). Refashioned property and marital relations in particular were not disturbed in the post-colonial nation-states; indeed in many countries, such as India, as we shall see below, nationalist leaderships participated in this refashioning of gender relations. It was the markings of modernity that were recognized by both the colonial and the nationalist elites in the rationalizing of patriarchal relations in inheritance, and in the quelling of 'uncivil' matrilineal marriage systems by both the colonial and the nationalist elites.

Under colonialism, modern capitalist relations required a 'rational' systematization of property relations; the inclusion of colonized states into the world economy necessitated recognizable property relations that could not be achieved without disturbing the 'alien/ uncivil' social relations. For example, in British India, the *zamindar*, the traditional landholder and tax-collector, was given property rights under the Permanent Settlement Act of 1793. Taking the model of the 'improving landlord' from the English context, the *zamindar* was given the same status and responsibilities. While this was a break with the earlier traditions of the *zamindar*'s position as dependent upon the feudal *nawabs*, the English colonial administration insisted that the Act was 'restoring institutions of the country'. Though even the English establishment soon became disillusioned with the Settlement, as the *zamindars* became the new rentier class uninterested in investing time and money in the improvement of land and continued to depend upon smallholders and their taxes, the idea was not repudiated by the colonial government. This was because it 'concealed a commitment to a European, and Whig, conception of the proper ordering of society.... The ideas of property and "improvement" which defined it remained central to the Raj of the nineteenth century' (Metcalf, 1995: 21). The resulting commercialization of Indian agriculture led to profound changes in rural social relations that resulted in the exclusion of women from the economic sphere. The sequestration of common lands meant women had little access to an important means of economic survival. Under the Permanent Settlement, as cash replaced kind in the payment of taxes, the production of cash crops necessitated changes in the patterns of agriculture production, and the division of family labour between the production of cash-crops and the provision of food (see Sarkar, 1983; Desai, 1989; Shiva, 1989; Mackenzie, 1995). Women's labour became increasingly concentrated in provision of food for the family, invisible and unaccounted for within the new financial arrangements. The male contribution to the family income took on greater visibility.

In Africa, too, the expansion of merchant capital worked against women. In particular, colonial institutionalization of land tenure and usage systems left women tied to the land, unable to take advantage of rural–urban migration, but also deprived of control over land resources (Chazan, 1990: 187). 'Colonial gender stereotypes, which identified men as farmers and women as wives and mothers, exacerbated this inequality by leading colonial officials to provide training and credit to male farmers' in Zambia (Munachonga, 1990: 130).[12] Further, the position of male elders was reinforced through codification of customary marriage laws and therefore underlined the centrality of women for the reproduction of labour, and the need for maintaining control over this resource (Lovett, 1990; Geiger, 1997: 25). In terms of rural–urban migration, women were almost completely excluded. This, argues Geiger, was because of the colonial state's preoccupation with controlling African women's sexuality and their reproductive capacity. In Tanganyika, for example, the 'problem of women' was posed by colonial bureaucrats in terms of 'rights, needs, and responsibilities of men in relationship to their dependants' (1997: 23).

Modern capitalism also required the increased reach of the state in garnering resources, and pushing out the narrow boundaries of market economies in the colonies. The first meant the exploitation of nature – terracing, logging and irrigating became widespread as colonialism became more confident. As Mackenzie points out, 'For the European, political expediency in the promotion of a policy of land alienation demanded both the creation of a conceptualization of African agriculture as "backward" and "inefficient", and the privileging of environmental knowledge based on Western experience' (1995: 102). Capitalist relations in agriculture led to an increased

---

12 It is important to note, however, that the colonial state also provided opportunities for women to register their protest against the traditional social relations in Africa. As Bayart notes, 'Neither "women" nor "minors" submitted passively to the law of the elders...women were feared for the efficiency of the sorcery....' However, 'their actions were not "revolutionary", and they were as often individual as collective' (1993: 112–13)

sense of 'improvement' of land through both changes in property relations and increased state intervention. The latter often took the shape of conservation and infrastructural projects – the 'management of nature' through western scientific knowledge to increase the productivity of land. Often these large infrastructural schemes were created and maintained through the forced labour of men and women of the colonies. While resistance to such exploitation of labour was widespread, it was also gendered. In cases such as the *Chipko* movement in India, or the renegotiations around use of the traditional Matengo pit system of cultivation in Tanganyika, 'the boundaries of gendered knowledge altered... in the context of changing relations of power' (Mackenzie, 1995: 105; also see Shiva, 1989).

Such refashioning of property relations and land management altered the relations between the peasant and the landholder. It also altered the position of women within agrarian societies. These new social realities were then given a frame of law. For example, the British never abandoned the idea of the 'rule of law' as their central contribution to the 'improvement' of the colonies. Through the codification of laws the colonial states, in particular the British colonial state, were able to combine, on the one hand, the utilitarian principles of liberal philosophy sanctifying capitalist relations and, on the other, 'traditional' sacred texts to ensure that the disturbance brought about through the revolution of economic relations could be contained within recognizable social frameworks, through supporting traditional social hierarchies (see also Liddle and Joshi, 1986; Parpart and Staudt, 1990a; Mackenzie, 1995: 108).

The Nationalist Response

In his book *The Intimate Enemy*, Ashis Nandy, like Frantz Fanon before him, has argued that the reach of colonialism encompasses both the political economy of the colony and the mappings of its culture and its selfhood as expressed by its political elites: 'Colonialism is also a psychological state rooted in earlier forms of social consciousness in both the colonizers and the colonized. It represents a certain cultural continuity and carries certain cultural baggage' (Nandy, 1983: 2). In political terms this translates, as Sartre (1990) so evocatively put it, into an attempt by the colonizers 'to fabricate an indigenous elite: they selected adolescents, branded them with the principles of western culture, stuffed their mouths with grandiose words which stick to the teeth.... Their living lies no longer had anything to say to their brothers.' However, 'all borrowings are also acts of reappropriation and reinvention' (Bayart, 1993: 27). On the one hand, the violation of selfhood that the male elites experience through the process and administration of colonization leads to a '[p]articulately strong...inner resistance to recognizing the ultimate violence which colonialism does to its victims, namely that it creates a culture in which the ruled are constantly tempted to fight their rulers within the psychological limits set by the latter' (Nandy, 1983: 3). The penalty of crossing these limits often is marginalization within the nationalist political process. On the other hand, colonial constructions of dominant modes of civility posed difficult issues for nationalist elites and movements. Chatterjee has called nationalism of these elites 'a project of mediation' (1993a: 72). This involved, as we shall see below, the appropriation of the popular – the innocent and the wise 'common man' rooted in the 'timeless truth of the national culture'; the 'classicization of tradition', which started with colonial disturbance and then fixing of culture as law; and, finally, the 'structure of the hegemonic domain of nationalism...where it sought to overcome the subordination of the colonized middle class' (Chatterjee, 1993a: 72–5).

Nationalism and 'social reform' was a particularly thorny issue for elites in colonial countries; no unified response was available (Parpart and Staudt, 1990a; Uberoi, 1996). These elites, who were significantly to influence the trajectory of post-colonial development, were divided on the question of social reform. To one section the need for social reform tied in with their modernist conviction that the country needed to look 'forward' – westward – to regain its independence and its place in the world, and that ancient customs needed modification, and sometimes to be rejected, if a modern nation-state was to take shape. The liberal modernists found much in common with the Marxists during the early phases of nationalist movements, which secured in many colonial countries the dominance of a linear, structuralist perspective. The alliance between the two was particularly visible during the early twentieth century, when the Leninist intervention in Marxist theory gave legitimacy to nationalist struggles through the trope of 'self-determination'. As Hobsbawm points out, 'Nationalism thus acquired a strong association with the left during the anti-fascist period, an association which was subsequently reinforced by the experience of anti-imperialist struggles in colonial countries' (1991: 148; see also Bianco, 1971; Sarkar, 1983). To the other nationalist section, social reform was part of the discourse of colonialism – an attack on ancient tradition, on the one hand, and a reminder that the peoples of the country were not free to refashion their own social and political system, on the other. In the hierarchy of issues, independence came before the need to re-examine social mores; social reform should be undertaken in the privacy of the home/national space and not in the glare of colonial dominance and internal discord (Kandiyoti, 1991b).

While there was no unity among the male nationalist elites in responding to the colonialist attacks upon 'rude cultures', for all sections, the nation took shape through nationalism. Nationalism was an essentialist discourse – of empowerment, of inclusion, but also of exclusion. The demarcation of the 'self' and 'other' that had been at the heart of the colonial encounter needed to be sustained for the nation to be secure in its borders. Nira Yuval-Davis has emphasized the need to distinguish between different types of nationalisms – cultural, ethnic and civic – because '[d]ifferent aspects of gender relations play an important role in each of these dimensions of nationalist projects and are crucial for any valid theorisation of them...' (1997: 21). While agreeing that these distinctions were critical to the political projects of nationalist elites, I would argue that whichever form nationalism took, the processes of 'othering' remained central to it (Giddens, 1987: 117). The creation of the nationalist 'self' required a universalist language of self-determination and equality that allowed nationalist elites to stake a claim to freedom. Nationalism could, thus, provide an ideal for anti-colonial elites that was based upon a complex recognition of glories past and the contemporary degradation, but also the promise of resurgence and self-determination (Said, 1978).

The language of idealism was very often used to describe the nation in the making, and frequently this description was imbued with notions of sanctity and sacredness. As the Turkish nationalist Ziya Gokalp asserted, 'This sacredness, even before it has reached consciousness, exists in an unconscious state in the psychological unity of the social group. So far it has remained a hidden treasure... [but] with all its halo of sanctity.... The emergence of an ideal means its rise from the subconscious to the conscious level' (Kedourie, 1970: 199). Gokalp speaks of 'hidden treasures' that invest the past with legitimacy while at the same time ensuring that the process of recovery is allowed through the mobilization of nationalists imbued with idealist visions of a sacred homeland. The nation itself became symbolic of familial relations by being called either 'fatherland' or, more generally, 'motherland', 'for whose sake people shed their blood. Why is it that all other lands are not sacred, but only that which is called fatherland?' asked Gokalp. By familializing the nation, the home becomes critical in the discourse of nationalism. Nothing is more imagined than this community of people subscribing to a singular idea of the home. As Papanek has pointed out, 'certain ideals of womanhood are propagated as indispensable to the attainment of an ideal society. These ideals apply to women's personal behaviour, dress, sexual activity, choice of partner, and the reproductive options.... [W]omen [are] the "carriers of tradition" or "the centre of the family" especially during periods of rapid social change' (1994: 46–7). However, what is also demanded at this time of crisis is that women's 'actions and appearance should alter less quickly than that of men, or should not be seen to change at all... [and that they should] conform to prescriptive norms of a *collective* identity that is seen as advancing the goals of the group' as a whole (p. 47). In this context, the ideals of society get attached to notions of appropriate behaviour of women, and the restoration of social order becomes a process of imposition of stringent controls over women rather than addressing the structural issues leading to and arising from conflict.

As Liddle and Joshi (1986) have shown in the context of India, this concept of the ideal home and the ideal woman within the home was very much an upper-caste/class idea of familial space and relations. Systems of social interaction that underpinned the upper classes were made on the basis of a 'national' understanding of social relations through both colonial acceptance and their use by the dominant nationalist elites. So what was a limited, and contested, terrain of social relations was then translated into the norm through the systems of laws and constitutions. Moghadam argues that this move became possible when, in line with Anderson's analysis, nationalism came to be viewed not simply as an ideology but as akin to kinship and religion (1994a: 4). According to Anderson, nationalism allowed the secular transformation of fatality into continuity – something that only religious discourses had articulated before the rationalizing thrust of Enlightenment (1991: 10–11). As continuity demanded reproduction of future national generations, of national/cultural values, and stability of social forms, as well as the reproduction of the national populations, the family became critical to this new secular articulation of the nation, and the idea of the nation came to be symbolized in the family.

This imagined home/nation symbolized many things – security, familiarity, tradition. It was a space that remained open to the male elites as their domain, untouched, in most part, by the colonizer, who structured public life so ruthlessly. Indeed, the autonomy of patriarch within the home was allowed by the colonial state in the hope of undermining anti-colonial resistance. As Martin Chanock

argues, analysing the cases of Northern Rhodesia/Zambia and Ny-
asaland/Malawi, the male elders allied themselves with colonial
rulers to re-establish control over women through a contrived 'Customary Law' (cited in Parpart and Staudt, 1990b: 7; also Mackenzie,
1995). Some of the bitterest opposition to the British rule in India
came from nationalists such as Bal Gangadhar Tilak when the colonial state sought to refashion dominant familial relations through
legislation on age of consent or on *sati*. The modernist nationalists,
on the other hand, supported these interventions as they became
part of the story of the contemporary degeneration of the Indian
society and its need for regeneration through secular nationalist
revolution (Sarkar, 1983; Uberoi, 1996). The relations within the
home, then, were very much part of the nationalist discourse; the
home/nation was the authentic space but was under threat. This
threat came not only from without – the colonial state – but also
from within – the traditionalists who opposed change and thereby
endangered the future, or the modernist who argued for a refashioned space without regard to the resultant pollution of authentic
culture. Moreover, this authenticity was firmly attached to the body
of the woman within the home/nation (Mani, 1993; Kandiyoti,
1991b).

The contours of the woman within the home were very particular:
'...only the women of the nation are the beautiful ones. Other
men's/nation's/state's women...are not "beautiful like the home/
national woman is"' (Pettman, 1996: 51). National identity was in-
separable from notions of boundary, purity and chastity; threat to
this identity came if women's role within the boundary of the
home/nation was compromised. The woman created the future generations and she ensured continuity of cultural traditions through
her own appropriate social conduct and through the religious and
cultural education of her children. The woman was thus seen as the
stable entity in periods of change. While male elites argued about
the need for change to the outer garb of the woman, her inner core
was conceded by all nationalist sections to be chaste and immutable,
as was the idea of the nation. This double move in imagining the
female figure allowed the discourse of modernity to encompass the
woman, but at the same time leave enough untouched within the
parameters of the home. In this way the nationalist Janus resolved
the 'woman question'. The tension between identity/culture and modernity was harmonized by making and endorsing the classical distinction between the scientific/technological and culture/tradition. The
Chinese modernizers of the eighteenth century, for example, formu-
lated this tension by distinguishing between *it* and *yong* – the thinking

and doing, the philosophical and mechanical (Grieder, 1981).[13] And in the African context President of Senegal and African poet Léopold Sédar Senghor wrote: 'Negro-African reason is traditionally dialectical, transcending the principles of identity, noncontradiction, and the 'excluded middle'. Let us...be careful not to be led astray by the narrow determinism of Marxism, by abstraction' (1995: 269). Whereas western science was needed for the economic sphere, traditional national values were central to maintaining the authentic 'self' so important to the stability of the new nation. By this account, while the regeneration of the new nation required the harnessing of western science, it also required protecting the 'traditional' norms and values that were endorsed by history, and recognizable as common to all those who called themselves nationalist. As Stacey (1983) has so powerfully argued in her critique of the Chinese communist movement, this distinction allowed a compromise between the communist elites and the peasantry on the 'woman question'. It resulted in the communists pursuing the project of nation-building with the support of the peasantry, and allowed patriarchal social relations to remain stable in a reconfigured space under the communist regime. Thus, the modernist discourse was constantly being disturbed from within nationalist movements.

The debates about the characteristics of the new nation and the refashioning of gender relations within its boundaries became accessible to increased numbers of people in the colonies through the spread of print capitalism and the consequent undermining of the earlier administrative languages of the elites with the growth of the vernacular press (Hobsbawm, 1991: 141; Anderson, 1991: 44). The vernacular presses carried the nationalist message across the colonial territories and 'created unified fields of exchange and communication' (Anderson, 1991: 44). One of the important currencies of this communicative exchange was the delineation of the woman. Modern or traditional, home-bound or participative in the nationalist struggles, bearer of authentic values or challenging both inherited and imported boundaries and positionings – the vernacular presses of nationalist struggles are full of struggles of meaning around the body of the woman. Vernacular journals also, for the first time, carried the voices of women themselves, and became the vehicles of the first feminist articulations that challenged both the colonial and the nationalist/patriarchal delineations of women's positions in society (Talwar, 1993; Geiger, 1997). The importance of this feminist

---

13   In India the cultural articulation of *ghare/baare* (inside/outside) served the same purpose (Chatterjee, 1993b).

challenge to the nationalist elites' views of the national community and women's position within it varied enormously from country to country. It would, however, be fair to say that in no context did feminist voices gain equality with male agendas within the discourse of nationalism. One of the reasons for this might be that feminist voices needed to keep hold of 'the woman' as a recognizable and stable entity as much as did the nationalist elites. Recognition of diversity was not part of the challenge at this stage. The struggles centred on the constructed woman and the space she occupied. The struggle over the space within was, then, very much a struggle over the contours of social relations with the figure of the woman central to it. However, print capitalism did allow for the voice of women to be heard, and in many cases to be mobilized in the nationalist cause. This mobilization, whatever its premises, became the basis of the first demands that women made in their own articulated interests.

The struggles over meanings within the nationalist movements regarding the place and role of women are important for understanding the alternative visions of post-colonial development that the nationalist elites put forward. These debates also indicate an acceptance by these elites of the powerful rhetoric of modernity that the colonialist powers had thus far monopolized. This acceptance of modernity and fashioning of alternative modern visions for new nations was also the basis upon which a new legitimacy was constructed by nationalist elites. It is by accepting norms of modernity that the nationalist elites asked, first, for the return of sovereign power to the national elites from the colonial centres, and, then, for the trust of the people of the country, and for a recognition of the centrality of political elites to the process of development.[14] I will return to this issue in the next chapter.

In the twentieth century, in most countries, bourgeois liberal nationalist elites became dominant in nationalist struggles.[15] As a consequence, their imaginings of 'the woman's' place in the new

14 In the case of Kenya, for example, the link between nationalism and African socialism was made on the premise that all Africa had a single traditional culture, 'that of communalism. The common colonial experience, it was argued, subdued communalism and exploited resources in Africa for the benefit of non-Africans. To achieve post-colonial economic advancement or progress, rational planning of resources would be required' (Cowen and Shenton, 1995: 316). The role of the state elites thus remained central to the project of African socialism.
15 For analysis of Marxist regimes, see below. The political situation in post-colonial Latin America was also different.

nation-state became dominant; as Jayawardena notes, upon this view, 'the women of the peasantry were...proletarianized, those of the bourgeoisie were trained to accept new social roles in conformity with the emerging bourgeois ideology of the period' (1986: 9). The constitutional reforms that were put forward in the post-colonial period remained largely political: equality for women within the legal processes; rescinding of obviously discriminatory practices; right to the vote, to education and in most cases to property; and laws prohibiting violence against women.[16] As the following example illustrates, both class and gender disturbed the stability of the new social relations that were normalized through nationalist political discourses and later through post-colonial constitutional and legal mechanisms.

In 1938, years before India gained independence, the National Congress set up a National Planning Committee. It was chaired by Jawaharlal Nehru and sought to draw the developmental map of the new India. One of the nine sub-committees established by the NPC was on 'Woman's Role in the Planned Economy' (Chaudhuri, 1996: 211). The sub-committee was to deal particularly with issues of equal opportunities and rights for women and access to the world of economic production, which was identified as key to resolving the unequal status of women (p. 213). The individual (woman) was the central figure for the Committee, while the 'social' largely represented the hindrances, in the form of custom, that prevented the individual from participating as a 'useful citizen' in the life of the new nation (p. 219). The debates within the Committee suggested that the nation was the only social unit that was liberating for the Indian woman and the liberation of the Indian woman was important to the functioning of the modern nation within the global order (p. 223). However, from the beginning there was a tension evident in the discussions of the Committee. While the 'social' as custom was suspect, the Committee was also concerned with maintaining customs and 'traditions': 'It is not our desire to belittle in any way these traditions, which have in the past contributed to the happiness and progress of the individual and have been the means of raising the dignity and beauty of Indian womanhood and conserving the *spiritual attributes of the Indian Nation*' (WRPE, 1947: 32–3, emphasis in the original; also Rai, 1998b). The converging lines of womanhood and the spirituality of the Indian nation within this document reveal

---

16   In countries like China where Marxism was embraced by a major part of the oppositional elites, class politics subsumed economic rights of women, while the political agenda was similar to the one outlined above (Evans, 1997).

the fraught nature of the enterprise upon which the Indian modernizing elites were embarked. As I have argued elsewhere: 'There was a constant redrawing of the social and historical map around the body of the woman to keep hold of the convergence that had been created; this was a project which could not reconcile the tensions with the affirmations of culture' (Rai, 1999: 243).[17] Thus, we see nationalism's 'capacity to appropriate, with varying degrees of risk and varying degrees of success, dissenting and marginal voices' (Chatterjee, 1993a: 156). We find, therefore, that the report of the Committee is scarcely mentioned after formal citizenship rights are granted to women in the Indian constitution in 1950.

Nationalism as Development

The successful post-colonial nationalist elites saw themselves as participants in the regeneration of their countries through gaining independence from the colonial rulers and envisioning a 'progressive', 'modern', 'industrialized' state. Indeed the role of the state, of planning, of regulation and of rationality was constantly emphasized in the nationalist rhetoric (see Nyerere, 1973; Nehru, 1990).[18] This was evident in liberal, socialist and Marxist states (Mao, 1965). Such visions of modernity had direct consequences for structuring gender relations in post-colonial states. The emphasis on industrialization, for example, meant that the focus remained on male employment; the acceptance of commercialization and mechanization of agriculture meant the marginalization of women's work in rural societies; and the 'taming of nature' by construction of dams across rivers – which Nehru called the 'temples of modern India' – for the

17 For an analysis of similar debates on culture and constitution in Algeria, see Bouatta and Cherifati-Merabtine (1994). The arguments about Islamic property and citizenship rights of women are discussed, as is the eventual compromise between the FLN and the Muslim clerics in the shape of the Family Code of 1984. Also see Mehdid (1996).
18 Nehru writes in *The Discovery of India*:

The very thing that India lacked, the modern West possessed and possessed to excess. It had the dynamic outlook. It was engrossed in the changing world, caring little for ultimate principles, the unchanging the universal.... Because it was dynamic, it was progressive and full of life, but that life was a fevered one and the temperature kept on rising progressively.... India, as well as China, must learn from the West for the modern West has much to teach, and the spirit of the age is represented by the West. (1990: 384–5)

production of electricity meant the displacement of populations, resulting in particular vulnerabilities for women. The equation of 'modernization' with the preferred political system was at times crude and explicit – 'fertilizers would enable increased agricultural output. [This] in turn, means socialism' (Nyerere, 1973: 46) – and narrowed the spaces from within which women could challenge their marginalization. Indeed as Heng points out in the context of China, 'the "modern" and the "Western" [were] conflated[, which]... meant that a nationalist accusation of modern and/or foreign – that is to say, Western – provenance or influence, when directed at a social movement, [was] sufficient for the movement's delegitimization' (1997: 32). Other than in the Marxist nationalist states, private property was taken as given. However, women could rarely inherit under recognized or accepted 'cultural' regimes, and this further supported the 'traditional' or modified colonial legal arrangements.[19]

To recapitulate my argument thus far. To the colonized male elites the nation came into view through the lens of anti-colonial struggles. Through these struggles the colonized peoples and elites experienced nationalism. The nationalist elites were able to convey to the colonized peoples the image of the nation (Anderson, 1991) in freedom together; they were able to visualize the possibility of articulating their own norms and rules of governance rather than being humiliated by working to the rules – hated and imperfectly understood – of the colonial state (Gellner, 1983). While all these images of the nation were deeply gendered, there was little acknowledgement of this. There was no recognition of women's interests as different from the constructed nationalist interests: this was considered essentially divisive. In the political hierarchy of issues, nationalism secured primacy, while 'the woman' continued to have a shadowy existence on the periphery of nationalist consciousness – mobilized in its cause but confined within the home that was also the nation. Through gaining independence, a separate identity and a new home/nation would be created upon the foundations of the old, recovered one, said the nationalist message. Within the boundaries of the new nation both men and women would move to a civic nationalism symbolized as much by a new universal citizenship as by a new economy.

---

19 While in principle Islam provides women with the right to inheritance in the father's property, in practice the right is often overlooked in favour of male heirs (Ali, 2000).

Nationalist Movements and 'Self-Determination' of Women

Jayawardena has shown convincingly the importance of the link between nationalist and feminist struggles. She emphasizes the link between 'women's participation in feminist movements for emancipation and their simultaneous involvement in struggles for national liberation and social change' (1986: 23). She seeks to discover the roots of Third World feminism in the participation of women in nationalist struggles. She argues that the economic and political challenges thrown up by the anti-colonial struggles allowed women to be constituted by, and to make demands upon the nationalist agendas. The development of capitalism in the Third World brought women into the labour markets; the restructuring of agriculture fundamentally altered their position within the village community and the local economy; the administrative changes that created new political stabilities under colonial rule brought forth questions of local versus national identity for women, especially in the context of increased mobility and migration to urban conurbations. Vernacular print newspapers circulated information and became a vehicle for articulations of discontent and the proposing of alternative visions by women. The nationalist response to the challenges posed by colonialism opened up the debates on women's social status and created new spaces that women could occupy and use. However, nationalism also posed significant challenges to nationalist women.

The biggest challenge posed by nationalism to women's consciousness was that of unity – the fight against imperialism demanded discipline and sacrifice. The nationalist movements – liberal as well as Marxist – spoke not in the name of particularistic groups but for pan-national interests. 'Particular interests' were regarded as threats that would only disturb and dislocate the coalescing of national agendas. As Helie-Lucas has commented, 'This is the real harm which comes with liberation struggles. People mobilize against such a strong, powerful and destructive enemy that there is no room for practical action in mobilizing women at the same time. But worse, liberation struggles erase from our mind the very idea of doing so, which is seen as anti-revolutionary and anti-nationalist' (1991: 58).[20] Second, unity meant keeping all

---

20 In China, Mao Zedong wrote 'On Contradictions' (1965), which systematized the Communist Party's demand for loyalty. He stressed that in each context, in each period, each crisis, the role of the communist leadership was to

sections of nationalist opposition on board. Here the element of sacrifice became paramount – if in the interests of unity certain rights of particular groups were compromised, this was not expediency but strategic bargaining. Recognizable social relations were the cement for political unity, and what could be more immediately recognizable than the figure of the woman within the home? For women's groups these issues of unity and sacrifice posed serious difficulties. On the one hand, most groups accepted that the urgency of the nationalist struggle must give it primacy; on the other hand, they were also aware of the particular constructions of the nationalist agendas, which marginalized their interests. On the one hand, the goal of non-gendered citizenship beckoned; on the other was the reality of differentiated experiences of the public and the private lives of men and women. Being cast as victims of their own society, women's groups rebelled against such delineations and asserted their cultural identities; being recast as 'new women' of a new nation-state, they were aware of the gaps between the political rhetoric and social reality. While self-imposed and self-regulated codes of silence (Crenshaw, 1993; Papanek, 1994) protected their communities from the attacks of the imperialist western powers, women's groups also remained uncomfortable with the nationalist leaderships' articulations of women's place within the national movements. In the demands for unity lay the key to future agenda-setting, but often women's groups were unable to intervene in time because of the ways in which the burden of solidarity was placed upon them. '[A] power structure was being built on our mental confusion: a power structure which used the control of...women as a means to get access to and maintain itself in power....During this crucial period, women had been assigned a place in society which could not be challenged without questioning both the past and the future...' (Helie-Lucas, 1991: 58).

If the demands for unity posed a dilemma for women's movements, this was compounded by divisions within women's groups on two issues: the first was modernism versus culture; the second that of differences among women. Most women who became heard during nationalist movements were bourgeois women – educated and well connected, promoted by their politicized families, symbolic of a new modernity, and even shared more intimate aspects of

---

identify the main contradiction, and devote all resources at the command of the Party to its resolution. All other (secondary!) contradictions were subordinate to the primary contradiction. Any disturbing of the hierarchy of contradictions identified by the Communist Party was therefore divisive and unacceptable.

their life experiences: as Geiger comments on the lives of Tanzanian women activists, 'At the time of mobilization, the TANU activists were ... divorced ... "middle-aged" by Tanganyikan cultural norms ... were freer than young women ... had very few children. Many had only one. Several had none ...' (1997: 68).[21] And yet, the tension between modernity and tradition formed the backdrop of their activism as much as that of the men's. This was because of the need felt by women to rescue cultural practices that could be owned by them, which would be self-representational as well as empowering in the context of colonialism and nationalist struggles. To be defined out of the cultural trope would risk marginalization and delegitimization. Motherhood in this context occupied an important contested place. As Malathi de Alwis has argued within the Sri Lankan context, '"Motherhood" ... can be defined as not only incorporating the act of reproduction ... but also the nursing, feeding and looking after of babies, adolescents, the sick, the old and even grown women and men, including one's husband' (cited in Maunaguru, 1995: 160). In this role, women were able to occupy particular public spaces; the acceptance of the place of women within the 'natural' order of family allowed them access to oppositional politics against the colonial state perpetrating violence on their homes and children. In doing so, however, the constructed motherhood of the nationalist discourse allowed a homogenizing and essentializing power; motherhood was contained within the boundaries of recognizable family forms that were validated by the nationalist elites. Issues of class, ethnic diversity and religion therefore became blurred and later emerged as real divisive issues for women's movements.

The anti-imperialist mobilizations led to what Kandiyoti has called 'the era of patriotic feminism' (1991a: 28). In Turkey, Kandiyoti points out, 'no less than a dozen women's associations [were] founded between 1908 and 1916, ranging from primarily philanthropic organizations to those more explicitly committed to struggle for women's rights' (p. 29). The same phenomenon could be seen in other countries engaged in nationalist transformations. However, in many cases women's organizations were established by and with the support of male nationalist elites; in others already existing women's groups were co-opted into dominant nationalist parties. The dilemmas that were posed by these co-options can be illustrated by the example of Turkey under Mustafa Kemal's regime in the 1920s. On the one hand, the 'new woman' of the Kemalist era became

---

21 Similar personal characteristics continue to define women politicians today. For India, see Rai (1997), and for Chile see Waylen (1997b).

symbolic of a break with the past; on the other, the paternalist be-
nevolence of the Kemalist regime hindered women's autonomous
political initiatives. Kemal refused, for example, to authorize the
founding of the Women's People's Party in 1923. Instead he advised
women's groups to establish a Turkish Women's Federation – an
association rather than a party. Even this was disbanded in 1935, a
fortnight after it had hosted the 12th Congress of the International
Federation of Women. The official reason given by the president of
the Federation was that Turkish women had achieved complete
equality and full constitutional rights, and that, the goals of the
Federation having been achieved, its continued existence could not
be justified. However, what was also clear was that the Kemalist
regime felt compromised by the pacifist speeches made by the British, American and French delegates to the conference; at a time
when the Turkish army was gearing up for conflict, Turkish feminists' stand on disarmament was seen as a grave embarrassment
(pp. 40–1). Thus Kandiyoti concludes, 'the republican regime opened
up an arena for state-sponsored "feminism" but at one and the same
time circumscribed and defined its parameters' (p. 42)

The Turkish example poses questions about the relationship between nationalism and feminism in two different ways. The first is
about the primacy of the dominant nationalist agendas in contrast to
the concerns of the women's movements. The second, is the difficult
relationship between different feminisms – national, local and international.[22] As Kandiyoti notes, 'Turkish nationalism could be perceived as divisive in a situation where other ethnic minorities were
restive, . . . for whom the notion of a Turkish nation constituted a
threat to the Islamic *umma*' (p. 33). Similarly, the dominant Brah-
manical codes of social interaction were naturalized as Indian social
codes by the British in India, thus erasing the different regional and
caste-based norms (Liddle and Joshi, 1986). Women who subscribed
to the secularization of social and public life often supported such
hegemonic positions, becoming vulnerable to the charges of cultural
ignorance, insensitivity, class bias and a slavish mentality in
accepting western ideas on religion and secularism. The support of

---

22   Bereswill and Wagner, writing on the women's peace movement in Europe
during the First World War, quote the leader of the Federation of German
Women's Organizations, Gertrud Baumer, who said, 'For us it is natural that
during a national struggle for existence we, the women, belong to our people
[*Volk*] and *only* to them. In all questions of war and peace we are citizens of our
country, and it is impossible to negotiate in an international circle...' (1998:
236).

women's groups for one articulation of nationalism could be presented as denying other identities, which made the identification of feminisms with western ideologies easier within the context of the home/nation.

Further, feminist interventions from the outside, especially from western feminists, created difficulties for local and national feminisms. Ramusack and Sievers (1999) identify the approach of most western feminists of the time as 'maternal imperialists'. They saw themselves as the agents of civilization and progress; they 'sought power for themselves in the imperial project, and used the opportunities and privileges of empire as a means of resisting patriarchal constrains and creating their own independence' (Liddle and Rai, 1998). While most nationalist feminists rejected such delineations of women in their own countries, their acceptance of the liberal values that western feminists espoused made them easy targets of traditionalists' attempt at delegitimizing their struggles for women's rights. Also, their anger at maternal imperialists' complicity with imperialist discourses of Orientalism meant that fruitful transnational alliances of solidarity were not possible; solidarity of western feminisms came at a price unacceptable to nationalist feminists. The national boundaries thus continued to delimit the space within which nationalist women's groups could organize, mobilize and negotiate. And the tensions within nationalisms and discourses of culture continued to pose significant challenges for women.

Codifying Nationalism

These challenges were, however, least visible at the very moment when a nationalist movement made the transition from being an oppositional movement into being the dominant political force in an independent nation-state. At the cusp of historical change, most women's groups remained convinced of the nationalist transformative agendas and were reluctant to seek 'special' political dispensations from the state. In India, for example, three women's organizations (the All-India Women's Committee, the Women's Indian Association and the Central Committee of the National Council of Women in India) wrote to the Chair of the Minorities Committee on the status of women in the proposed new Government of India Act, 1935, demanding equal political rights with men. They also insisted that they would resist 'any plea that may be advanced by small individual groups of people for any kind of temporary concessions... [for] securing the adequate representation of women in the legislatures....To seek any form of preferential treatment would be to violate the integrity of the universal demand of Indian women for absolute equality of political status.' Women's groups within most nationalist movements saw themselves as freedom fighters, and as citizens of a free country. Liberal ideas of individual freedom were very attractive to women who participated in the nationalist struggles, even though they were mediated through the ideologies of nationalism. However culturally bounded, the freedom of the individual found its political form in the figure of the citizen.

The early conversations about nationalism helped demarcate the boundaries within which citizenship was operationalized. This concept was translated in very particular ways in order to stabilize new polities. Different visions of the future of the nation-state, and of its citizens, determined where women were positioned within this discourse in different political systems. In liberal political systems, a civic nationalism became the hegemonic political rhetoric. A pan-nationalist discourse of a citizenship tolerant of differences was developed to tie in the various groups, ethnicities and religious communities that formed the new nations. This was important for political stability, which in turn was essential for economic development. In this context, women continued to be regarded as markers of non-secular group identities and at the same time became individualized as citizens of the new nation. The Indian case[23] is a good one to reflect upon here. As citizens women were equal to men. However, as women they were deemed to be markers of identity first, and individuals later. Thus, in the interests of political stability after the trauma of the partition of the country at the time of independence, Muslim women were denied many of the rights that Hindu and Christian women were granted. Thus, the 'traditions' of Islamic family law were accepted, maintained and endorsed through the Indian constitution, whereby Muslim men could marry more than one woman, and divorce proceedings, claims of custody of children, maintenance of the divorced wife and division of property and inheritance were decided according to Islamic rather than 'Indian' constitutional law.[24] As most successful nationalist movements

---

23 For a discussion of contradictions arising from the co-existence of African customary law and nationalist, secular legal regimes, see Stewart (1993).

24 The Shahbano case, which involved a Muslim woman seeking judicial intervention to claim an appropriate amount of maintenance at the time of divorce from her husband, opened up the debate on women's rights and cultural rights in the 1990s. It also showed the intractability of this constructed binary on the basis of 'ideal' home/nation (see Pathak and Sunder Rajan, 1992).

were led by urban male liberal elites, the equality legislation fulfilled their commitment to democratizing gender relations. However, the process of reconciling the two impulses of social and political order and ideology and cultural traditions has, for example, resulted in very painful consequences for women in Algeria. The revolutionary state tried to maintain both a 'socialist' and an 'Islamist' identity. Unable to placate the fundamentalists and to deliver economic goods to the people, the political situation careered out of control, with tragic consequences for the country and for Algerian women in particular (see Bouatta and Cherifati-Merabtine, 1994; Rai, 1996a).

In non-democratic political systems, such as Nigeria under military rule, for example, we find a 'strategy of exclusion rather than of unequal incorporation. Until recently,... military rulers (much like colonial administrators) pursued a policy of purposeful female neglect' (Chazan, 1990: 190). The nearly total masculine membership of the military and the army-led public bodies left women marginalized within the formal power structures. Further, owing to the inaccessibility of these formal institutions to women, women were also largely excluded from the patron–client relationships that took the place of more visible political participation (Mba, 1990; Chazan, 1990).

In Marxist states the concept of citizenship became subsumed under the categories of class while cultural nationalism was aligned to the modification of ideology – the state and nation became blurred, with seepage of some of the dominant cultural norms into state policies, and the suppression of others through state power. Evans notes that 'the subordination of gender to the supposedly more substantial matters of economic development and political power has been a recurring feature of the party-state's approach to woman-work since the early days of community control' (1997: 31). Construction of socialism in the 1950s in China required producing children for the development of society, and as a political commentator in 1953 suggested, 'having children was a social duty, failure to observe which "should be severely criticized by the party"' (p. 44). However, as Stacey has observed in the context of China, the 'new democratic morality linked sexuality not with procreation, but with felicitous marital relations, and, thereby, with the construction of socialism' and the maintenance of a social order where concerns about women's appropriate behaviour within the family were implicitly accepted and given succour through policy-making and implementation (1983: 188). In all three political contexts – democratic capitalist, socialist and non-democratic – the articulations of nationalist aspirations remained crucial to the setting of political and economic development agendas. In the moment of victory, whatever the ideological framework of decolonized nation-states, women seemed to be shut out of the institutional design.

It is in this context that the ideological framing of women's aspirations – as patriots, nationalists and citizens – becomes important for an understanding of the places they occupied in development agendas. First, while social reform was considered a priority by all post-colonial elites, it was also emphasized that the 'essential distinction between the social roles of men and women in terms of material and spiritual virtues must at all times be maintained. There would have to be a marked *difference* in the degree and manner of westernization of women, as distinct from men, in the modern world of the nation' (Chatterjee, 1993b: 243). Second, the above distinction was made but not acknowledged. This non-acknowledgement took different forms but the assumptions about the social placing of men and women were built into the constructions of these concepts, and then naturalized through law and state policy. As Smart has argued, 'we can begin to analyse law as a process of producing fixed gender identities rather than simply as the application of law to previously gendered subjects.... Woman is a gendered subject position which legal discourse brings into being' (1992: 9). The language of equality was used in most post-colonial states to firm up the contours of citizenship, while citizenship remained differentially constructed for men and women. The legitimacy of the state rested upon social and political reform, and upon the assembling of the values of citizenship in constitutional design. The hegemonic language of nationalism made it difficult for minorities and other marginalized groups to challenge this location of citizenship values in a universalized 'citizen' – bourgeois or socialist. Nationalist elites took this universalized (male) citizen as both the agent and target of policies of development agendas, while women remained very much targets and not agents. As we shall see in the next chapter, the particularities of the post-colonial nation-states and this universalized ideological framing of women were a powerful combination in the marginalization of women in development.

In Conclusion

It is perhaps for this reason that increasingly women and feminist scholars have become convinced that the nationalist project is incompatible with feminism (Moghadam, 1994a: chap. 1).[25] However, this growing distance did not, and does not, address the painful issue of women's political participation. Disengagement from nationalist movements also has costs. The struggles to shift the meanings of the nation and nationalism have only been partially successful – as much to do with the struggles over these meanings within and outside the women's movements themselves as to do with the contexts in which questions about the form of nationalism are raised. In no contemporary nationalist movements for sovereignty do we find the 'mainstream' programme of national development being systematically gendered in its programme. The story of nationalism is thus not an entirely happy one for women. However, in the first phase of nationalist struggles against colonialism, women did find a place in the public arena, which, in its popular imagery as well as wide participation, was unique. And access to this space allowed the further development of feminism, which has ironically made nationalism more incompatible with women's concerns for equality. In chapter 2 I build on this discussion about gender and nationalism to query the emerging discourses on development from a gendered perspective.

---

25   For a 'colonization' of nationalism to women's agendas in the form of the radical idea of a women's nation, see Andrea Dworkin's *The Jews, Israel and Women's Liberation* (2000a). In an interview Dworkin argues, '...women cannot be free of male dominance without challenging the men of one's own ethnic group and destroying their authority. This is a willed betrayal, as any assault on male dominace must be.' She comments: '...it is an incredible thing to overlook as a possibility. We've never dealt with the issue of sovereignty...' (2000b).

2 | Gender and Development
Theoretical Perspectives in Context

> What can be seen in a field of knowledge is a function of the way the field is conceived, the way knowledge itself is conceived, and what can be seen also determines what must remain unseen.
>
> Christina Crosby, 'Dealing with Differences'

Introduction

In the previous chapter I examined the impact of colonialism, nationalism and the processes of decolonization on the construction of discourses of gender and development and the ways in which these framed the positionings of women and men in national economies and societies. In this chapter I begin by focusing on the international contexts within which decolonization proceeded, and the alternative models and discourses of development that were shaped within these contexts. I do this not only to contextualize the debates on development but also to reflect upon why feminists, and women's movements, asked certain questions about development and not others. A comparative and historical perspective allows us to understand the differences and commonalities that women and feminists faced within the developmental framework.[1] I then explore why the women's movements in most decolonized nations participated in

---

1 For a similar argument on the concept of difference, see Tripp (2000). Tripp argues, 'We may want to inquire under what political and historical conditions do contrasting conceptualizations of difference emerge... how varying cultural

and subscribed to the early articulations of the nationalist elites' development models, even though the nationalisms in question framed 'the woman question' very differently. In the second section I trace the major debates on development that took place in the context of decolonization, on the one hand, and the Cold War, on the other, and examine the gendered critiques of these debates. I argue that feminist engagements with theoretical debates and development policy-making structures secured a valuable and critical space for women within development projects. Both western and Third World feminists participated in these debates and broadened our understanding of the practical and strategic needs of women in different contexts. I suggest, however, that women in development/ gender and development literature largely continue to work within the liberal framework, and that this makes certain strategies of women's empowerment feasible while at the same time closing off alternative spaces. A focus on power relations within any socio-economic system would need to address not only issues of empowerment for women but also the power relations within which both men and women work and live.

The Contexts of International Development

The process of decolonization took place within two overlapping contexts. The first was that of the Second World War and the emerging post-war world order, with the deepening ideological fissures between the socialist world and the western capitalist world. The second was that of the particular national movements, and of the process through which these achieved nationhood. Both these contexts had important implications for the post-colonial state formations, and for the debates on national development strategies and the ways in which these framed gender relations.[2]

---

perceptions of identity render different understandings of the problem of difference' (p. 650).

2   See Enloe (1989), where she argues that 'the vision that informed these male officials' foreign-policy choices was of a world in which two super-powers were eyeball-to-eyeball, . . . a world in which taking risks was proof of one's manliness and therefore of one's qualification to govern.' Enloe concludes, 'To accept the Cold War interpretation of living in a "dangerous" world also confirms the segregation of politics into national and international' (pp. 12–13). As we have seen in chapter 1, 'danger' is not only confirmatory but also constitutive of the nation and of nationalism.

The International Divide

If the close of the First World War had seen the emergence of a significant challenge to capitalism in the shape of the Soviet Union, at the close of the Second World War China posed a similar challenge. Its leaders were able to harness the power of nationalism to the cause of socialism. On 1 October 1949 China declared itself to be a 'People's Republic'. While the new regime tried to hold on to the politics of alliances based on nationalism through its commitment to 'New Democracy', it soon became clear that it would not be able to stand back from the growing fissures on the international scene between the two superpowers. China joined the socialist camp with its Treaty of Friendship with the Soviet Union. However, as events unfolded, it became clear that the socialist camp was not a homogeneous group of countries (Christiansen and Rai, 1996: ch. 2). By the 1960s China came to symbolize an alternative model of development – alternative to both capitalism and Soviet-style socialism. Mao's rhetoric at this time 'resonate[s] with contemporary notions of alternative development which are also very pertinent to the questions of women's emancipation' (Prazniak, 1997: 24). It is interesting, however, that this alternative model of development is absent from the debates about development that became increasingly important in the post-war period, especially within the UN system. One reason, perhaps, was the absence of socialist China from international fora; Taiwan (Republic of China) took the 'Chinese' seat in the Security Council of the United Nations. A second reason for a refusal to engage with the Chinese model of development was its challenge – in terms of both rhetoric and politics – to both capitalist models of development and the Soviet-style centralized model. As an international pariah, China and its leadership were not taken seriously by either camp in the Cold War-dominated world.

The challenge of socialism was real for western capitalist states. The (in)famous 'Domino Theory' was the political articulation of this perceived threat, while at the economic level there was a recognition that the question of poverty would have to be tackled in response to this challenge. The Labour victory in the UK in 1945 and the Marshall Plan were also clear signals of the aspirations of the people in the post-war new world order, on the one hand, and the serious competition for influence to shape that world, on the other. Through the 1950s, as the post-colonial world took shape, political alliances were based on the growing clash of ideologies. Revolutionary movements were automatically seen as potential allies of the Soviet

Union. As the case of Cuba shows, destabilization of post-colonial revolutionary leaderships became the focus of US international politics, while ensuring their survival became the task of the Soviet government. Aid packages and trade regimes were often tied to perceived security concerns, making the attempts of the newly emerging nation-states to articulate their development plans contingent upon international politics. This state of affairs continued until 1991,[3] when the Soviet Union imploded, and with it also collapsed its satellite states in Eastern Europe.

The ideological divide and the resulting security concerns led to different outcomes, reflected in the institutionalization of the international economic and financial regimes. The Bretton Woods Conference was held in 1944, as the first phase of decolonization was about to begin with the independence of India in 1947. It resulted in the establishment of the two institutions that have played a central role in crafting development agendas in direct and indirect ways: the World Bank and the International Monetary Fund (IMF). These institutions were set up to promote stable exchange rates, foster the growth of world trade and facilitate international movements of capital. Their concern was to avoid the shortcomings of the pre-war international economic system, such as protectionism and competitive devaluations through the regulation of international financial markets. In the post-war period, the development focus of these institutions remained Europe and Japan. Their voting systems gave clear control to the larger contributors – the western industrialized countries – thus marginalizing the emerging post-colonial nations. India's forthcoming independence was recognized, but, like the other Latin American countries, its presence was marginal, and its voice largely ignored (South Commission, 1990: 27). The Bretton Woods system was as much a response to the failures of the past as to the challenges of the present. The western capitalist nations came together in an unprecedented way in order to counter the claims of socialism and of the Soviet bloc countries. For the Soviet Union, the concerns of security were no less relevant than for the western bloc. While it advocated a break with the capitalist system, a look at its policies during the 1950s and 1960s show how flexibly this break was interpreted. India, Tanzania, Egypt, all got the support of the Soviet Union despite the varying political rhetoric of their elites. The

---

3 Thus, even in the 1980s, Crush points out, 'Chief Mangosuthu (Gatsha) Buthelezi of the Inkatha Freedom Party was usually far more welcome than the [African National Congress] in Western capitals. He, at least, spoke "the right language"' (1995: xi).

focus of Soviet aid policies was a country's distance from the USA. Within the socialist bloc, however, the Soviet Union wanted higher levels of conformity, and the failure to do so resulted in attempts at destabilization, and the withdrawal of aid, as shown by the examples of Yugoslavia, China and Albania (Christiansen and Rai, 1996: ch. 7).

In sum, the Cold War between the two superpowers, and the two ideological configurations, had a direct impact on the alternatives that post-colonial elites felt able to consider and pursue. As we shall see below, these alternatives were embedded in deeply gendered understandings of development that focused on a masculine sphere of work, without acknowledging the important contribution to the national economy of informal and private spheres where women's labour predominated. However, there were also some similarities between the two sides in their approaches to development. First, both believed that development was a purposeful project – with 'resources, techniques and expertise...brought together to bring about improved rates of economic growth' (Kabeer, 1994: 69). Economic growth was the target of both ideologies, and development agendas were geared to increasing its levels. There is a linearity that marks both types of development processes too.[4] For the socialists, development would accrue when a country moved from a capitalist form to a socialist form of social relations, from the anarchy of the market to the certainty of planning. For the liberals, development would occur when human and physical resources developed through the force of rational individualism and the development of market-regulated competition. Second, for both, economic growth was tied to industrialization and urbanization of economies and societies. Whether the policies were of state planning and nationalizing, import substitution or export-led growth, it was accepted that only industrialized countries are developed. Mechanization of agriculture, the building of dams and a general valorization of science were common to both ideological camps. Both liberal and Marxist theories have in common elements of a reductionist methodology, with its determinate outcomes, its linearity, and hierarchies of knowledges leading to constructions of regimes of Truth. All these features, together with the political systems and ideologies arising out of this rationalizing discourse on development, had consequences

---

4 To quote Nehru, 'Some Hindus talk of going back to the Vedas; some Muslims dream of an Islamic theocracy. Idle fantasies, for there is no going back to the past.... There is only one-way traffic in Time. India must therefore lessen her religiosity and turn to science' (1990: 391).

for the relations of power within the newly emerging nations – especially relations between men and women, and between marginalized communities and the dominant groups. This is not to suggest that the differences between the two ideological frameworks were cosmetic. However, the similarities in the two approaches did create an international consensus around what development meant, even though the route by which this definition was arrived at was ideologically specific. Development became a metanarrative, and at the same time a particular stage of economic viability.

Together with the emergence of two ideological camps in the period of the Cold War, there also emerged 'Three Worlds'. The polarized worlds of the western and the Soviet blocs were called the First and Second worlds, and the non-aligned countries trying to chart their own models of development, such as India and Tanzania, and later Yugoslavia, were the Third World. These latter countries came together for the first time at the Bandung Conference in 1955 to assert their identity, and to propose what we might today call a Third Way between capitalist and Marxist development models. The name Group of 77 also described these states at the time of the setting up of the UN Conference on Trade and Development (UNCTAD) in 1964. However, the unity between these countries could not be maintained for long as pressures of ethnic, religious and cultural historical divisions led to conflict. Increasingly, in the 1970s, the term 'Third World' came to mark post-coloniality, and also economic position within the world-system. GNP per head became the determinant of which of the Three Worlds a country belonged to, with the lowest GNP per capita economies placed in the Third World category. What the countries belonging to this category shared, then, was a history of colonial exploitation that allowed them to identify with each other. However, different colonial histories and processes of decolonization also led to fracturing of a sense of solidarity among these nations.[5]

---

5 I use the term 'Third World', as well as the more recently crafted term 'South', to denote post-colonial and poor countries of the world. This is as much to indicate their economic position as to acknowledge their evolving histories. Naming of groups is never an unproblematic process – it conceals as much as it reveals. It is purely a political position that I use the term 'Third World', and an acknowledgement of changes following the collapse of the Second World that I use the term 'South'. It has also been argued that neither term reveals the 'worlds within' these categorizations – that first and third worlds exist within the Third World/South (Mohanty, Russo and Torres, 1991; Thomas and Wilkin, 1997; Hoogvelt, 2001).

Development and Its Critics

While philosophically and methodologically the two conflicting ideologies of liberalism and Marxism had a common root in the traditions of the Enlightenment, the differences that marked the two were fundamental. The issue at the heart of their struggle was an understanding, acceptance and maintenance of certain power relations in society. When these ideological and political frameworks came to bear upon development discourses, theory and practice, radical differences appeared in the languages employed to identify, catalogue, describe and prioritize the assumptions, strategies and frames of development. While an emphasis on the *discourse* of development is recent in development studies (Crush, 1995; Escobar, 1995a; Cowen and Shenton, 1995), Berger (1976) referred to the differences in the terminology of development as 'clue concepts' that can be used to determine the ideological underpinnings of development frameworks. Whereas surplus, class, dependency, imperialism, neo-colonialism and modes of production, for example, characterized the writings of the Marxists, modernization, efficiency, integration and nation-building were the liberal key concepts. In the capitalist world, development took shape as liberalism.

The first UN Decade of Development (1970–80) saw an emphasis on two sets of initiatives by the United Nations and First World countries. The first was aid, which was tied to the expansion of markets, and supporting export-oriented economic projects within the poor countries. International market rationality was at the heart of aid projects in this context. Technical training, capital-intensive investments, mechanization of agriculture, building of communications infrastructures, formed the list of priorities.[6] The impact of these policies would be, the story went, the 'trickle-down' effect of development. So Paul Hoffman, Managing Director of the United Nations Special Fund and the fourth President of the Society of International Development, wrote in 1959:

> Poor people are bad customers. As these countries produce more they trade more, and in the process we all gain.... My optimism is based ...on the belief than underdeveloped countries are just that – underdeveloped, not (or only in few cases) inherently poor. They are

6 For an analysis of the way in which cotton-based mono-cultural economic development was encouraged in Egypt by both US and Soviet aid, and, despite some land reforms and state help to farmers, led to increased dependency of the country on both the western and eastern blocs, see Toth (1980: 127–47).

underdeveloped because their resources, both physical and human, are not being used to anything approaching their full potentialities. (1997: 22)

The second set of initiatives resulted from a welfare agenda in the context of crises – aid to tide over Third World countries coping with natural disasters, famine or wars; to ameliorate the worst of the hunger and disease that made Third World countries poor participants in the international economy (Burnell, 1997).

In the first UN Decade of Development, the major international institutions of development took shape within the liberal capitalist framework. Further, these institutions worked within the framework of diffusion politics – in effect the task was to tie the Third World nations into international capitalist trade regimes. The promise was that the 'trickle-down effect' that sustained growth in the metropolitan economies would be duplicated in the 'developing world'. Aid became an important means for this process of integration.[7] Building of economic infrastructure in Third World countries and direct capitalist investment were other planks of this modernization model of development.

Women in Development

In the debates on development in the first Decade, women became visible as a group only in specific contexts. This is evident in the ways in which the growing body of UN Conventions focused on the liberal welfare conception of women's rights. Thus, the UN Conventions of particular concern to women during this period were the 1949 Convention for the Suppression of Traffic in Persons and the Exploitation of Prostitution of Others; the 1951 Equal Remuneration for Men and Women Workers for Work of Equal Value; and the 1952 Convention on the Political Rights of Women (Wallace with March, 1991: 1). As far as development strategies were concerned, women appeared most prominently in debates on population control. They were the 'targets' of most population control programmes sponsored by national and international agencies. Their education

---

7 Bayart points out that in Africa aid fuelled the corruption within the state and its elites. Considerable amounts of aid were channelled through private interests, and state-imposed duties on even humanitarian aid were used to increase the revenue of the state. The one exception to such corruption was Tanzania under Nyerere (Bayart, 1993: 79–81).

became an issue also in this context, as did their health needs. In most other respects, women, like other marginalized groups, were aggregated with 'the people' of the Third World. Their visibility in some contexts was not accidental – constructed gender relations framed them; they were primary workers in the reproduction of labour, and as such important to the ways in which they fitted in with the nationalist and international agendas for population control (Davin, 1992). However, there was on most questions an assumption of sameness between men and women that rendered the latter invisible in the political discourses of the time. Given what I have argued in the first chapter – the close relationship between the articulation of nationalist aspirations and the structurings of gender relations – this invisibility might seem predictable. The metanarratives of the Nation and nationalism articulated through political elites rested upon normalizing the aspirations of the dominant classes and elites. In chapter 1 I briefly discussed why nationalist women found it difficult to resist the nationalist discourses on development during the struggles for independence. In the next section I expand on the dilemmas that faced women as post-colonial development agendas took shape.

Hopes and Hierarchies of Development

One can identify several reasons for the absence of women's agendas at this stage of national development and international policy-making. First, women, too, were living in an age of hope. Nationalist successes, after the processes of decolonization, demanded forbearance. The defeat of imperialism and regaining of sovereignty conjured up vistas of 'progress', but also realistic assessments of the developmental tasks ahead. Most Third World countries inherited huge problems of economic and political chaos, in some countries of infrastructural devastation. Reconstruction was the primary task at hand, and the hopes of most marginalized groups were tied to this overarching project. The language of development encompassed men and women alike. Constraints on national economies were painfully evident – illiteracy, traditional cultural practices, mass poverty in most cases, and economic 'underdevelopment'. To bring down the entire edifice at one time could lead to political instability. As Nyerere cautioned the Tanzanian socialists: '... the amount of cultural change required should not be greater than they [the people] can accommodate' (1973: 3) – prioritization of the most urgent tasks seemed sensible as a strategy for development.[8] Second, in most Third World countries, this hope was based upon some immediate benefits accruing to women, in the shape of political citizenship. To be enfranchised and therefore be able to participate in the reshaping of a country's political system and future agendas was enormously empowering. Political citizenship did not necessarily mean that civic and social citizenship rights accrued to women and men equally (see chapter 1). Neither did it focus attention of women's labour – in the home and in the workplace. However, political rights could form the basis of real claims upon the state.

Of course, the language of rights was not employed in similar fashion by all post-colonial states. In state socialist countries, such as China, the focus remained on redistribution of economic resources, on the one hand, and on opportunities of employment for both men and women, on the other. While political rights were not emphasized for either men or women, state planning and control of resources meant real changes in the ways women were situated within social and economic spheres. Land redistribution in China, for example, meant that women were allocated land in their own right for the first time. Further, the Marxist analysis of the 'woman question' meant a commitment to women's employment, resulting in public provision of education, health and child-care facilities so that women could become economic actors (Rai, Pilkington and Phizacklea, 1992). The quality of these facilities was generally poor, however, and the system of job allocation by the state meant that women were often placed in traditionally acceptable roles as schoolteachers, nurses and industrial workers in light industry (Rai, 1991: ch. 6). While in agricultural communes, all members – men and women – earned work-points and were paid accordingly, for the first time disaggregating the income of women from the 'family income', work roles were gendered and women's work paid lower rates (Wolfe, 1985). The early acceptance of dominant gender roles, which I discussed in chapter 1, now came to bear upon post-revolutionary opportunities for women. An added issue for women was the lack of political space in which to organize their own varied interests (Croll, 1978; Johnson, 1983; Wolfe, 1985). In the first phase of national reconstruction in China, women thus formed part of the army of labour, but on terms that retained, despite the egalitarian political rhetoric, a gendered hierarchy supported by the state. Nevertheless, in the first flush of independence from imperialist rule, the gains seemed to far outweigh the problems for most women, even though

8 See also chapter 1, fn. 20 on Mao.

sceptical voices, such as the author Ding Ling, were heard very early on (see Evans, 1997).

In liberal states political rights premised on enabling individuals to become active in the public sphere limited themselves to equal opportunity discourses, which did enable some women to enter the world of public employment. In Kenya, for example, African socialism was defined to assert 'that community, because it was natural and therefore amenable to another form of content, should become a necessary part of capitalist development' (Cowen and Shenton, 1995: 317). While capitalist relations would allow both women and men access to the sites of production, the idea of 'the community' could be seen as the stabilizing influence within the new economic regime. The focus of the liberal discourse on individual freedom and equal access meant that men and women were made responsible for their success in taking advantage of opportunities provided by the capitalist market regimes and party-based democratic systems. In the words of Bibi Titi, a woman political leader in Tanzania, 'I am not satisfied to see you, my friends in East Africa, not playing any part in the government or in the political parties. This is your own fault; you are not joining parties' (cited in Geiger, 1997: 180). The role of the state, in this context, remained important in laying down the infrastructure that might make such enablement possible – education, training and most important political rights fell into this category.[9] This was especially so in the first phase of post-colonial development.

In this context, some states consciously modified the individualist ethic of liberalism to accommodate what were seen as historical social and cultural discriminations by creating separate regimes of enablement for different groups. There was an acknowledgement, for example, in India that the caste system among the predominant

9 The post-colonial states' role in stabilizing social relations through law also formed an important part of this infrastructure-building. 'Upon independence the Zimbabwean Government adopted a law reform strategy aimed at gender and race neutralization through substantive, procedural and institutional legal unification' (Hellum, 1993: 258). This neutralization reflected attempts both to create a new African moral community as part of the ideology of African socialism, and to build on the traditions of traditional African community-based culture. The state's role was set up as an arbiter between the old and the new moral communities in many African states, such as Kenya. The state rewarded efforts and punished 'those who refuse to participate in the nation's efforts to grow. "Sending needed capital abroad, allowing land to lie idle and ... misusing the nation's limited resources ... are examples of anti-social behaviour that African socialism will not countenance"' (Cowen and Shenton, 1995: 326).

Hindu community meant that the lowest castes or outcasts had been systematically discriminated against. In order for this group of Indian citizens to take advantage of the new opportunities of either the free market or of political independence, it would need special provision in terms of protected access to public life. Some, though less systematic, special provision was also made on the grounds of culture and religion. Muslim personal law was left untouched by the reformist state (see chapter 1), and certain restrictions were placed on the federal state in its dealings with the government of Jammu and Kashmir – the only Muslim majority state in India. Individual right to buying property was also curtailed in this context – people residing outside the state could not acquire land there. The point here is that individualism, though the predominant feature of the liberal discourse, was interpreted and tailored to the articulated development needs of post-colonial elites. For women, liberal regimes posed different issues. In countries where women had been active and visible during the national movements, political citizenship became a starting point for waging other struggles, despite the fact that they, too, were faced with the dilemmas posed by the politics of prioritization. In countries where the process of decolonization had been dominantly either a male or elite affair, women's political rights reflected their marginalized position.[10]

National Identities, Orientalism and the World System

Another reason why women continued to assent to the forming of overarching national agendas was their growing disquiet about the place they occupied in the 'world-system' as citizens of post-colonial nations. I have already commented on the marginality of Third World states to the refashioning of the liberal post-war world. This marginality was institutionalized through the Bretton Woods system, in particular as the World Bank and the International Monetary Fund became more important in policy-making, as well as through aid regimes. Together with this marginality within the international capitalist system, the discourse of modernity affected the

---

10 For a discussion of the position of women in law in Pakistan, see Ali (2000). She points out that the Islamization of the law in Pakistan posed a dilemma for the state. As the Shariat law gives the right to property to Muslim women, this was 'contrary to the interests of the landlord-dominated [legislative] assembly, which ventured to delay its adoption'. Women were able to invoke Islam in this debate, while the state struggled with maintaining the dominant property relations in the region of Punjab (pp. 43–4).

relations between the Third and the First worlds. One of the strengths of the rhetoric of liberal democracy is the language of equality. To be identified as powerless or excluded creates a sense of inferiority that is unpalatable. While the nationalist movements of many Third World states had created an optimism based on the discourse of equality, and these states sought to join the community of nation-states as equal members, the language of development and modernization ensured that they were constantly characterized as 'underdeveloped', 'undeveloped' and essentially a 'problem' that needed addressing and managing. This language built upon and fed the cultural constructions of the colonial world, which have been analysed in the work of Edward Said as 'Orientalism' (1978). Women occupied a central though particular place within this discourse (Spivak, 1988; Enloe, 1989; Mohanty, 1991; Liddle and Rai, 1998). They were the victims of barbaric cultures as well as their markers. The social relations that enmeshed them were barbaric, and therefore threatening to the civilized world. The problem of the Orientalist discourses is not simply of essentializing, dichotomizing cultures as old and new, traditional and modern, but also one of invention. As Staudt has pointed out, 'British colonial officials in Africa sought to establish the principles of "customary law" from what was in reality a very fluid complex of indigenous legal systems. They turned to male elders, who contrived a "blend of tradition and wishful thinking" for the Native Courts that were established' (1991: 46–7; also see Hobsbawm and Ranger, 1983, and Liddle and Joshi, 1986). Further, the overpowering imagery of colonial/Third World woman as oppressed through segregation, early marriages, denial of education, and constantly under pressure to produce children was homogenized across cultures and national boundaries, and even continents. As Staudt asks: 'And how frequent is marriage? In Cameroon, more than a third opt against it' (1991: 47).

These Orientalist constructions of the Third World influenced the ways in which development agencies included women in their formulation of the problem – rescue of hapless women – and the solution – enabling women so that they could escape the traditional roles imposed on them. Women were 'objects that need[ed] help, not subjects who could be active participants in the development process' (Chowdhry, 1995: 33). This construction of cultures and of Oriental women was then infused within the development discourses. For Third World women this posed significant problems of identity and struggles. On the one hand, they were faced with making difficult choices within national boundaries in terms of pressing their claims upon the national states. On the other, they did not want to be seen to be participating in any validation of the Orientalist and racist discourses that were part of the development policies and regimes. The 'codes of silence' that Crenshaw (1993) has written about in the context of black women's choices in the USA also operated in the worlds of Third World women. The nationalist elites in most cases brought up the question of national cultures under threat, and of women as representatives of authenticity of these cultures, in order to secure political support and stability within their borders and to resist pressures from international organizations such as the UN and international Conventions such as the Convention for the Elimination of All Forms of Discrimination Against Women (CEDAW) (see Ali, 2000).[11] The question of culture often also became one of national loyalty – to insist upon recognition of women's oppression within the patriarchal organizations of the nation-state was unreasonable, and even undermining of national stability. For western development agencies, which were either oblivious of these dilemmas, or chose to ignore them, women's silence on issues of cultural practices reinforced the Orientalist imagery of oppressed women waiting to be rescued through new development initiatives.

As Moser (1993) has categorized it, the first initiatives of international development agencies aimed at women, particularly the World Bank, were welfarist in nature. This is not surprising, given the political and ideological biases of the Bank and the aid community. This approach was 'premised on the assumption of women as "others" performing childrearing tasks, [and] identified women solely in their reproductive roles' (Chowdhry, 1995: 32). Programmes of birth control, and nutrition projects for women and children and for pregnant and lactating mothers were the focus of aid programmes. Huge populations that eroded the benefits of growth, rather than the patterns of ownership and control of means of production, were thus considered to be the problem.[12] Despite

---

11 Amartya Sen has argued in *Development as Freedom* that 'in the freedom-oriented perspective the liberty of all to participate in deciding what traditions to observe cannot be ruled out by the national or local "guardians"...nor by political rulers...nor by cultural "experts"...' (1999: 32). The discussion about codes of silence, however, points to the structural framework of racism, anti-Semitism or ethnic dominance within which communities operate, and therefore suggests that a conception of individual-based freedom is unable to address some of the issues of participation and agency in the public political sphere.

12 For a critique of the Ehrlich equation $I = PAT$ (where I is impact of any human group on the environment, P is population, A is affluence and T is technology), see Hartmann (1997: 293–302). Hartmann argues that the 'main

significant changes in this approach by the Bank, 'ten of the eleven [projects] approved in fiscal 1989 . . . addressed such basic matters as family planning . . . and maternal and child health care' (World Bank, 1990b: 15). Patriarchal and liberal discourses, at both nationalist and international level, left unchallenged the question of gender relations in society, and often made these attendant upon a sexual division of labour and individual negotiation within the family. The welfarist approach remained dominant in the first phase of development practices.

Challenging the Growth Agenda

While the liberal paradigm was predominant within the capitalist world during the 1960s, this predominance was continually challenged both by internal liberal critics and by the alternative development model of state socialism. After the optimism of the 1960s, the 1970s saw the western capitalist economies slow down considerably. The oil and debt crises led to intensive dialogues between western and Third World states, and emphasized the interdependence of economies and states within the world-system. The oil crisis also focused attention on the issue of consumption of non-renewable natural resources, and the UN World Food Conference in 1974 focused the need to address the question of food production rather than the production of tradable cash-crops. Development programmes based on the needs of small farmers were discussed, and in this context attention was paid to health and education programmes for all, including women. The old certainties of the 1960s were no longer sufficient to address the fact that violence, hunger and poverty were showing no sign of abating in the Third World. The spectre of social revolution seemed real in many parts of the world, and for the western alliance, security once again became a live issue. Considerations of international politics thus combined with challenges to the modernization paradigm to produce a shift in thinking about development.

The challenge to the liberal western agendas of development continued to develop during the 1970s and 1980s from three different quarters. The first was from within the liberal framework. The International Labour Organization initiated the work on the basic needs

---

problem with the equation . . . is what it leaves out, namely the question of social, economic and political power, . . . [which] underlie P, A, and T, and the interaction between them' (p. 295).

approach to development, which sought to shift the focus of development from growth to fulfilment of basic human needs. This concern was further developed in the 1980s by Amartya Sen in his work on poverty and the concept of human entitlements and capabilities, (1987a; see also Nussbaum and Sen, 1993). During the 1980s there also emerged the discourse of sustainable development (see below). This became the particular concern of ecologists, ecofeminists and environmentalists addressing questions of degradation of the earth's resources because of the unreflective march of economic development. Also within the liberal framework, the women in development (WID) approach was first articulated during the 1970s and became a starting point for serious feminist engagements with development as discourse and as practice. The second source of challenge, from Marxism, emerged from two different sources – from alternative models of state-led development, especially in China but also in Cuba, and from Marxist theorists who focused on the role of the post-colonial state in development. The latter were successful in locating the post-colonial state as a major economic actor in the Third World countries, and in stressing the importance of self-reliant development (Amin, 1976; Alavi et al., 1982; Sen, 1982). The politics of state institutionalization and localized class struggles in international contexts was the focus of this challenge. Marxist feminists critiqued and contributed to these debates. Another source of challenge came from post-structuralist critics, who in the 1980s engaged in a sustained questioning of development as a narrative of progress, and as an achievable enterprise.

In the following pages, I examine the impact of these critiques on the state of the discipline and on development strategies at the national and the international levels.

Access and Enablement: The First Critiques

The optimism that characterized development regimes in the 1960s was not universally shared. The Swedish economist Gunnar Myrdal, writing in 1963, warned: 'Without a radical change in policies in both these groups of countries [the rich and the poor], the world is headed for an economic and political cataclysm, even though nobody can foresee the exact nature of what would then happen' (1997: 27). Myrdal identified several issues that he thought important for addressing the growing gap between the rich and the poor countries: an 'ominous population trend'; low productivity of the workforce, 60–80 per cent of whom were engaged in agriculture;

widespread illiteracy; lack of capital; and finally the fact that '[m]ost of the underdeveloped countries have inherited an inegalitarian social and economic order that is difficult to break down, but which must be removed in order to clear the desk for efforts to economic progress' (p. 27). How this inegalitarian order could be removed was less clear. Myrdal's hopes were pinned on 'assistance from the rich countries' through aid and credit. Though the concern for the poverty and hunger prevalent in the Third World was clearly driving this reformist agenda, it is also clear that this liberal concern was not challenging the basic paradigm of capitalist development. Indeed, population control, education, liberalizing trade regimes and encouraging imports, which were endorsed by Myrdal in his assessment, were the planks of development policies of the first UN Decade of Development. While identifying the issue of inegalitarian political and economic vested interests, this liberal analysis said little about *how* this change might come about other than through shifts in the policy-making agenda through elite institutional lobbying. The declaration of the first Decade of Development did not mention women specifically. However, in 1962 the UN General Assembly asked the Commission on Women's Status to prepare a report on the role of women in development. It was only in 1974, four years after its original publication, that Boserup's pathbreaking study on *Woman's Role in Economic Development* was 'discovered' when the Society for International Development's Women in Development group put together the first bibliography on WID (Boserup, 1989; Tinker, 1997: 34).

The work of Ester Boserup was a liberal feminist challenge to the early patterns of modernization as development – it was a combined argument for equality and efficiency and therefore a powerful political statement in the interests of women. Boserup argued that women's status varies with the nature of productive activity and their involvement in it. She argued that women are marginalized in the economy because they gain less than men in their roles as wage workers, farmers and traders. Focusing on rural production, Boserup contended that mechanization of agriculture, generally equated with economic development, has resulted in the separation of women's labour from what is characterized as agricultural labour, which in turn undermines their social status. She pointed to shifting agriculture and irrigated agriculture as economic regimes where women's participation in production as well as their social status was high. Tinker (1997) reinforced Boserup's analysis by suggesting that because western aid agencies exported gender stereotypes, modernization of agriculture led to the widening of the gap between men and women in economic and social terms. Whyte and Whyte (1982) reached similar conclusions, while at the same time citing 'culture' as a mitigating factor. So, while a system of irrigated agriculture in Thailand could mean an improved status for women, the presence of Islam mediates this form of agriculture in Bangladesh to give women a low social status. However, the key to women's social status remains their participation in agricultural production, which is largely calculated through empirical data.[13] Rogers (1982), writing a decade after Boserup, made a similar analysis of women's work and social status, but also emphasized the importance of women to the development process itself; it was not only women who would benefit from expansion of opportunity, but the development process itself would better achieve its targets by virtue of their participation. This was an appeal to efficiency as much as to a better deal for women. This analysis became the basis upon which the women in development agenda was crafted. The project was to ensure that the benefits of modernization accrued to women as well as to men in the Third World.

WID's focus on access – which was in line with its liberal theoretical approach – led to an under-emphasis on the social and political structures within which women were located and acted. As Beneria and Sen have argued, Boserup presumed that 'modernization is both beneficial and inevitable in the specific form it has taken in most Third World countries.... [S]he tends to ignore processes of capital accumulation set in motion during the colonial period, and...does not systematically analyse the different effects of capital accumulation on women of different classes' (1997: 45). As such, Boserup not only did not take into account the stratification of women along the lines of class, but also could not build into her analysis the negative impact of capitalist accumulation regimes on women as well as on men. Thus, Boserup's analysis could not hold in tension, on the one hand, the subversive aspects of capitalist modernization as it broke down traditional social relations and, on the other, the new forms of subordination created by it.[14] What Boserup and other WID scholars offered in terms of policy insights were the oft-repeated prescriptions regarding improving women's standards of education and

---

13   This standpoint has recently been endorsed by Amartya Sen in his work on gender and poverty (Drèze and Sen, 1989: 56–61; Sen, 1995).

14   For an alternative view that makes regimes of accumulation central to the analysis of women's work, and women's social status crucial to the workings of the capitalist regimes of production and accumulation, see Maria Mies's study of the lace makers of Narsapur (1982).

skills so that they might compete more vigorously with men in the labour market. The individual, rather than social categories, was the focus of such analysis; the privileging of the male productive norm – in which women, in this analysis, need to participate – led to a 'truncated understanding of [women's] lives' (Kabeer, 1994: 30). By 1980 feminist scholars were already criticizing this access-based framework. In Britain, the Subordination of Women collective argued for a comparative approach to issues of gender relations, rather than the assumption of 'women's interests'. It also questioned the eliding of gender issues with the practice of development agencies (Pearson and Jackson, 1998: 2).

Despite all its problems, however, the WID theorists' work made an important correlation between work and status, which had thus far been ignored by the development agencies and governments in the West. This analysis also resonated with the attempts of liberal nation-states like India to address the persistent gender gap in their societies by focusing on issues of access and equal opportunities as means of improving women's social status.

Meeting Needs, Developing Capabilities, Sustaining Development

The basic needs (BN) approach, which, as has been noted, was first articulated in the 1970s, was an important contribution to the debates on development. It queried the focus on growth and income as indicators of development. Methodologically, it challenged the dichotomous relationship between means and ends. It put forward the idea that poverty is not an 'end' that can be eradicated by the 'means' of a higher income (Kabeer, 1994: 138–40). BN theory thus built on the analysis that the liberal 'trickle-down' approach to development had not resulted in a reduction of poverty and unemployment. In 1969 the International Labour Organization (ILO) launched the World Employment Programme to address this issue. The assumption was that employment is the route out of the poverty trap.[15] However, at the World Employment Conference of 1976, the ILO had come to the view that 'creation of more and better jobs is not enough; employment issues are intimately connected to the

15 Such a starting point obviously had important consequences for the debates on the 'status of women'. The example of women in the socialist state was by this time no longer valorized – the problems of the 'double day' of women had already been theorized by socialist feminist scholars (see Molyneux, 1979; Treiman and Hartmann, 1981).

wider issues of poverty and inequality, and it is in this context that they need to be examined' (1977: 31). It was at this conference that the ILO proposed that *'development planning should include, as an explicit goal, the satisfaction of an absolute level of basic needs'* (p. 31, emphasis in the original).

It was argued by BN theorists that poverty is an indication of the inability of people to meet their basic needs. These needs are both physical – minimum levels of calorie consumption, for example – and intangible – what Sen (1987b) was to call 'agency achievements' – of participation, empowerment and community life. Thus, it was argued, development economics, in emphasizing the quantity of life (longevity) and neglecting the quality of the lives led, was found to be wanting (Crocker, 1995: 156). The BN theorists thus rejected the division between growth policies and income distribution policies: '...the problem of development must be defined as a selective attack on the worst forms of poverty.... We were taught to take care of the GNP as this will take care of poverty. Let us reverse this and take care of poverty as this will take care of the GNP,' argued Mahbub Ul Haq, the Chief Economist of Pakistan's Planning Commission, and later the head of the United Nations Development Programme (1997: 60). In 1977 the ILO looked to the year 2000 'as a target date by which the most essential basic needs should be met in all societies' (Grant, 1977: vii). However, as the ILO's own analysis showed, this target could be met only if two conditions were present: first, in every region except Asia, largely because of China, the share of the poorest 20 per cent of households would have to more than double, and in Africa it would have to treble; second, 'in every region except the medium-income countries of Latin America, the extent of redistribution that would be required would be such that social changes of this order of magnitude are unlikely to occur' (ILO, 1977: 43).

The BN approach shifted the attention of development agencies from actual or potential income earners. By making its focus the needs of all members – children, old people, the sick, the orphaned, the disabled, as well as workers and future generations – the approach posed a real challenge to the modernization orthodoxies. Upon this view, basic needs included two elements: first 'they include certain minimum requirements of a family for private consumption: adequate food, shelter and clothing are obviously included, as would be certain household equipment and furniture'; second, 'they include essential services provided by and for the community at large, such as safe drinking water, sanitation, public transport, and health and educational facilities' (ILO, 1977: 32). The family and the state were, then, the focus of BN theorists' attention. However, while this allowed for a context-bound analysis of labour issues, it was in itself embedded in a gender ideology that did not unpack the relations of power obtaining within families. Women's work, too, remained on the margins of ILO analysis, as attention remained on the welfare agenda of protecting women's health when they were at work. The ILO's approach was broadly supported by the reports of the Club of Rome (Tinberger, 1976) and the dialogues between the Third and First World countries at the UN World Food Conference, which focused on rural employment, improved food distribution and reduction of poverty. Finally, the BN approach focused on people's participation in development; people need to participate in making the decisions that affect their lives. 'Participation interacts with the two main elements of basic-needs strategy. For example, education and good health will facilitate participation, and participation in turn will strengthen the claim for the material basic needs' (ILO, 1977: 32). Linked to the idea of participatory development was the still broader framework of basic human rights, 'which are not only ends in themselves but also contribute to the attainment of other goals' (p. 32). As we shall see below, BN theory has revived in contemporary debates on human capabilities, and found reflection in the Human Development Index of the United Nations Development Programme through the work of Amartya Sen and Martha Nussbaum. In particular, this extension of BN has been used to examine not only quantitative data on employment, but also the quality of life issues attached to employment as well as the rights of women to the development of their basic capabilities (Nussbaum, 1999).[16]

Starting from a universalist concern defined as 'an elementary demand for impartiality – applied within generations and between them' (Anand and Sen, 1996: 3), Sen has argued that development means the enhancement of human achievements and capabilities: '... in analysing social justice, there is a strong case for judging individual advantage in terms of the capabilities that a person has, that is, the substantive freedoms he or she enjoys to lead the kind of life he or she has reason to value' (1999: 87). Upon this view, then, poverty is seen as 'capability deprivation', though it is also argued

16 Nussbaum makes a strong link between development, human rights and capabilities by arguing that '[t]he basic intuition from which the capability approach begins, in the political arena, is that human abilities exert a moral claim that they be developed' (1999: 236). For a discussion on women and human rights, see chapter 5.

that factors other than low income can result in such deprivation (p. 87). Equally important, the focus on individual freedom underlines the argument that 'preferences are not always reliable indicators of life quality, as they may be deformed in various ways by oppression and deprivation... [and that] resources have no value in themselves, apart from their role in promoting human functioning' (Nussbaum, 1995: 5).[17] Finally, Sen argues that there is a variable relation between low income and low capability among different communities, families and individuals. Public action can thus be an important means of altering this relation.[18] The fixation of development economics with opulence and GNP growth is therefore challenged through the focus on development of human capabilities. While Sen urges planners and the state to take account of what policies lead to an enhancing of human capabilities (Anand and Sen, 1996: 15), in focusing on increasing people's abilities to achieve, his theory also shows concern with 'the extent of the freedom that people have in pursuing valuable activities or functionings' (Drèze and Sen, 1989: 42). In making a distinction between 'commodity command and functioning ability,' the capability theory also addressed issues of concern to marginalized groups, such as the old, children or women: 'Women... have, in most societies, special disadvantages in achieving particular functionings. The roots of these problems can be social as well as physical, and the remedies sought have to take note of the nature of the constraints involved and extent to which they can be removed' (p. 44). Finally, the capability approach drew attention to the need to consider economic as well as non-economic inputs in determining functioning and capability: 'Nutritional achievements may be strongly influenced by the provision of a command over certain crucial non-food inputs such as health care, basic education...', which are as much dependent upon social mores as upon economic provision (p. 44). Building upon and extending this analysis, Nussbaum suggests that the following, when combined, are the central human functional capabilities essential for a human existence: life, bodily health and integrity, senses, imagination and thought, emotions, practical reason, affiliation, being able to live with other species, play, and control over one's

---

17 Kabeer (1999) has argued for the need for grounded analyses and to cross-check evidence on women's agency against outcomes of choices made or not made by women, in contrast to Sen's inference of agency from outcomes.

18 In sub-Saharan Africa, for example, the number of 'missing women' on grounds of mortality rates, under-nourishment and illiteracy is much less than in India and China (Sen, 1999: 99–107).

environment (1999: 235, 238). Nussbaum proceeds to use the idea of central human functional capabilities to argue for a cross-cultural (universal) understanding of women and equality that will not be undermined by specific traditional norms, but that is, at the same time, flexible enough to be translated into different cultural and social contexts.

Sen's work is important not only because of its sensitivity to gender relations, and as a critique of neo-liberal economics, but also because it attempts to move beyond an understanding of human needs and capabilities to a discussion of the required entitlements for the development of these capabilities. Following the work of feminist scholars such as Hannah Papanek, Sen challenges a 'culture'-based acceptance of women's entitlements, which, he argues, are internalized and reproduced as a culture of sacrifice. For Sen, the basic parameters of entitlements are 'endowment' (what is initially possessed) and 'exchange entitlements mapping' (which reflects the possible exchanges through production and trade). In terms of endowment, Sen makes the point that for the vast majority of people, it is their labour that is most important, and therefore the conditions of labour should be central to any analysis of entitlements. However, in Sen's recent writings (see Sen, 1995; 1999: 38–40) there is an extension of this concern with entitlements to include legal, political and human rights that govern the domain of freedom needed to maximize labour-based entitlements.[19]

Sharing, with BN, a perspective on needs also allowed human capability theorists to disaggregate household incomes and the different power positions of the various members of a household. Why were women and children showing greater deprivation as individuals and as members of groups than were men? The assumptions of altruistic family distribution of resources (Becker, 1981) could now be challenged.[20] Drèze and Sen argued that because of the limited access women have to the world of paid work, or control over family income and its distribution, their position within the family has been adversely affected. Indeed, the family was not, as

---

19 Sen argues that while these freedoms are instrumental to (means of) development, they are also an end of development, and therefore constitutive of it. The instrumental freedoms that Sen identifies as important to development are: political freedoms, economic facilities, social opportunities, transparency guarantees and protective security. These freedoms enhance individual capabilities, as well as support each other (Sen, 1999: 35–8).

20 As noted above, the ILO in the 1970s had assumed, in a rather unproblematic way, that the family would provide for the needs of its individual members.

Becker had delineated, an altruistic space of harmonious distribution of resources, but a deeply contested space where women suffered owing to the patriarchal social relations obtaining within the home and in the public sphere. The quality of life of women and girls within the family was therefore far worse, and more iniquitous, than Becker's altruistic model had recognized (Drèze and Sen, 1989: 56–61; Sen, 1999: 189–203). This analysis of the family followed feminist critiques of the family and the analysis of the way women negotiate spaces within it through making 'patriarchal bargains' (see Kandiyoti, 1988). The importance of such bargains, Sen suggests, is that an absolute increase in a family's resources (entitlements) brought about by the labour of the woman of the family will lead to the relative enhancement of the woman's share in these resources. Increased capabilities and quality of life of all groups of population, and a concern with intergenerational justice rather than increasing GNP, were the focus of this approach (Anand and Sen, 1996). By making the fulfilment of 'non-material' needs part of the development project, the BN approach also stressed the importance of the processes of development as well as the goals and outcomes. Participation of people in decision-making that affected their lives and self-management of development projects were an important part of the basic needs agenda. Focusing on participation also meant giving attention to the locale of people's lives – the context in which people were best able to participate were seen to be the local rather than the national stage. However, as Pearson and Jackson question, 'how do we conceptualise "gendered identities and subjectivities in a manner that avoids both essentialism and the unproblematic assumption of the self-determining individual"? Recovering a female subject risks essentialism; refusing a female subject risks erasing gender difference' (1998: 8).

Sustaining Development

Needs – economic and social, material and non-material – have also been the focus of later feminist critiques of development. Ecofeminist critiques have been wide-ranging, and have challenged both the policies of modernization and the paradigm of modernism. They have imbibed the sustainable development argument, but pushed it further to incorporate the relations between social and biological life, on the one hand, and the relations of power that structure these, on the other. Ecofeminism has an egalitarian basis that it shares with the ecology movement. It reasserts the 'age-old association' between women and nature (Merchant, 1980): 'It points to the exclusionary gender biases that are built into the new developments in biotechnology, which reveal the "anti-nature and colonial" dispossession of productive capacities held by women and inherent in nature' (Mies and Shiva, 1993: 16). It questions the trajectory of modern science and technology by making a strong link between patriarchy and arrogation of knowledge to science: 'It focuses on the costs of progress, the limits to growth, the deficiencies of technological decision making and the urgency of conservation...' (Merchant, 1980: xix). Its commitment to sustainable development is also a loyalty to future generations and to planet Earth, which is underpinned by women's nature and experience of being women (Diamond and Orenstein, 1990). Vandana Shiva (1989), in particular, has made direct links between colonialism and the degradation of the environment and of women's lives themselves in her work on the *Chipko* movement in India. She argued that when science was harnessed to the technology of war and trained against the societies that did not own such technology, Science waged war against Nature: 'Whenever women acted against ecological destruction or/and the threat of atomic annihilation, they immediately became aware of the connection between patriarchal violence against women, other people and nature...' (Mies and Shiva, 1993: 16). Thus, '[t]he "corporate and military warriors"' aggression against the environment was perceived almost physically as an aggression against our female body' (p. 16). Ecofeminism's anti-modernism provides a radical edge to its critique of growth. The alternative model of development that ecofeminists espouse is anti-patriarchal, decentralized, interdependent and sustainable (see Braidotti et al., 1994).[21]

The BN, human capability and ecofeminist theories all have an interest in sustainable development. The term became part of the alternative development discourse with the publication of the 1987 report of the World Commission on Economic Development (WCED), *Our Common Future*. It defined sustainable development as 'development that meets the needs of the present without compromising the ability of future generations to meet their own needs'

---

21 For a critique of Shiva's position on science and technology, see Nanda (1999), in which she argues that 'we should acknowledge the dismantling of scientific rationality into social and cultural discourses for what it is – a luxury that the supposedly "radical" critics of science, both in the West and in the Third World, have long indulged in.' She further argues that 'this genre of science-critique that insists on predicating the construction of all claims of objectivity of knowledge on power, gender identity or cultural discourses has succeeded in delegitimizing the very theoretical grounds for trans-cultural appropriation of modern scientific knowledge.'

(p. 43). It identified two key concepts – 'needs' and limits to growth – for sustaining environment's ability to meet future needs. In doing so it clearly built upon the BN discourse, but by focusing on the needs of future generations it also supported the ecological concerns of the long-term sustainability of our environment. Together with both BN and human capability theories, the debates about sustainability have sought to move the liberal debate on development forward from its concerns with growth. Together, these critiques have attempted to saturate the growth-oriented development discourses with concerns for justice and ethics, and to provide alternative ways of envisioning development.

The debates on sustainability have been a powerful challenge to the growth agenda. There is no doubt that these debates will become more influential in the years to come. Their attractions are manifold. First, they are challenges from within the liberal paradigm, even though they seek to shift fundamentally the parameters of the development discourse. In their concerns they are radical, but the means through which they seek change are familiar ones: persuasion; debate; policy activism of the state, of NGOs and of international bodies such as the UN. Second, in being challenges from within, they also speak in the language of feasible politics: NGOs can lobby; economists and philosophers can persuade; social movements can pressure and challenge dominant discourses. The attraction of feasibility is that it makes action possible for many in different political, cultural and social conditions. Third, perhaps the most attractive feature of these approaches is that they bring together the concerns and viewpoints of various social movements and positions on development. If there was an international hegemonic discourse built around economic development and its markers, then it is important that the challenging discourse has at least the potential for creating a counter-hegemonic consensus. By bringing together an array of important discourses under one umbrella of sustainability, this potential becomes visible.

However, while group-differentiated needs meant a disaggregation of requirements of development processes and outcomes, the disaggregated groups themselves remained relatively closed categories. So, for instance, women were one category while the disabled were another, without much regard to the overlaps between the two. In essentializing the relationship between women and nature, ecofeminism raises difficult questions for feminists and women activists (Agarwal, 1992; Nanda, 1999). Feminist scholars have also expressed a growing unease with the 'women, environment and development' (WED) articulation. They argue that 'it is the very separation

of women from the context of economic, social and political reproduction rather than their insertion into a notion of a sustainable future that differentiates a socially grounded feminist
analysis from a free floating "naturalistic" perspective which
equates women's realities with natural futures' (Pearson and Jackson, 1998: 9).[22]

Further, the focus of the sustainable development critiques, while
interrogating the growth agendas, has been limited in its challenge
to offering 'public action' for the provision of 'public goods' as an
alternative to the growing globalizing of market-led development.[23]
The sustainable development approach has remained tied to the
capitalist model, though the form that capitalism takes has been
brought into question. The politics of needs-based development was
one of liberal critique, of persuasion, of information and education
rather than any fundamental challenge to the prevailing social
relations. For example, in the late 1960s, the Chinese development
model, with its focus on labour-intensive, small-scale sustainable
industry, its emphasis on poverty elimination, primary education
and health, flexible but full employment, was often presented as a
way forward by BN theorists and practitioners. But these initiatives
were spoken of in parallel with a disregard of the challenge China
presented to the capitalist world. The Chinese development model
became depoliticized in a technical development debate about policy
choices: 'Of course, its political system, its isolation, its great size, its
ideological mobilization, all of these have contributed to the evolution of its pattern of development. But are there any lessons to learn,
even when we do not subscribe to its political system?' (Haq, 1997:
61; also see Anand and Sen, 1996).[24] A liberal view of politics has
remained at the heart of these powerful critiques of free-market
development strategies.

---

22 Consider here also the work of Agarwal (1997), who emphasizes gendered
interests in particular resources, such as land and land rights, and ecological
processes on the basis of the gendered division of labour, and argues for environmental concerns to be translated into the struggles against exclusions of
women from access to these resources.
23 For further discussion of public goods, see Kaul, Grunberg and Stern (1999)
and chapter 4.
24 It is not surprising, then, that now that the Chinese government has abandoned the socialist model of development, the Reports of the World Bank
(1999b, 2000) abound with references to the Chinese model of liberalization.
Also see Sen (1999: 41–3).

From Women to Gender: Feminist Analyses of Development

By the 1980s, not only had a women in development (WID) frame-work been critiqued by feminist scholars and activists, this critique had also led to a shift in focus from women to gender relations as the major concern. While some saw, and continue to see, this shift as depoliticizing and decentring the claims of women, gender and development (GAD) theorists have argued that a focus on the relation-ships that position women within society must be at the heart of political activity (see K. Young, 1997: 51–4). The major differences between WID and GAD theorists and activists can be broadly sketched out as illustrated in table 2.1.

A focus on the gender division of labour within the home and in waged work, access to and control over resources and benefits, ma-terial and social position of women and men in different contexts – all form part of the GAD perspective on development. Cynthia Enloe's work, for example, is a comprehensive exposition of the ways in which a whole series of international political economy issues, from debt servicing to the development of the tourist indus-try, are based upon particular positionings of women and men within patriarchal societies. She shows, for example, how national governments, international organizations, and many INGOs and NGOs are implicated in supporting these relations which means that, without it being acknowledged as such, 'Gender Makes the World Go Round' (1989: 1).[25] Enloe concludes, 'Making women in-visible hides the workings of both femininity and masculinity in international politics' (p. 11). Making men and women visible doesn't necessarily mean essentializing them. On the contrary, such visibility prompts an examination of the politics of femininity and masculinity between countries and within ethnicities of the same countries (p. 13). Operationalizing gender in policy analysis is therefore critical to the GAD discourse.

There is also an important focus in gender debates on what are distinguished as practical – more immediate – and strategic – or long-term and transformative – needs of women in their specific social and political contexts. Assessment of these needs is important to the spaces women have for negotiating for an enhancement of

---

25 'Thus the politics of international debt is not simply something that has an *impact* on women in indebted countries. The politics of international debt won't work in their current form *unless* mothers and wives are willing to behave in ways that enable nervous regimes to adopt cost-cutting measures without for-feiting their political legitimacy' (Enloe, 1989: 185).

Table 2.1 Comparing WID and GAD

	WID	GAD
The approach	Views the absence of women in development plans and policies as the major problem	Views unequal social relations between men and women and their 'naturalization' as the major problem
The focus	Women	Socially constructed, endorsed and maintained relations between women and men, with special focus on the subordination of women
The problem	The exclusion of women from the development process – an efficiency approach that focuses on the loss of half of developmental resources as a consequence of this exclusion	Unequal power relations, which prevent equitable development and women's full participation
The goal	More efficient, effective development that includes women	Equitable development with both women and men as full participants in decision-making
The solution	Integrate women into the existing development process	Empower the disadvantaged and women and transform unequal relations
The strategies	• Focus on women's projects, on women's components of projects and on integrated projects • Increase women's productivity and income • Increase women's ability to look after the household	• Reconceptualize the development process, taking gender and global inequalities into account • Identify and address practical needs, as determined by women and men, to improve their conditions; at the same time, address women's strategic interests • Address strategic interests of the poor through people-centred development

Source: Based on Parpart, Connelly and Barriteau, 2000: 141

their social status, and in their capabilities (Molyneux, 1985; Moser, 1993).[26] Increasingly this concern with interests is also being reflected in the debates about empowerment (Moser, 1989; Rowlands, 1997; Parpart, Rai and Staudt, 2002). While the GAD framework has become predominant in feminist development debates, this is not the case in development planning and in the work of many development agencies. Moser argues, for example, in the context of development planning, that '[b]ecause it is a less "threatening" approach, planning for Women in Development is far more popular. ...Gender planning, with its fundamental goal of emancipation, is by definition a more "confrontational" approach. Based on the premise that the major issue is one of subordination and inequality, its purpose is that women through empowerment achieve equality and equity with men in society' (1993: 4). I would argue, however, that while this challenge of 'gender and development' remains *potentially* a powerful one, in practical policy terms it has too often been used interchangeably with 'women in development'. While the GAD approach is theoretically a clearly 'feminist' approach, and therefore more challenging to existing social relations, we have only to see the way in which the major national and international development agencies have embraced the terminology of GAD to be aware of the dangers of co-option and the limits of its challenge.[27] Institutionalization of gender, as integration of women before it, poses critical practical and political questions for feminist activists and theorists (Baden and Goetz, 1997: 10). Perhaps the issue at heart is the question of power relations – among women and men, but also between women occupying different socio-economic spaces.[28] I would argue that the challenge before GAD is to take into account the relations of production and accumulation as well as of patriarchal relations if the disjuncture between GAD aspirations and its co-optation is to be addressed (see chapters 5 and 6).

---

26 For more on the debates on interests, see chapter 5.

27 The World Bank and even the IMF have taken on the GAD terminology. In the 'Gender Dimension of Development' in the Operational Manual of the World Bank (1999a), the Bank 'aims to integrate gender considerations in its country assistance program'. There is an increasing network of national machineries for women to address issues of empowerment of women (see Rai, 2002b), and there is an exponential growth in gender-focused NGOs (Stienstra, 2000) and a gender focus in the work of major international NGOs.

28 Another 'motherhood' term acceptable to all development agencies, and even private business, is 'empowerment' (see World Bank, 2000: part II). For a critical reflection on this term and the way it is being used within the GAD framework, see Parpart, Rai and Staudt (2001: Introduction).

Deconstruction and Representation: The Politics of Post-Development

Building on the WID/GAD debates, but extending them in different directions, there emerged in the 1980s and 1990s the postmodernist feminist critique of development. At the heart of postmodernism is what Lyotard has called 'an incredulity towards metanarratives' (1984: xxiii–iv). The growing acknowledgement of the fact that state-based strategies of development were not working, and that international agencies remained concerned with rather narrow development agendas, led to a disillusionment with 'the project of development' itself. Within this 'post-development' framework 'reason' and determinacy were questioned, and a more diffuse sense of power relations discovered by focusing not on binaries of western philosophy but on the multiple differences that we live with and within. The critique focused

> on the texts and words of development – on the ways that development is written, narrated and spoken; on the vocabularies deployed in development texts to construct the world as an unruly terrain requiring management and intervention; on their stylized and repetitive form and content, their spatial imagery and symbolism, their use (and abuse) of history, their modes of establishing expertise and authority and silencing alternative voices; on the forms of knowledge that development produces and assumes; and on the power relations it underwrites and reproduces. (Crush, 1995: 3)

Postmodern critics argued that '[d]evelopment has been the primary mechanism through which the Third World has been imagined and imagined itself, thus marginalizing or precluding other ways of seeing and doing' (Escobar, 1995b: 212). As such, development shares this framing characteristic with Orientalism.

Postmodern critiques of development thus placed themselves in opposition both to liberal theories of modernization and to Marxist discourses of transformations. The emphasis shifted from defining and managing modernization of countries and societies, to critique. The growing unease regarding the environmental crises enveloping the world in the wake of large-scale projects of industrialization and commercialization fed into this critique. The strong antagonisms of postmodernists to metanarratives questioned the primacy of science as a framework for problem-solving. The modern/traditional binary was rejected, as were articulations of planned development. Upon this view, state-led development is a problem of, not a response to, development. The dethroning of Science from the pedestal of Knowledge meant that other modes of thinking and analysis of our worlds became possible within the postmodern framework. These modes were no better or worse than the most systematized knowledge of western science, and thus found equal status within the post-development framework. 'The local' as a political and conceptual space then became important – not to be reconfigured by the nation-state but to be the site of multiple, life improving initiatives (Crush, 1995; Escobar, 1995b; for an analysis of 'the local', see chapter 6, this volume).

For feminists engaged in debates on development, participating in this critique of development opened up new spaces. The emphasis on 'difference' is what attracts many feminists to postmodernism, without abandoning the GAD framework. Feminists have long claimed that women have been constructed as the social 'other' in male-dominant worlds of philosophy and science. They have been denied their subjecthood within the traditional structures of knowledge/power. They have also, as noted above, struggled between the essentializing focus of WID and the potentially pluralistic understanding of gendered social relations. As Parpart and Marchand comment in their excellent summary of feminist debates on postmodernism, it is unsurprising that the feminist focus on difference and attraction to postmodernism coincided with the critique of middle-class, white western feminism by women who did not recognize themselves and their experiences in these early articulations of feminism (1995: 7). The displacement of Feminism by various feminisms was a starting point for a self-examination for many feminists, creating a space within which their subject positions came under scrutiny, as did those of others. For some Third World feminists this new space was not only one within which they could critique western feminisms, but also one where they could begin to examine the vexed issues of identity-based politics, which the nationalist discourses had either obscured or co-opted. The link between modernity, development and Orientalism that was made by post-development theorists has resonated with many feminists. The link with Orientalism in particular allowed feminists to open up the issue of differences among women of the Third World. Though this had been done within the Marxist framework of class, the intellectual complicity of modernizing elites was brought into focus by post-development feminists, as was the hierarchical relationship between donors and recipients of aid, the NGO worker and the 'clients' of the Third World. I have already discussed the critique of science put forward by ecofeminists. Other post-development feminists point to the empowering element of their approach, as one where women of the Third World find space to articulate their own needs and agendas (see Marchand and Parpart, 1995).

Two main questions have been raised about the postmodern critique and post-development. First, there is the question of agency. If there is no structure, if all power is diffuse and all hierarchies redundant, how are we to approach the question of political activism? The focus on difference rather than on the structural framing of men and women makes mobilization of opposition difficult. The question of organization – political, social and economic – also becomes unanswerable as the question of achievable goals is brought into question. Perhaps most pressing in this context is the relative value placed upon different standpoints (see Moghissi, 1999: 50–1). Is there nothing to choose between right-wing mobilizations of women claiming a 'motherhood' persona for them, on the one hand, and those struggling to find a public space for women to articulate their interests as individuals, or members of groups, on the other? Does not a postmodern perspective thus lead to political nihilism? To a stranded standpoint? Harstock points to the postmodern view of power as one 'in which passivity or refusal represent the only possible choices. Resistance rather than transformation dominates ... thinking and consequently limits ... politics' (1990: 167).

Second, there is the question of politics. Here, the opposition comes from various quarters – both liberal and Marxist. Amin, for example, asks the question 'Postmodernism – a Neoliberal Utopia?' to make the point that because it takes 'refuge in national, subnational, and ethnic communities ... [it] is a negative utopia (in contradistinction to positive utopias, which call for transformation of the world). At bottom, it expresses capitulation to the demands of capitalist political economy in its current phase, in the hope – the utopian hope – of "humanely" managing the system. This position is untenable' (1998: 101). Walby, on the other hand, argues that 'postmodernism in social theory has led to the fragmentation of the concepts of sex, race and class and to the denial of the pertinence of overarching theories of patriarchy, racism and capitalism' (1990: 2). Moghissi, discussing changing gender relations in Iran, notes postmodernism's 'well-advertised but fictitious radicalism, which rapidly dissolves into a celebration of cultural difference, its privileging of the "local" ... and in consequence, its curious affinity with the most reactionary ideas of Islamic fundamentalism' (1999: 52).[29] At the level of

---

29 Gray makes a similar point when he challenges the postmodern dismissal of the Enlightenment project, and asserts that the 'post-modernist stance is

development practice, Lehman (1997) asks the question: critique to what end? He suggests that the constant deconstruction of discourse leaves difficult questions of power relations, and immediate questions of crisis management, unanswered and unanswerable. Socialist as well as liberal feminists from Third World countries have also pointed to this issue. In her analysis of democratization struggles in Africa, Nzomo asks, 'What relevance...postmodernist discourse?' (1995: 131). She points out that the postmodernist critique 'would indeed dismiss the current strategies and visions of African women whose struggles for gender-sensitive democratization hinge upon universalist feminist ideals' (p. 141). From another standpoint, Udayagiri notes the 'curious silence about the political changes wrought by earlier resistance to modernization, in counter-discourses such as dependency theory...'. In this silence, she contends, lies the privileging by the postmodernist discourse of its own position (1995: 171). Further, it also raises the important question, 'has the relationship of policy to the scholarship on women in the South been a complete failure?' (p. 172). The question of feminist engagements with nation-states remains critically unanswered within postmodernist critiques (see Rai, 1995, and chapter 6 in this volume).

The Structuralist Challenge to Liberal Development

The structuralist opposition to the modernization model of development emerged early. In 1963 Raúl Prebisch was one of the first to articulate what came to be known as dependency theory. A.G. Frank took up this analysis and argued that the liberal development model was in fact the 'development of underdevelopment'. This caught the imagination of the neo-Marxists working in the field of development. The argument was that while colonial countries were undeveloped before western capitalist penetration, the Third World became underdeveloped after its incorporation into the international capitalist system. What development took place was a *dependent* development with the metropolitan economies structuring satellite economies as well as ensuring an outflow of surplus from them (Frank, 1969). This understanding of 'development' has very different points of reference from the liberal optimism of the modernization theorists. While dependency theory resonated with the Marxists, it did not emanate from a Marxist analysis of colonialism and imperialism.

---

typically one which rejects Enlightenment reason while (like the Romantic movement) retaining its commitment to a humanist emancipatory project – a shallow and ultimately incoherent perspective' (1995: 146).

What dependency theorists were able to do was to disassociate (and even counterpoise) capitalism and development, in particular at the global level. In doing so they presented an enormous challenge to the liberal development institutions that had taken shape in the West in the Bretton Woods tradition. What was less clear was what this analysis offered in terms of feasible politics and incremental development. Upon this view, opting out of the global capitalist system was the only strategy that Third World countries could pursue; social revolution, though an ever-present possibility, did not translate into reality very often. There were other problems too. The Third World countries were constructed entirely as hapless non-actors in a tremendously structured world with no agency to act, subvert or negotiate. As Bayart argues, 'unequal entry into the international systems has been for several centuries a major and dynamic mode of the historicity of African societies, not the magical suspension of it. ... Of course the concept of dependence still keeps its meaning, but it should not be dissociated from the concept of autonomy ...' (1993: 27). Further, and perhaps more important, the focus shifted to the world capitalist system and away from local struggles of the working peoples of Third World countries. It also did not allow for an analysis of the post-colonial states and how their specificities affected their position within the international capitalist system. The interests of all, except the capitalist and bureaucratic elites of the dependent countries, were assumed to be the interests of the working classes, the poor or the deprived. There was no attempt to distinguish between the marginalized within societies on the basis of ascriptive, gendered or non-economic indicators.

In the 1970s Immanuel Wallerstein developed the 'world-system' theory, which identified a three-tier system composed of the core, the periphery and the semi-periphery. While the first two categories corresponded to dependency theorists' characterizations of the world economic hierarchy, the third was a group of 'emerging markets' – a half-way house between the state of underdevelopment and development. Wallerstein placed greater emphasis on the role of politics, ideology and the state in the working of this three-tiered world-system. The concept of relative autonomy of the state was used by Wallerstein to suggest that states that were strong played an important role in striking the best bargains, while those that were weak had to accept unfavourable terms of trade. However, semi-peripheral states could have strong states that allow them to play the system maintenance role – politically, by endorsing the modernization discourse, and economically, through pursuing the growth agenda (Wallerstein, 1979). Following Wallerstein, some neo-Marxist theorists, writing in the 1970s and early 1980s, further explored the role of the national state elites in development (Amin, 1976; Alavi et al., 1982). Their argument was that Third World states arose out of particular historical struggles, and at specific historical moments; that these struggles and moments of transformation created configurations of state and economic elites that were specific to these countries. Taking their cue from Marx's analysis of the 'Asiatic Mode of Production', these authors argued that the state elites played an important economic role in post-colonial societies.[30] This role arose from the weakness of the indigenous capitalist classes, which were incapable of investing in the large infrastructural projects needed for laying the basis of economic growth, or disinclined to do so. This allowed the state to be both a monopolizer of political infrastructures of violence and coercion, and an economic actor. The historical weakness of landed elites and the industrial bourgeoisie of Third World states meant that state elites were able to mediate between these two sections. They were also able to intervene in conflicts involving economic elites and the oppositional classes – the working class and the peasantry. As a consequence of these two facts – the state's economic role and the weakness of the capitalist classes – the state occupied a critical position as an agenda-setter, mediator and arbiter of class relations in the post-colonial societies Marx, 1973; O'Leary, 1989). While modernist in its framework, this critique of the post-colonial development process took issue with the linear assumptions of modernization theory. The argument was that the post-colonial state could not deliver modernized economies, enmeshed as they were in a world-system of international capitalism, which induced dependency and created a core, a periphery and a semi-periphery within the world-system. In challenging the state, as an actor within the dominant international capitalist world-system, these theorists posed important issues for development. They argued that international capitalism depended upon the exploitation of cheap resources of the Third World; that the opening up of the post-colonial states to international capital would lead, not to enhanced development, but to increased dependency and exploitation; that the post-colonial state elites were not simply dependants within the world capitalist system, but actors with considerable agency as

---

30   For a critique of Frank's analysis of capitalist and feudal modes of production, see Laclau (1971). He argues that the causality of dependence lies in the system of production, and not of exchange, that obtains in both capitalism and feudalism. Brenner (1977) criticizes what he calls the lack of a class analysis to the periphery in the work of Frank.

they sought to position themselves to ensure their own survival and that of the dominant classes within international capitalism. However, the neo-Marxist framework of this critique, with its dismissal of the state elites of the Third World as simply self-perpetuating and ultimately tied to international capital, prevented these theorists from fully developing the political implications of their own analysis (see Amin, 1997).

A strong intervention was made in the structuralist debate by Marxist and socialist feminists. Writing of women as 'the last colony', a group of German socialist feminists (Mies, Bennholdt-Thomsen and von Werlhof, 1988) argued that primitive accumulation remained essential to capitalist growth, and that international and national capital and state systems exploited the Third World and women in their pursuit of profit. They identified several commonalties between 'women and the colonies': 'First, both are... placed within – or more accurately demoted to – the "realm of nature", because prior to capitalism the idea of a supposedly "backward" nature did not exist.... [Further,] they are treated as if they were means of production or "natural resources" such as water, air, and land ... the relationship between them is one of *appropriation*' (pp. 4–5). They argued that capitalist exploitation of wage labour was based upon the male monopoly of violence in a modified form; that patriarchal violence at home and in the public space was intrinsic to the lives of women and to their exploitation. They suggested that this patriarchal dominance was maintained through the agencies of the state, which institutionalized the 'housewifization' of women's labour within marriage and through work legislation. It was not in their suggestion of the super-exploitation of Third World labour that they differed from Marxist interpretations, but in their conceptualization of the work of the housewife: '...in the Marxian schema of accumulation these milieux and classes had no place' (p. 6). As an alternative, Mies and her colleagues argued for a society based on a feminist conception of labour that was based upon a direct relationship with nature and was not mediated by technology, where women exercised autonomy in all areas of their lives, especially in the area of reproduction, and where both men and women were engaged in the economy of care as well as that of subsistence. Again, while this was a powerful critique of existing social relations, and its focus on the gendered nature of capitalist accumulation provided a critical development of structural analysis, its utopian radicalism remained politically essentializing of women, and its rejection of any engagement with the state made it difficult to translate this critique into policy agendas of development. As I argue later in this book, the question of feminist engagement with structures of power remains central to the challenge of feminist politics.

Taking on this challenge of 'transforming practice' have been an increasingly influential group of feminists who have drawn early inspiration from Marxist critiques of capitalist development, but have been largely eclectic in their theoretical approach. They have consistently participated in the debates on modernization and development and have argued not only against the 'male bias in the development process' (Elson, 1995), but also for initiating an engagement with institutions on the 'inside' of the policy processes – at both national and global levels (Elson, 1998). The focus of this body of literature has been how the differential positions of women and men in development processes are integral to the fashioning of modern capitalist economies and technologies. Two areas have been at the core of this critique of development: women's work, and the gendered nature of structural adjustment policies of the 1980s and 1990s (Waring, 1988; Elson, 1995). In insisting upon opening up the area of work to economic analysis, these feminists have posed difficult issues for development economists and the development establishment (see chapter 4). They have built upon Sen's critique of the altruistic family to show not only how the life chances of women are affected by the gender relations obtaining within the family, but also how their contributions to family income are being appropriated without acknowledgement. In disaggregating the impact of structural adjustment policies on the family, and focusing on the disproportionate burden of the privatization of social welfare that women are being forced to carry, this powerful critique has resulted in some important shifts within the economic discourse of international institutions. These feminists have built as much upon the Marxist understanding of the bases of gender inequality as they have upon the liberal concepts of equality and equal opportunity. They have also further developed the interventions of Third World feminist and development groups, such as DAWN, that have advocated a strategic engagement with the policy community, and with state and international economic institutions, in order to challenge the assumptions of neutral goals of development (Sen and Grown, 1985). Because the focus of this group of feminists has been the achievable, and because they have engaged actively with policy machineries, especially at the international level, their influence in the field of Development Studies, and their interventions in the debates on development, have been growing considerably since the 1990s.

In Conclusion

To weave a path through these debates is salutary. It reminds us of how much and how little the development agendas and concerns have moved. In the 1999/2000 World Bank Report we find a more modest claim for the liberal economic agenda – 'a broad pragmatism' is the framework that is put forward by James Wolfensohn, the President of the Bank (World Bank, 1999b: III). There is also an explicit acknowledgement that 'trickle-down' development does not work, and that 'development must address human needs directly' (p. 1). Further, in the post-Cold War world, the Bank is also able to assert that 'no one policy will trigger development; a comprehensive approach is needed' (p. 1; see also Sen, 1999: 126–7). On the other hand, in this era of 'broad pragmatism' an examination of the economic and human indicators of development reveals that the number as well as the proportion of the poor in Third World countries rose in the 1990s. For example, in Latin America the number of people living under the poverty line 'rose from 22.0 percent of the population in 1987 to 23.5 percent in 1993, and in Sub-Saharan Africa it increased from 38.5 percent to 39.1 percent' (p. 25). The same Report also notes that '[o]ne study has found that a 10 percent increase in female literacy rates reduces child mortality by 10 percent' (p. iii) while increased male literacy rates have little affect. However, it has been amply demonstrated that with the pressure on the national state to reduce public expenditure on education, female literacy rates are going down wherever parents have to make choices between male and female children to invest in education (Seager, 1997: 74).[31]

The debates discussed above did influence policies of both international agencies and particular countries directly and indirectly. The alternative vision adopted by the United Nations Development Programme of measuring 'quality of life' rather than simple economic growth rates and per capita income reflects the strength of the arguments put forward by BN theorists. The disaggregation of economic data by gender now found in many national statistical data and in the Human Development and the World Development Reports shows the impact of WID/GAD theorizing and research.

---

31 Education has, of course, long been regarded by development institutions as a panacea for improving the social status of women (see World Bank, 1990b, 1999b). For a critique of this position, see Stromquist (2002) and Patricia and Roger Jeffrey (1998).

The various world conferences on women, from Mexico to Beijing, organized by the UN allowed gender and development agendas to be articulated, reassessed, critiqued and pushed forward. Bi- and multi-lateral aid and various programmes of assistance have been affected by these wider debates on development, though major issues of gender-blindness and power relations among the donors and recipient countries remain (Staudt, 2002).

It is also useful to note that until the 1990s the debates on development took place largely in the context of the nation-state. In the next chapter I address the changing context of development and the issues arising out of the growing pressures of globalization, where the nation-state seems under threat, and influence of remote economic actors is being felt not only at the national level but also at local levels. Christopher Lasch (1995) has argued that in the globalized world national elites have been able to break the link of responsibility (of social compact) with the national states that have sustained them thus far. Kothari (1995) has warned of the dangers of fragmentation of the nation-state, especially for the poor. Is this just nostalgia for the days of certainties within national boundaries? Or does this convey anxieties about governability, responsibility and accountability in development processes? If we examine how women of the Third World experienced the nation-based development of the 1970s and the 1980s, we might be able to understand these anxieties better. Interrogating the theoretical debates on gender and development in the context of world politics allows us to reflect upon the complex and often contradictory nature of these debates, and therefore the impact that these have on policy and institutional issues. In the next chapter we examine the changing world of development in the context of globalization, and how these changes reflect and affect the relationships between men and women.

3 | Globalization
New Agendas for Gender and Development?

The rules of globalization are undermining the rules of justice and sustainability, of compassion and sharing. We have to move from market totalitarianism to an earth democracy.
> Vandana Shiva, Reith Lecture 2000 on Poverty and Globalization

...pragmatic globalism does not force a selection between false choices: modernity vs. tradition, contrast vs. uniformity, globalism vs. localism, reflexivity vs. withdrawal. Rather, it aspires for an overall sanity that endures through all the conflicts and contradictions that beset our daily, global life.
> Kimberly A. Chang and L.H.M. Ling, 'Globalization and Its Intimate Other'

Introduction

If becoming a nation-state was equated with the possibilities of becoming 'developed' in the post-war world of the 1940s, under globalization that nation-state seems under threat. Its survival seems dependent upon whether it finds a new role for itself within the globalized economy, which seems to be growing at an inexorable pace. As such, nation-based development, too, is brought into question. As we saw in the previous chapter, postmodern critiques of development have grown in tandem with the changes to capitalist economies. There has also been a shift within the liberal discourse on development from growth-oriented to sustainable, human development. If the course of nationalist movements and the accession to power of new nationalist elites had a profound impact upon the structuring of gender relations in the post-colonial states, how is the fragmenting of the nation-state affecting these relations?[1]

In this chapter I examine the ways in which globalization is shaping the material world of economy, together with the changing contours of social and cultural worlds. I reflect upon where and how men and women are situated within these changing and yet familiar worlds. I consider the various debates on globalization and argue that we need to anchor these in a *gendered* analysis of the shifts in the social relations of production under globalization. This would allow us to bring in the politics in a debate that is often descriptive (Burnham, 1999; Peterson, forthcoming). I assess the gendered dimensions of the processes of globalization conceived of as a distinctive expansion of capitalist relations of production that requires a restructuring of the role not only of the national state, but also of international relations, political vocabulary, the institutions of governance, as well as the idea of the community. If the nation is an imagined community, so, I would argue, is the 'global village', and both are deeply implicated in gendered power relations. I will examine these in three different contexts: markets, the nation-state and governance. All three are central to the understanding of globalization, and to the transforming relations of production and their regulation.[2]

---

1 The situation is further complicated when we examine the emergence of the new nations in the post-Cold War era. The visions of development of the post-colonial nations took shape in contexts very different from those of globalization; the Eastern European nations are confronting the problems of state-building and pressures of globalization together (see True, 2000).

2 I will build upon this understanding of globalization in chapter 5 to analyse political resistance to globalization, and the forms that this resistance takes. While gendered production-based analyses provide us with grounded empirical evidence of the consequences of global production, (such as value chain analysis, poverty and inequality levels, and the changing nature and character of work – see Jackson and Pearson, 1998; Chang and Ling, 2000; Carr, 2002), distribution-based analyses allow us to insist upon issues of public action for the provision of public goods and mobilize around these demands. Analytically, a distribution-based assessment of globalization focuses on public policy and strategies of empowerment, but a production-based assessment points to the limits of such empowering engagements. In the following pages I will argue that both need to be held in tension with each other (see also Peterson, forthcoming).

Globalization and Convergence

There is a vast literature on globalization that has been spawned in the last decade. As one would anticipate, there is no consensus about the meaning of the term, its novelty, its causality or its normative consequences. Attempts have been made to provide some systematic accounts of the main thematic elements of these debates, which I discuss below.

Debating Globalization

Scholte (2000) sketches out five other usages of the term: internationalization, liberalization, universalization, westernization and deterritorialization. Held et al. (1999) make the following distinction between the various positions on the nature of globalization: First, there are the hyper-globalizers, who see globalization as a process driven by capitalism. Both liberal and neo-Marxist scholars argue from this position, though, of course, with very different analytical and normative frameworks. Second, there are the sceptics, who deny any structural break with the past globalizations and argue that indeed globalization of the economy is less secure today than it was in the earlier phases, with regional blocs emerging as counterfoils to globalization.[3] Finally, there are the transformationalists, who characterize contemporary globalization – which is conceived of as a transformative force responsible for a massive 'shake-out' of societies and economies – as the central driving force behind socioeconomic changes that in turn underpin globalization (pp. 2–29).

Pieterse (1997) maps out and comments on four different lenses through which globalization is examined: post-Fordism, globalization, the Bretton Woods institutions and development policies. Post-Fordists are further distinguished into neo-Schumpeterians, regulationists and those focusing on flexible specialization (Amin, 1994). The globalizers, too, are divided, between those who debate one form of globalization against the other (Robertson, 1992; Hirst and Thompson, 1996). Then there are those who focus on the failures of

---

3 Hirst and Thompson (1996), among others, point out that globalization as a process that gave 'a cosmopolitan character to production and consumption in every country', so that 'in place of the old local and national seclusion and self-sufficiency, we have intercourse in every direction, universal inter-dependence of nations', was described by Marx and Engels over a hundred and fifty years ago in the *Communist Manifesto* (Marx, 1973).

Bretton Woods institutions and the collapse of the state-based economic system and alternatives to these, not only as an organizational response but also a normative response to rethink development (Griesgraber and Gunter, 1995, 1996). Finally, there are those who argue for 'Limits to Competition'[4] as part of a normative agenda to address growing inequalities, ecological damage and the growing power of unaccountable economic units such as multinational corporations (Group of Lisbon, 1995).

Globalization theorists also take positions on the issue of modernity and postmodernity. For example, Giddens and Castells examine the impact of 'informational technology' and suggest that the global economy is both capitalist and informational (Giddens, 1990; Castells, 1996;[5] see also Lash and Urry, 1987; Beck, 1992). Castells argues that the development of a 'network society' is making capitalism distinctively global through 'the application of... knowledge and information to knowledge generation and information processing/communication devices, in a cumulative feedback loop between innovation and the uses of innovation' (1996: 32–3). This distinctive capitalism then leads to distinctive politics. Giddens makes the distinction between the (old/modern) emancipatory politics, which involves transformatory political engagements to bring about equality and justice, and the (new/reflexive) life-politics, based on 'self-actualization' and identity. Others, like Albrow, have linked globalization to reflexivity in the postmodern world, a reflexivity that is a 'challenge... to the idea of ever-expanding modernity, and hence to the nation-state' (1996: 4). There are, Albrow signals, at least five major ways in which globality has taken us beyond the assumptions of modernity. They include: 'the global environment and consequences of aggregate human activities; the loss of security where weaponry has global destructiveness; the globality of communication systems; the rise of a global economy; and the reflexivity of globalism, where people and groups of all kinds refer to the globe as the frame for their beliefs' (p. 4). For feminist theorists and activists, arguments about modernity and postmodernity have been explorations of identities, critiques of linearities and universalized certainties, and challenges to masculinized versions of rationality and action (chapter 2).

It is, of course, interesting (perhaps predictable?) that feminist scholars figure hardly at all in the traditional international relations

---

4 This follows from the Club of Rome reports on 'Limits to Growth' (see chapter 2).
5 For a reflective critique of Castells' *The Information Age*, see Bromley (1999).

and international political economy accounts of globalization. However, feminists have engaged in and extended the debates on globalization from different perspectives, and continue to do so (Sen and Grown, 1985; Mies and Shiva, 1993; Chang and Ling, 2000; Shiva, 2000; Peterson, forthcoming). Faced with new challenges, feminists have also sought to examine and theorize how globalization is changing political activism both at grassroots level and at the level of global institutions (Stienstra, 1994; Basu with McGrory, 1995; Cockburn, 1998). In terms of political activism, feminist scholars have built on and stretched further the ideas of 'borders' and a 'borderless world' through studies of women's migration (Pellerin, 1998; Kofman, 2000), world communities such as those based on religion (Moghissi, 1999; Karam, 2000), and by examining the growing density of women's networking through informal and formal organizational structures (Meyer and Prügl, 1999a; Stienstra, 2000).

While some feminist scholars have focused on communicative expansion that has been brought about by globalization (Eisenstein, 1998), others have been concerned about global economic regimes. In particular, global production and structural adjustment policies that are affecting women's lives directly and indirectly reshaping gender relations within the home and in the workplace (Afshar and Dennis, 1991; Elson, 1995; Jackson and Pearson, 1998; Beneria, 1999; Grown, Elson and Cagatay, 2000) have been the focus of attention, as have issues of security and insecurity and of well-being (Blumberg et al., 1995; Elson, 1995). Most, however, would agree with Peterson (forthcoming) when she analyses global political economy as the interaction of reproductive, productive and virtual economies. She includes in reproductive economy intergenerational, social/cultural/institutional reproduction as well as continuity and change in power relations within and outside the family and, finally, non-waged labour/informal sector activities. Such a perspective on the 'productive' economy of globalization allows us to map the gendered nature of production[6] (which includes a critique of the traditional economic and political divisions between the public and the private spheres) and to stretch the boundaries of what is considered

---

6 Beneria and Shelley (1992), for example, have shown that women's activity in four areas of labour is routinely overlooked: subsistence production; unpaid work; domestic production and related tasks; and voluntary work. The strength of the feminist critique of labour, and women's struggles, is evident in the radical new pensions legislation in the UK (December 2000), which enables (largely) women who have not worked for wages to have, and contribute towards the maintenance of, pensions.

the appropriate domain of the 'global'. Postmodern as well as insti-
tutionalist feminists have examined the changing understanding of
borders – in relation to the changing forms of masculinities and
femininities – as well as the consequences for local communities and
politics as national borders become more porous and regional
boundaries more secure (Weber, 1995; Zalewski and Parpart, 1997;
Kofman, 1998; Staudt, 1998a; Ling, 2000; Marchand and Runyan,
2000). Feminist scholars have examined the changing form and
nature of the nation-state in the context of globalization (Moghadam,
1996; Rai, 1998a; Peterson and Runyan, 1999) and made a political
and normative case on the environmental damage being done in the
name of free markets (Mies and Shiva, 1993; Shiva, 2000). Both theorists of global political economy and of changing identities in a
global world have paid attention to the idea of convergence.

The term 'global' as an analytical category suggests convergence –
of economic policies, value-systems or political ideologies – and an
understanding of universal human needs, which can then be translated into public policy. What we mean by convergence is of course
again contested – in terms both of the idea itself, and of its extent. In
its political form, convergence takes the shape of liberalization and
democratization, and in its economic form, the expansion of
markets; then there is the convergence of cultures – 'Americanization' or 'westernization' – and, as we shall see below, also a convergence of identities.

Globalization as Convergence

The collapse of the Soviet Union had an important effect on the
expansion of both the visions and possibilities of western governments' spheres of action. Economic liberalization and political conditionalities became routine, as international financial institutions
became involved in the restructuring of Eastern European economies
and polities (see chapters 4 and 5). Concomitant with liberalization
of the economy there has also been the erosion of the role of the
state, celebrated in particular in Eastern Europe and Russia owing to
the disbanding of authoritarian power that states had enjoyed in the
region. The collapse of authoritarian regimes and the transition to
the market economy and a multi-party political system took place in
very different contexts, and these differences influenced the trajectories of political and social development, although the variations
were largely obscured from view in the early period after the 'fall of
the Wall'. Such variations have particular resonance for gender relations in these transitional societies. As Rueschemeyer puts it, while

'very few people, men or women, would chose to return to life in the authoritarian systems of Eastern Europe...important expectations associated with the role of the state [have been] threatened, and women especially feel that threat' (1994: xii).

Three texts have been influential in the political debate on convergence, as it developed after 1989. These are: Fukayama's 'end of history' thesis (1991); Huntington's vision of the victory of Christian liberal ethic over the Islamic in a clash of civilizations (1995); and Barber's lament for the undermining of democracy by global capitalism and Islamic (and other) fundamentalisms, and his evocation of a revitalized liberal democracy within the national state structure (1996). In all these three sketches of the world in the twenty-first century, liberal values triumph over others; aspects of western civilization over other cultures; and modernity's concerns are resolved through these triumphs. Struggles within the parameters of other cultures, religions and ideologies, upon this envisioning, are doomed to failure unless they recognize the impossibility of reform from within. The logical conclusion, then, is that a liberal world is the only future that we can 'rationally' look forward to if we wish to live civilized, non-violent and democratic lives.

For Development Studies and the policy sector, envisioning of liberal futures world-wide has obvious importance. In this context we see a new conditionality emerging – one based on the liberal conceptualization of ethics and human rights, with the individual at its heart. The enthronement of possessive individualism allows a consumerist ethic finding voice even in the foreign policies of western countries (see DFID, 1998). Agency devolves to the western consumer, who becomes an actor in the global civil society and a participant in reconfiguring recalcitrant, unaccountable nation-states (see chapter 5). On the other hand, the post-Cold War international context allows the international economic institutions to deploy conditionality in the name of governance (see, for example, World Bank, 1994) in order to pursue the policies of liberalism through national bureaucracies, which are projected as unaccountable if they refuse. In this conception of governance, non-governmental organizations, especially the international NGOs, play an important role in a space that is supposedly being vacated by the nation-state. All these shifting or strengthening frameworks of capitalism and modernity have particular meanings for men and women, and for gender relations.

Some see the convergence of culture – 'westernization', 'Americanization' – as a juggernaut crushing before it the variety in our lives with crude consumptionist urges (Tomlinson, 1999). Some, like

Halliday (1999), have argued for the contemporary pertinence of imperialism as economic globalization creates inequality in the social, political, legal and cultural spheres, among others.[7] However, some see the global space encouraging cultural diversity as metropolitan cultures become 'indigenized' and as national imaginations are radically disturbed by imagined 'worlds': '... it is worth noticing that for the people of Irian Jaya, Indonesianization may be more worrisome than Americanization...' (Appadurai, 1990: 295). Feminist debates about the relationship between women of the North and South, white women and women of colour, and colonial and postcolonial discourses and imaginings of 'the feminine' and of the 'Third World woman' have reflected some of these arguments about globalization (Marchand and Parpart, 1995; Liddle and Rai, 1998). Work on consumer resistance and changing consumer habits has also reflected the importance of taking seriously the cultural dimensions of globalization – integrative as well as challenging (Barrientos, McClenaghan and Orton, 2000; Klein, 2001).

Identities – as consumers and producers, as femininities and masculinities – have also been the focus of feminist theorizing on globalization.[8] Theorizing changing femininities and masculinities under a converging globalization, Ling evokes the concept of hypermasculinity (characterized by Davos Man[9]), first developed by Ashis

---

7 Halliday provides a five-point argument on imperialism: (1) the inexorable expansion of capitalism as a socio-economic system on a world scale; (2) the necessarily competitive and war-like character of developed capitalist states; (3) the unequal character of capitalist expansion, and the reproduction on a world scale of socio-economic inequalities; (4) the creation of inequality also in the social, political, legal and cultural spheres; and (5) the generation of anti-imperialist movements (1999: 5).

8 Ryan described femininity as follows:

> A constellation of ideas found in every society which ascribes certain traits of character almost exclusively to women and conspires to dichotomize the human personality according to sex... femininity does not stand alone but is always rooted in a second universal structure of societies: the division of labor, power and privilege by sex... [and] evolves in tandem with the organization of material life, of which capitalism represents only one stage. (1979: 151)

Ling's work challenges this 'exclusivity' ascribed to femininity, though she 'roots' this shifting identity in historical processes of production and exchange (Ling, 2000).

9 According to *The Economist*, he is the new male actor of the globalized economy. Davos men 'hold university degrees, work with words and numbers,

Nandy (1983) in his study of colonialism as the glorification of aggression, competition, accumulation and power, to explain the developmentalism of the East Asian states (see also Hooper, 2000). She suggests that in these states the nationalist elites replay the relationship of hypermasculinity's dominance over a feminized society by enmeshing it in public patriarchy and political authoritarianism. 'Women in the [East Asian societies], as the most feminized of feminized subjects, suffer the most extensive exploitation and silencing' (Ling, 1997: 10; also 2000). Ling argues that 'globalization serves as a venue for the mutual reconstruction of both global and local forces, precisely because identity is open, organic, and unpredictable'; that it allows for 'the convergence of global and local patriarchies that underpin East Asia's oft-cited "economic miracle".' In terms of feminist politics, Ling asserts, the analysis of global and local convergence of masculinities means avoiding a flattening of the Third World woman's identity by pointing to the participation of the national elites of East Asian countries in the privileging of masculinist regimes of discursive and political power. In terms of the debate on globalization, the convergence of patriarchal control is best studied, as Ling points out, 'across cultural, spatial, and systemic divides' (1997: 9; see also Chang and Ling, 2000). The converging media play a significant part in this construction and legitimization of a masculinized consensus, as do varied access of men and women to the various 'scapes' – techno-, finan-, ethno-(Appadurai, 1990). The representations of femininity find clear reflection in the recruitment of female labour into the labour markets, the differential wage systems, the denial of property rights, and through structural adjustment-inspired cutbacks in public provision, and the increased burden of women's work within the family (see chapter 4).

One could argue that debates about convergence are being had today because of the one important convergence that occurred in the 1990s – the conversion of the former state socialist systems to capitalism following the collapse of the Soviet Union. As Pieterse notes, 'If we would try to find a common theme among the disparate debates that are taking place...capitalism remains the single framework that would be able to organize them' (1997: 367). The possibil-

---

speak some English and share beliefs in individualism, market economics and democracy. They control many of the world's governments, and the bulk of its economic and military capabilities.' It is, upon this view of new global masculinity, 'the beauty of Davos Man that, by and large, he does not give a fig for culture as the Huntingtons of the the world define it' (1997: 18). As such, this figure symbolizes the subordination of society to the economic system.

ity of alternatives to capitalism has shrunk dramatically. Equally, one could argue that alternative visions of development have proliferated once liberated from the confines of a bi-polar world.

In the following section I will examine how the globalization/convergence of markets poses new questions for women and men.

Embedded Global Markets

Globalization has been characterized by the '[m]arket, or at least ideologies of free trade and open markets,...[and] the increased *potential* for...flows [of international market transactions] resulting from the reduction or elimination of national and local barriers to all kinds of trade and investment' (Picciotto, 1996: 3). International trade flows, measured as the share of exports in GDP, provide evidence of the globalization trends in markets. Between 1950 and 1996, the volume of world exports increased sixteen times while total world output increased only six times (DAW, 1999: 2). Trade has actually grown more quickly than the world economy with the Third World states showing a huge increase in manufactured exports through the 1990s (World Bank, 1999b: 5; Crafts, 2000: 26).[10] Moreover, the composition of world trade has also changed substantially. There has been a significant decline of primary products and the rise of manufactured goods since the 1950s (Crafts, 2000: 26). Private capital flows to Third World states now far exceed official flows. In 1998, for example, the net official capital flows to developing countries were US$45 billion while foreign direct investment was US$150 billion (World Bank, 1999b: 6–7). This increase in trade world-wide has been underpinned by the liberalization of Third World economies, under what came to be called the 'Washington Consensus'.[11]

In the following section I analyse the gendered nature of the market itself, as well as the ways in which the gendered labour market is taking shape under globalization.

---

10   This underscores my concern with an analysis of globalization that is embedded in relations of production. The outsourcing of production to the Third World continues at a rapid pace. As such, the deepening levels of exploitation of labour need to analysed, as do changing gender relations as constitutive of and reacting to these productive relations.

11   This included fiscal discipline, tax reform, market-determined interest rates, competitive exchange rates, trade liberalization, opening up to foreign direct investment, privatization of state enterprises, deregulation and legal security for property rights (World Bank, 2000: 63).

Gendered Marketplaces

If markets are crucial to the understanding of globality – through the mechanisms of global production and exchange, of regulation that spans not one country but regions and (with the increased role of international economic institutions and the World Trade Organization) the globe; through the use of technologies that so enhance the flows of monies and make instantaneous financial transactions across the globe possible; through breaking down the political resistance of nation-states to liberalization and opening up of their internal markets to global competition – then we need to analyse the impact of gendered roles for women within markets. As table 3.1 shows, and as feminists have argued, markets are socially embedded institutions and roles 'within market systems are structured by non-market criteria' (Harriss-White, 1998: 201).

Two main points need to be made here. First, markets are very often presented as discrete, technical and economic spaces where exchange of goods and services takes place. Increasingly they are presented as arenas where trade and finance predominate, while the labour market is entirely ignored, or spoken of only in connection with the disciplining of labour unions as a prerequisite for the proper functioning of markets (Burnham, 1999: 38). Thus, I would argue that a gendered mapping of markets needs to take place in the context of a theoretical understanding of markets as embedded in wider social and cultural frameworks rather than as rational and impartial mechanisms for resource allocation, as characterized by neo-liberal economics (see Polanyi, 1944). Second, this gendered mapping of markets also needs to signal the changing form of labour markets world-wide, where we have seen a sharp rise of women's employment (see below).

The definition of labour markets has been traditionally problematic for women because their work, being unwaged, was excluded. It was only in the 1970s that the ILO began to define 'informal' labour markets, and research shows that women are concentrated in this sector: for example, 43 per cent in the Republic of Korea and 79 per cent in Indonesia (DAW, 1999: 11). While the informal and the informal markets have been linked by subcontracting, the measure of the informal sector remains difficult to assess because of lack of sensitive indicators. This in turn has various implications for public policy. First, without gender-sensitive indicators, the allocative process cannot be an efficient one. Second, lack of gender-sensitive indicators fails to recognize the importance of the role of women in the labour market, leading to inequities that are overlooked and not

Table 3.1 Gender-based distortions in (financial) markets

Type of gender-based distortion	Transaction costs for credit institution	Transaction costs for female borrowers
Information constraint	Information-gathering might go through male intermediaries; women are perceived as risky, not creditworthy enough	Women have lower literacy rates and are less mobile, which results in lower access to financial market information
Negotiation constraint	Women have less experience in taking formal credit, which requires more time from bank personnel	Women may need husband's permission; have higher opportunity costs to travel to a bank; women may face a discriminatory attitude by bank personnel
Monitoring constraint	Women's economic activities may be more difficult to monitor since they are often in different and smaller-scale sectors than men's activities, which are financed through credit	Women may find it difficult to control their loans in the household when other family members (particularly men) find it in their right to exercise control over this money
Enforcement constraint	Women often lack formal property rights, which makes it difficult for creditors to claim collateral when a loan is not paid, and underscores the initial reluctance to provide credit to women	Women may be more susceptible to pressure, intimidation or violence from creditors or their agents

Source: Adapted from van Staveren, forthcoming

addressed by policy-making (DAW, 1999: 7). Third, perhaps one of the novelties of globalized markets as we enter the twenty-first century is the much enhanced possibilities for finance to flow across the world, while at the same time the flow of human labour across national frontiers is being systematically reduced.[12] In this context

12 The impact of globalization of labour markets in this particular way has, of course, enormous implications for women's work and migration.

gender relations are being affected within local spaces, and gender is affecting the mobility of labour at the global level (chapter 4). Fourth, the development discourse under globalization, in which the individual market agent is central, also requires us to take seriously the ways in which men and women are able to access and play the market in order to enhance their life-chances, or standards of living. And finally, the role of the state needs to be emphasized in the study of markets. Far from being a passive victim of the global market, the state, I suggest, needs to be seen as an active player not only in restructuring the national gendered labour–capital relations in response to new pressures of globalization, but also in reorganizing its own regulatory and political boundaries to protect its position within the globalized political economy (Burnham, 1999, and below).

In discussing the dimensions of market power, White comments: '...the substance of market politics is characteristically about a number of issues: about the position of an agent or agents in relation to others within a market and their differential ability to extract resources through exchanges with other market participants; about the rules of the game and the nature of market institutions; and about the boundaries of the market' (1993: 5). The participants in the market include the state and organizations such as trade unions, consumer groups, business associations, market networks and firms, as well as individuals. The functioning of the market depends upon the politics of state involvement, the politics of market structures and the politics of social embeddedness – of the state and of the market (White, 1993: 6–10). In such a patterned market system, participants come to specific markets with unequal capabilities and bargaining capacities and resources, which results in widely different market structures, regulated by different state formations, and characterized by more or less unequal power. (Class and gender are two bases for unequal power relations operating in the market.) Bhaduri comments that the market mechanism is 'better understood not in terms of its allocative efficiency, but as the mechanism for extraction of surplus by one class from another', which he terms as the 'class efficiency' of markets (1986: 268). Evans argues that 'the power to threaten or disrupt economic relationships beyond the parameters of principal–agent relations is the kind of extra-economic coercion or influence that the neo-classical model fails to make explicit' (1993: 25). It thus fails to take into account the embedded nature of markets. It does not query that individuals can pursue their economic self-interests in ways that have nothing to do with the 'best price'. Neither does it question the 'degree to which self-interest places economic goals ahead of friendship, family ties, spiritual considerations, or morality' (Block, 1990: 54). Nor, indeed, does it consider how reproductive roles might change in the playing out of market roles (Harriss-White, 1998). Finally, there is an assumption that instrumentality in decision-making goes hand in hand with obedience to rules, and with maximizing interests, rather than being a set of signals that can lead to conflictual economic and social behaviour in different groups of populations. The social embeddedness of markets is therefore not considered, other than as a distortion, by neo-classical economists.[13]

For men and women, the socially embedded market operates differently at both the local and national/international levels. For example, the caste regime in India means the exclusion of women (and other deprived groups) from certain areas of work (Bardhan, 1983). On the other hand, the colonial state in Africa 'rationalized' the production and sale of alcohol by erasing women from the market, while in West Africa today, marketplaces have been 'identified as female domains, as sites for the exercise of female autonomy' (Parpart and Staudt, 1990a; Harriss-White, 1998: 200; Women Working World-wide, 2000a). Much work has also been done on the ways in which employers – state and non-state – use culturally based norms to justify the restriction of women's employment to certain (low-paid) sectors (Mies, 1982; Ong, 1987; Truong, 1990; Hart, 1991; Chang and Ling, 2000). Structural adjustment and the privatization of important sectors of state activity have also resulted in the casualization and feminization of certain labour sectors, resulting in tensions within the family for women as gender relations get reconfigured (Honig and Hershatter, 1988; Dennis, 1991; Einhorn, 1992; Kabeer, 1994; True, 2000). Of course, the market allows access to different women differently. Race and class intersect to provide different opportunities to women from upper and lower classes within the matrix of the market. White professional women inhabiting the world of international finance or involved in international bureaucratic machineries are positioned very differently to white Russian women looking to improve their life-chances by consenting to become 'catalogue brides', and still more differently from Filipina domestic workers in Canada. However, there is also evidence to show that gender cuts across race and class and is one of the crucial factors in ways that markets allocate resources and jobs (see Rai, Pilkington and Phizacklea, 1992; Barlow, 1993; Gilmartin, Rofel and White, 1994).

Markets pose another issue for men and women. Globally, women own about 1 per cent of the world's property; therefore, they are

---

13 See chapter 4 for feminist critiques of neo-classical economics.

involved in the globalization process through their access to labour markets rather than through their participation in financial or investment markets. They are the providers of services – sexual, domestic and increasingly as workers in export production – and are employed in lower-paid work; they are not in control of the huge financial and export flows in a globalized economy. The family power structure and the consequent gender segregation of work thus affects the ways in which markets operate and how women and men operate within these. The public–private divide is as much constitutive of markets as the markets consolidate this binary between men and women's place in the economy.

Another important issue here is that, despite the rapid increase in women's participation in both formal and informal labour markets, occupational gender segregation remains widespread (DAW, 1999: 16). Behavioural aspects of the market become particularly important to the language of neo-liberal discourses on globalization. For feminists, articulations of globalized masculinities in an increasingly market-dominated world, as discussed above, pose crucial questions about the role that women are expected to play in the expanding markets, and the terms upon which they do so.

The concept of hypermasculinity, discussed above, makes a contribution towards opening up the debate on gendered regimes of market access as well as of market operations. A hypermasculinized marketplace is a hostile space for women, especially as women are largely having to enter the marketplace within the framework of survival or only marginal improvement in their quality of life rather than to make huge profits. However, while the concept of hypermasculinity allows us to examine the historical significance of gendered identities of political and economic configurations, it once again seems to set up binaries – though historically shifting – of male/female, state/society. The feminine/feminized is characterized as powerless; women and the feminized are viewed as without agency, constructed and unchallenging within the discursive and structural framework of developmental capitalism. This ignores the fact that women's access to markets can be crucial to their survival, given the other structural constraints that they are functioning under. Thus, struggles over the withdrawal of child-care and health provisions under the regimes of structural adjustment are also struggles for continued presence of women in the marketplace; their earnings in the market are an important contribution not only to their individual survival but also to that of the family. The feminization of casualized labour markets, while undermining of organized labour struggles, has allowed women the space to earn wages that are crucial to the survival of their families. Further, the new forms of labour relations have led to explorations of new types of labour organizations, such as the SEWAs (Self-Employed Women's Associations), and have also forced a recognition of the importance of this feminized labour force on the agendas of the trade union movements.

Thus the nature and functioning of markets are brought into question by women's specific positioning within them and by feminist and socialist critiques of them. Attention needs to be directed towards the values and behaviours that they generate and the controls and mechanisms of accountability that are required in order that, in Polanyi's terms (1944), the 'disruptive strains' and 'varied symptoms of disequilibrium' (unemployment, class inequalities) and 'pressures on exchanges' and 'imperialist rivalries' do not go unchallenged.

Gendered Labour Markets

Owing to the reasons discussed above, assessing the position of women in the labour markets under globalization is not easy. Many have argued that generally the position of women improves with paid employment.[14] Women's employment rose dramatically between 1950 and 2000. For Third World countries, for example, the figure for women in the age group between 20 and 54 years in employment rose from 55 per cent to 68 per cent, while the trend world-wide has been from 46 per cent to a massive 81 per cent. And except in Africa, women's employment has risen faster than men's since 1980 (DAW, 1999: 8). However, the gender segregation of labour markets has concentrated women's work in certain areas. Export-oriented growth state policies have shown the greatest increase in women's employment. 'In general, the stronger the concentration of exports of labour-intensive goods, such as clothing, semiconductors, toys, sporting goods and shoes, the higher tends to be the proportion of women workers' (DAW, 1999: 9). Export-Processing Zones (EPZs) are dominated by female labour, as table 3.2 shows.

---

14 Chang and Ling point out in the context of Filipina domestic workers in Hong Kong that

> [w]hile they can earn up to six times what they would make at home, ... [they] often find themselves incarcerated within [a] regime of 'labor intimacy.' They discover that the larger community often links their domestic work with sexualized service ... women turn to prostitution when domestic contracts are prematurely terminated and/or crippling debts are owed to recruitment agencies in the Philippines. (2000: 35)

Table 3.2 Total employment and share of women in employment in EPZs in selected Central American and Caribbean countries, 1997

Country	No. factories	Workers in textiles and clothing (%)	Total employment	Women in total (%)
Costa Rica	250	70	50,000	65
Dominican Republic	469	65	165,571	60
El Salvador	208	69	50,000	78
Guatemala	481	80	165,945	80
Honduras	155	95	61,162	78
Nicaragua	18	89	7,553	80
Panama	6	100	1,200	95

Source: DAW, 1999: 10

However, much of this employment is in national subcontracting factories, rather than in global companies.[15] It is here that the role of the state becomes critical in providing the legal and policy framework within which subcontracting, export-oriented manufacturing can take place. 'The state actively structures, facilitates, and sustains a globalized service economy. The Philippines government, for example, supervises, regulates, transports, and taxes its overseas contract workers with various state agencies organized under the Department of Labor' (Chang and Ling, 2000: 35). Labour unionization has been one key area of state regulations, together with the enforcement of labour standards more generally (see chapters 4 and 5).

In agriculture, too, the effects of globalized production on women in the labour market have been visible. In Latin America, for example, the emphasis on commercial cropping has displaced women from permanent agricultural employment to seasonal employment. On the other hand, in Kenya, Uganda and Zimbabwe, women dominate work in the non-traditional agricultural economy (DAW, 1999: 11–12). In China, food production is increasingly carried out by women, while cash-crops and small-scale industry in the countryside also absorb considerable female labour (Rai and Zhang, 1994; Jacka, 1996).

Globalization of markets has also opened another area of employment for women: the sex industry (Truong, 1990; Pettman, 1996). As

---

15 Foreign direct investment employment accounts for only about 2 per cent of total wage employment in the Third World (DAW, 1999: 9).

the report by the Women's Environment and Development Organization (WEDO) points out,

> [w]ith the opening of borders and markets, and the accentuation of inter-regional and inter-class disparities, growing numbers of women, and increasingly very young boys and girls, are falling victim to an ever-widening and deeply entrenched flesh trade.... The criminal exploitation of women fostered by the forces of economic globalization makes a mockery of their hard-won recognition as equal partners with men in development...' (1998b: 6)

With this expansion of the sex trade, we also witness an expanding market in pornography. For example, '[t]he pornography industry will soon reach third place in Russia after illegal weapons trade and drugs' (p. 6). These industries are, of course, built on violence against women, and also expand in areas dominated by violent conflict, especially where there is a strong military presence (Enloe, 1989; WEDO, 1998b).

Labour markets are also flexible under globalized production. One of the myths of labour market analyses has been that women prefer flexible work. What is of course not questioned is the basis of this preference. According to a Statistics Canada survey, the major structural constraint for the wage gap in the country is the presence of children: 'In 52% of families in which both partners had full-time paid employment, the female partner was responsible for all the daily housework...' (CRIAW/ICREF, 2000: 3). In countries with less visible and strong women's movements, this figure would be even higher. The disadvantage to women is compounded by the general low pay and poor career development prospects in this area of employment. It is not surprising that flexible work, which includes home-based work and part-time work is dominated by women.

Furthermore, we find that risk has increased in the markets with the rapidity with which capital flows are able to respond to economic conditions. While this characteristic is most visible in financial markets, it is also perceived in foreign direct investment patterns, and in reversal of investment flows or capital flight.[16] The adverse

---

16   A typical scenario is outlined by DAW in this way:

> Large capital inflows lead to a rapid expansion in bank credit, leading to a subsequent increase in economic activity which eventually tends to spur inflation. As a result, domestic currencies become overvalued. This causes exports to decline and imports to rise, giving rise to a trade imbalance.

effects on women of such capital flight and the resulting financial and economic crisis[17] are amplified due to the unequal gendered labour markets and to policy prescriptions – such as stabilization measures (see chapter 4) – that affect family finances and security, which women, more than men, have to deal with. The cooperative conflicts within the family that we discussed in chapter 2 then become operative with gendered consequences for the entitlements and well-being of different members of the family.[18] The independence of state policy-making institutions is also called into question when an economic crisis hits the economy, underlining the strength of what Strange (1995) has called 'casino capitalism' and the impotence of national states in the face of the globalized power of such capitalism.

Globalization and the Disempowered State?

With the focus on globalization of the world economy, the national state has come under scrutiny. There is a growing literature that assumes that globalization and the marginalization of the national state go hand in hand. The argument has been most cogently put by Strange (1995). She makes three points to put her case. First, the nature of competition between states in the international system has changed – from competing over territory to competing over markets. Second, as the form of competition between states has changed, so has their nature, with trade and finance policies becoming more important than defence and foreign policies. Finally, Strange argues that 'authority over society and economy is undergoing another period of diffusion, after two or three centuries in which it became increasingly centralized in the institution of the state' (p. 55). Strange's analysis has been challenged. As Cable argues, 'The nation-state

---

Foreign investors then begin to expect a currency devaluation and their eventual reaction to the weak macroeconomic 'fundamentals' – rising inflation, trade deficits and overvalued currency – precipitates capital flight. (1999: 48)

17 According to Joseph Stiglitz, 'Crises have become more frequent and more severe, suggesting a fundamental weakness in global economic arrangements' (2000: 1075).

18 The UNDP's (1998) report on the Asian financial crisis, for example, has asserted the importance of the human-centred development in which three key elements – human rights, human development and human security – must form part of any schema of socio-economic change.

has "lost" sovereignty to regional and global institutions and to markets but has also acquired new areas of control in order to promote "national competitiveness"' (1995: 23–4). Governance, too, has been cut loose from the nation-state. Brought into political currency by Rosenau and Czempiel in their book *Governance Without Government* (1992), the term 'global governance' is increasingly being used to emphasize 'the implications of a widespread reorientation of individuals' political skills and horizons' (Hewson and Sinclair, 1999: 5).

One of the most innovative analyses of the national state in the era of globalization is that of Robert Cox, who argues that what we are witnessing is not the demise of the nation-state but its 'internationalization'; not its destruction but its transformation. In brief, Cox argues that, from being bulwarks against global intrusions into national economies, today's states are becoming adapters to and mediators and negotiators with the global political economy. To perform this changed role they have to reconfigure the power structures of government, giving far more emphasis to the role of finance and trade in economic regulation rather than industry and labour, for example. The state's role, therefore, becomes one of helping to adjust the domestic economy to the requirements of the world economy (Cox with Sinclair, 1996). In a sympathetic critique of this position, Burnham points out that Cox's analysis 'underplays the extent to which "globalization" may be authored by states and regarded by state agents (both liberal market and social democrat) as one of the most efficient means of restructuring labour/capital relations to manage crisis in capitalist society' (1999: 39). In this context the nostalgia for a benign, or at the very least powerless, nation-state is clearly misplaced. Burnham, following Polanyi, argues, instead, that '[n]ational states exist as political "nodes" or "moments" in the global flow of capital', and that their development is part of the crisis-ridden development of capitalist society (p. 41). Upon this view, then, the recent changes in the global political economy are analysed as being predominantly about reorganizing states rather than by-passing them, with 'state managers' actively attempting to restructure, and respond to, 'a crisis of labour/capital relations' (p. 41). If the state is a participant in the reconstitution of its own relations with the global political economy, then it continues to be a focus for the struggles against this changing relation – whether it is from (dis)organized labour in the urban or the rural context, or from other social movements.[19] An example of the complex relationship

---

19 It is fascinating to note how global economic institutions such as the World Bank are clearly recognizing this participating state in particular political ways.

between the nation-state and global economic actors is the ENRON case in India.

ENRON and Electricity

Since its liberalization policies were put into effect, India has attracted US$289 billion in foreign investment, of which about 39 per cent is in the power sector (Pavri, 1997: 1). ENRON, the giant water and electricity corporation, secured a contract from the ruling Congress Party government in 1992 to manage the world's largest – though non-viable – electricity-generating plant in Dabhol, near Bombay. While ENRON had promised to invest US$3 billion, it was agreed that this would be repaid through tariff, which was set so high that the company would receive US$26 billion in return. 'The unnecessary plant needed vast amounts of agricultural land, which was obtained by compulsory purchase. Its discharges threatened fisheries. Enron also required 8,338 litres of fresh water a minute to keep Dabhol generating and by 1996 formerly lush villages found their wells and rivers had emptied' (Cohen, 1999: 35). An enquiry into the whole affair was set up in 1995 by a newly elected BJP government as it was felt that corruption was at the heart of the deal. The inquiry concluded that ENRON had 'padded the cost by about 25 per cent' (Pavri, 1997: 5), and that the deal 'should be cancelled because of corruption, lack of transparency, high costs and the failure to prove that the state needed the plant' (Cohen, 1999: 35). The threat of a legal challenge by ENRON, the prohibitive costs of such litigation in another (UK) country, and the lack of political will by the Maharashtra state government to withstand the pressure from such a powerful economic actor meant that the contract was renegotiated, and the plant was allowed to be built. When local rural people organized, '[w]omen in their eighties were beaten and dozens were held in the Enron compound, which at this, and 30 other demonstrations in 1997, doubled as a private prison. Police wages were met by Enron...' (Cohen, 1999: 35). This, and the example of the neem tree campaign (see p. 140), shows how global

---

Thus, the 2000/1 World Development Report clearly states: 'Poverty is an outcome not only of economic processes – it is an outcome of interacting economic, social and political forces. In particular, it is an outcome of the accountability and responsiveness of state institutions' (World Bank, 2000: 99). The economic forces, then, get depoliticized, while the state becomes associated with maladministration (non-accountability) as well as with politics (lack of responsiveness to its 'clients' interests).

restructuring is affecting directly the lives of people in rural communities by shaping and reshaping, privatizing and destabilizing local environments, and undermining national state governments either through corruption or through severe economic pressures.

However, this account of the reconfiguration of the nation-state is incomplete if we do not take into consideration 'the ways in which social subjects understand themselves and their relations to social structures, structures which are in turn constituted in and by social practices informed by intersubjective understandings' (Laffey, 1992: 2).[20] A gendered reading of the state thus becomes important if we are to understand the processes of change through which the nation-state is passing. Pringle and Watson, for example, have argued that 'we can conceptualize the state, not as an institution but as a set of arenas; a by-product of political struggles whose coherence is as much established in discourse as in shifting and temporary connections' (1990: 229). They further argue that 'group interests do not pre-exist, fully formed, to be simply "represented" in the state... they have to be continuously constructed and reproduced. It is through discursive strategies, that is, through creating a framework of meanings, that interests come to be constructed and represented in certain ways' (pp. 229–30). In the context of globalization, the articulation of women's varied interests mediate between the reconstituting of their and others' interests, on the one hand, and the ways in which the state incorporates, makes visible, speaks to and frames interests of various groups, on the other.

This more layered reading of the role that the state plays in national development allows for further explorations of the state as embedded in different cultural contexts. If we take the state to be an economic participant through its direct and indirect interventions in the sphere of economy, then Polanyi's concept of 'embeddedness'[21] serves as a useful tool with which to analyse not only the market but also the state. In this context of embeddedness it becomes important to exam-

---

20 Laffey also argues that Marxism is a regional account of the world, taking for granted a set of western modernist categories and universalizing them, and that this 'prompts questions about the capacity of Marxism to cope with difference' (1999: 4).

21 Polanyi (1944), of course, sets up a dichotomy between pre-capitalist embedded markets and the unembedded capitalist price-setting market of a 'modern society'. However, the idea of the embedded market is now widely used to understand the different ways in which different sectors and regions experience the market, and how markets are 'distorted' by or enmeshed in cultural and historical spaces (see also Braudel, 1985).

ine how different state fractions relate differently to each other, and to other civil and economic groups in different cultural milieux. I would argue that 'embeddedness' of state institutions in the gendered power relations imbuing society, while supporting the goal of economic development, can and does also act against the interests of politically marginalized groups, including women (Rai, 1996b: 14). This is because the relationship between a modernizing state and a civil society within which it is configured is a complex one. While for some groups the mutual reinforcing of bureaucratic capacity and social connectedness becomes the key to the effectiveness of the developmental state (Charlton and Donald, 1992: 7), for others, including women, the reinforcing of bureaucratic capacity by social norms can be a terrifying combination.[22] In this context, to view the state as a unitary entity becomes paralysing, and regarding civil society as 'a space of uncoerced human association' perilous (Rai, 1996b: 17–18).

Embeddedness also raises another issue for the analysis of the nation-state in the context of globalization. If the human economy is embedded in the non-economic (social) institutions as well as the economic, then an understanding of the complexities of these institutions is needed to assess their limits and potential. The nation-state as the focus of developmental struggles allows historical knowledges of traditions, cultures and political contexts to be mobilized with greater facility than is available to the amorphous 'international economic institutions', peopled by shadowy figures not visible to the local oppositional struggles. The frustrations of local struggles when they are unable to hold the international elites accountable for the disasters brought upon them also fuels the lament for the nation-state.[23] Women's movements have been grappling with this changing role of the state. As the sites of production and reproduction shift within states, as new regimes of production make for different forms of work – part-time, flexible, concentrated in EPZs, migratory – women are having to organize differently. As global capital's presence is felt directly, less mediated through the

---

22   The example of the Taliban government in Afghanistan comes to mind here (see also Moghissi, 1999).

23   For a critical analysis of feminist engagements with the World Bank, see chapter 5. There is also now a growing interest in what is called 'corporate citizenship' in an attempt to underscore the accountability of private economic institutions to the communities (as opposed to the nation-states) within which they operate (see Andriof and MacIntosh, 2001). The accountability of private corporations is also raised in the discourse of 'ethical trade' and 'codes of conduct' (see Barrientos, McClenaghan and Orton, 2000; for a critical evaluation, see chapter 5).

state, and as local spaces are opened up to the forces of the market, the challenges to global economic forces and organizations are also posing issues of political discourse and mobilization for women. While the state continues to be a central focus of women's mobilization on various issues, supra-territorial strategies are being increasingly employed in order either to counter the state, to delegitimize its position, or to mobilize global discursive regimes in their interests (see chapter 5).

Global Governance and GAD: New Challenges for Development?

Since the 1990s, together with, and sometimes in response to, the perceived threat to the nation-state, the system of global institutional politics has come under scrutiny. On the one hand, there is an attempt to provide the UN with an increased relevance – not as an organ of supra-national global governance, but as an organization representing collective action of states in an 'issue-specific' rather than generalized manner (Higgott, 1998: 34). On the other hand, the UN is generally considered to be ineffective, bureaucratized and unrepresentative of the rapidly changing world. The US has led the crusade for a refashioning of the UN machinery, and a great deal of emphasis has been given to making the UN more accountable to its members. The UN, for its part, has had to deal with newly emerging powerful competing institutions of governance in the World Trade Organization, and has seen the Bretton Woods institutions – the World Bank and the IMF – making increasing inroads into the social and political arenas. 'Good governance' is on the agenda of the economic institutions and is being made part of the conditionality of aid. This has resulted in a demand by the donors upon the recipient nations 'for democratic pluralism, for the rule of law, for a less regulated economy and for a clean and non-corrupt administration... for greater decentralization...' (UNDP, 1994: 76).

A discussion of levels of governance and issues raised by the shifting boundaries of the local, national and international leads us to view the current debates on governance and how they imbricate with the agendas of engendered development. 'Governance' has been defined as 'a vantage point to the sources and political implications of global change' (Hewson and Sinclair, 1999: 5). It has come to denote 'a shift of location of authority in the context of both integration and fragmentation' (p. 5). Feminists, too, are engaged in this debate as they see a 'general broadening of the field of international reorganization from a preoccupation with describing the output of intergovernmental organizations, their formal attributes and processes of decision-making to a concern with structures of governance'. These include organizations such as the UN and NGOs, as well as social and political movements in a 'global civil society' (Meyer and Prügl, 1999b: 4). A concern with issues of governance also helps explode the myth of consent that is a feature of the earlier globalization literature – a consent that is often juxtaposed with the inevitability of globalization and therefore conceals the power relations within which the process is developing (Newell, Rai and Scott, 2002b). However, one could argue, as Palan does, that 'the language of global governance, with its attendant rather unflattering insinuations about the functions, legitimacy, and aptitude of the state (and society)…makes sense only once an agreement is reached about some prior, if normally undeclared, common human goals, political functions and so on' (1999: 67). These *a priori* notions are themselves markers of closures – not the same as those that operated under nationalist regimes, but new closures that make for new winners and losers – in both the public and the private spheres, and take both national and local/global forms.

In terms of governance as political practice, we can distinguish different patterns. The two most dominant today are the 'liberal' and 'critical' governance strategies. The liberal strategies 'seek to work within the current economic system, to improve the way in which it functions' (Newell, 2000, p. 124) and to offset the worst excesses of development. The examples of such governance would be the consumerist movements; collaborations between civil society groups, NGOs and economic organizations (see chapter 5); lobbying for codes of conduct within markets (see Women Working Worldwide, 2000b); and lobbying for private firms to draw up and implement their intra-company/organization codes for managing economic recourses. Critical governance, on the other hand, could be described as regulation through opposition. It involves the exposure of policies and practices of economic organizations; challenging the rationale and moral premise of global legal and economic regimes such as the World Trade Organization (see chapter 4); consumer boycotts with a political message, such as the Shell boycott after the execution of Ken Saro-Wiwa, the human rights activist in Nigeria (see Yearly and Forrester, 2000); and propaganda and 'counter-information' to challenge the advertised claims of transnational corporations (Newell, 2000; see chapter 4 below for further exploration of the latter strategy).

There are several important issues to be raised here. The first is that at the beginning of the twenty-first century we find the fundamental issues of governance and development relatively unchanged – security and the enhancement of our life-chances still preoccupy us most. Is this a failure of development strategies pursued, or an indicator of the limitations of our imagination? Second, we find ourselves living in a world without an ideological divide writ large in international politics. There is a sense of lack of alternative to the liberal ideology, which is resulting in the emergence of strategies of governance – liberal and critical – to be developed. Alternatives to capitalist development seems utopian and therefore politically of little use. Third, we find ourselves living in a world that is clearly seen to be one, and yet where the individual competitive ethic is predominant. We can see this contradiction when we hear talk of sustainable development, on the one hand, and of sustainable growth, on the other, when interdependence and the free market go hand in hand, and where technologist solutions predominate at the expense of redistributive ones. In this new/old context, how are the feminist development agendas shaping up? What are the demands of the feminist movements regarding development? In the next section I briefly sketch out the ways in which globalization is addressing issues of security, equity and democracy, and follow this by an assessment of some of the dilemmas faced by feminist movements addressing issues of governance in a global age.

Security, Equity and Democracy

One of the mantras of 1980s neo-liberal economics was that market-led growth is the only viable route out of world poverty. While many are now arguing that such market-oriented growth has only resulted in increasing inequalities between the rich and poor people and countries (Chossudovsky, 1998), others have suggested that poverty and inequalities have increased due to the non-successful implementation of market reforms (World Bank, 2000: 62). The debate, according to the World Development Report, is not about markets, but about 'how reforms to build markets can be designed and implemented in a way that is measured and tailored to the economic, social and political circumstances of a country' (p. 62). Two issues have been identified in this Report. First, that market reform is a staged process, with the 'first-generation' reforms – stabilization and liberalization – leading to 'second-generation' reforms – institutionalizing and good governance (p. 64). The hope is that with the second stage completed, the full impact of market-led growth will be felt in poor economies. The second issue is that of assessing the impact of growth on the lives of the poor, even when market-led growth is visible – what, in short, have been the human development indicators of market reform of the global economy?

According to the survey by WEDO, for example, '[w]omen...pay a disproportionate share of the costs of economic globalization while being excluded from its benefits' (1998a: 1). The indicators used by WEDO for an assessment of gender impact of macroeconomic policies under globalization are: women's rights and access to land, property and credit, employment, the environment, education, health and housing (p. 1). Scholte (2000) raises three issues as indices of the 'state of globalization': (in)security, (un)democracy and (in)equity. How various groups are experiencing these under globalization is one way of assessing the normative assumptions of globalization, and its efficiency in dealing with these as a source of its legitimacy is another.

Therefore, the concept of global governance – supra-territorial delivery of the orderly conduct of social and economic activity – needs to translate into global policy-making through global institutions and through a replacement of the national infrastructural state (Mann, 1986) with de-territorialized infrastructures of governance. In terms of process of governance, the concept of global governance thus raises the issue of power: 'Effectiveness signals two kinds of power: first, to "build upon and influence decisions taken locally, nationally and regionally"; second, to "draw on the skills and resources of a diversity of people and institutions at many levels"' (Mann, 1986: 533). Who are the actors in global governance is as important a question as who are not included in the process of governance. At the level of institutional actors, states, corporations, economic and social institutions, and civil society organizations and NGOs are all participants at different levels of governance. A glance at the gender balance of all these institutions would reveal a highly masculinized governance process and machineries. But gender is not the only axis of exclusion – class and race, religion and sexuality, rural/urban are the others.

It has been argued that under globalization we have seen a shift from the traditional concerns of security – of national borders – to an expanded definition of security, including environmental security, economic security and security from violence (Scholte, 2000). One could argue that the picture is mixed as far as a gendered reading of security is concerned. While environmental movements and ecological discourses and governance mechanisms make us aware of the connectedness of locales and the need for their protection, consumption of natural resources shows no signs of reducing, and indeed continues to be an indicator of development.[24] Women of the industrialized world and elite women everywhere are an important part of this ever-widening circle of consumption, raising questions of the growing gap between the lives of those who produce and those who consume. Violence has long been a concern of feminists and women activists. From violence in the home to violence as war between states, women have been in the forefront of debates and movements. Insecurity resulting from violence is thus an important indicator of whether global governance works. While there is an increasing acceptance of the illegitimacy of war, wars abound. Women have been suffering horrific violence at the hands of the army or militants in several 'theatres' of war such as Algeria, Afghanistan, East Timor and Sudan, to name but a few (WEDO, 1998b: 6). The rape of women in Bosnia, as well as in Rwanda, also tells a grim story. Cynthia Cockburn notes that '[t]housands, perhaps tens of thousands, of women were raped [in Bosnia Herzegovina]. The rapes had both a meaning specific to the ethnic and patriarchal relationships of this war and a meaning common to rape everywhere and at all time' (1998: 222). Global institutions were unable to contain conflict and reduce the insecurity of the Bosnian peoples. With fragmentation of old states and the structural adjustment of economies, one could also argue that violence against women becomes a particular problem. In 1995, for example, nearly half of all murder victims in Russia were women murdered by their male partners (Seager, 1997: 27).

Issues of economic security and equity have also not provided global governance with good press. The pressures of structural adjustment policies, of cutbacks to the welfare state, and of market competition have resulted in increased inequalities between nations and classes, and between men and women. Women's access to health is endangered by these cutbacks to social budgets. In Sri Lanka, for example, as part of fiscal austerity, food subsidies have been replaced by food stamps, with a consequent increase in the levels of malnutrition among poor women, thus jeopardizing the future health of children through an impoverished diet during pregnancy (WEDO, 1998a: 7). Unemployment, insecure employment and employment with few rights or protections have meant that the gap between the rich and the poor, and between men and women, is

---

24 The World Development Report, for example, provides us with data under 'Distribution of Income or Consumption' as if the two are interchangeable categories.

escalating. The World Development Report shows that women's share of formal employment did not increase very much between 1980 and 1998 – a world average from 39 per cent to 41 per cent, with low-income countries showing only a 1 per cent increase from 40 per cent to 41 per cent, while the high-income countries showed an increase from 38 per cent to 43 per cent (World Bank, 2000: 235). On the other hand, women's unemployment averages 70 per cent in Armenia, Ukraine, Russia, Bulgaria and Croatia. While millions of women have joined the labour force under these insecure conditions, it could be argued that they have joined the 'race to the bottom'- feminization of labour has meant impoverishment of jobs and lives. Feminist scholars have also observed that, although often celebrated, the globalization of communication networks has not led to greater access to these networks for women, and that global institutions, especially the corporate institutions, remain dominated by men (Peterson and Runyan, 1999; Youngs, 2002).

Markets are thus differently accessed by women and men. Women are having to bear a triple burden of work in the home and outside, and also of care as welfare provisions of health and education are whittled away under structural adjustment (see Beneria and Feldman, 1992, and chapter 4). In its report to the World Summit for Social Development, the United Nations Research Institute for Social Development (UNRISD) pointed out that

> [n]early one third of the population in developing countries lives in absolute poverty...in 1992, six million children under five years of age died of pneumonia or diarrhoea. The livelihoods of nearly one billion rural residents are at risk as a result of environmental degradations....Over the past decade, 80–90 million people were displaced by programmes to improve infrastructure (dams, roads, ports...) and the number of years that girls in developing countries spend at school is approximately half that of boys. (1995: 24)

As economic pressures bite, the rates of 'missing women' continue to grow (Drèze and Sen, 1989: 56–9).

Under such conditions of insecurity and inequity, has democracy been at least one gain of globalization? China, Chile and Uganda are examples of successful liberalizing states that are also to varying degrees in the processes of democratization. If we take seriously the point made by Amartya Sen (1999), that famines do not occur in democratic states, then perhaps there is hope for development in a global context. Democratization has also led to an increased space for political mobilization, and global networks of communications have made for an increased reach of these social movements. Critical strategies of governance require an extension of the democratic infrastructure at both the national and global levels. Some feminists have pointed out, for example, that '[m]ost western feminist organizations are on-line today. The Global Fund for Women fights for women's human rights...FemiNet Korea promises an electronic space for women which challenges the male privilege of the information society...cyberdialogues exist between the cracks of mainstream news reporting and people's everday lives'; and that 'communication allows for diasporic publics to connect with one another and initiates new alliances with people "outside" any one geographical region' (Eisenstein, 1998, p. 42; also Youngs, 2002).[25] Movements for human rights, and for women's rights, for the environment and against racism have benefited from the convergence of political discourses around individual rights, even though these are premised historically in the much criticized liberal tradition (Charlesworth, Chinkin and Wright, 1991; Ali, 2000). The institutions of global governance have given prominence to some of the important agendas of these various movements. The Beijing Conference, the World Summit on Social Development and the Rio Summit on the environment have created political spaces that have allowed for discursive political mobilizations.

However, even in this area there are those who have pointed out that globalization has allowed the elites to become uprooted from their local spaces, leading to a culture of 'economic raiding' and a disinvestment in local communities that is antithetical to democracy (Kothari, 1995; Lasch, 1995). Global financial markets, and the major actors in these markets, are unaccountable either to national states or to institutions of global governance, except in the once-removed regulatory sense, and yet can prove terribly destabilizing of economies and polities, as was evidenced in the 1997 crash of the East Asian economies. Further, the expanded role of the multinationals in domestic economies of the nation-state has led to further attacks

---

25   It is perhaps pertinent to point out here that, as with other resources, communication networks, too, are unevenly distributed among and accessed by the rich and the poor, men and women. While there are 135 internet hosts per 10,000 persons in industrial countries, the figure for the poor countries is 0.9 (UNESCO, 2000). Even among the poorer nations, the unevenness is marked. In China (excluding Hong Kong) there are 8.9 personal computers per 1,000 people, and in India, 2.7 (Sachdev, 2000). As the figures for education show, gender gaps are often greater for the poor. This also affects the access of women to communication networks.

upon workers' organizations. The conditions of work in EPZs, for example, continue to raise issues for the mobilization of women workers (see chapter 4). As for the notion that the media help to keep elites accountable, Barber has pointed out that the concentration of this industry in very few hands could 'privatize politics and replace deliberative debate in public with the unconsidered instant expressions of private prejudices' (1996: 270). Thus, as O'Hearn argues, 'globalization has made access to, and control over *meanings* of, technologies and resources more unequal than ever. The rise of supranational global institutions and market-oriented global networks has increased the power of core capitals to subjugate peripheral regions...' (1999: 114). For many, therefore, globalization has spelled a 'global disorder' (Harvey, 1993) rather than any benefits of global governance, and is antithetical to development (Raghavan, 1996; Hoogvelt, 1997).

Where does all this leave women's movements and groups? Are women to be victims, bystanders or participants in the processes of globalization? Palan writes, 'Beliefs that we inhabit closed entities accompanied the rise of the nation-sate in nineteenth-century Europe. Such beliefs have not disappeared. Instead they are being refocused, in part by global governance thinking...' (1999: 68). What role can and do feminists and women's groups play in this refocusing of social closures and challenges to these?

Global Governance and a 'New Design for Development Cooperation'

Starting in 1990, the UN Development Programme has brought out annual Human Development Reports that reflect a new approach to measuring development in the light of debates in Development Studies on sustainable development, empowerment and human capability (see chapter 2). Development has been regarded as enabling people to make, have and enlarge life-choices. Considerable attention has been paid to disaggregating development data for both men and women. What is absent in these reports, however, is a serious consideration of *how* these choices are to be enlarged for both men and women, given the structural constraints imposed by existing power relations in societies, and *who* is going to exercise them (Nijeholt, 1992: 15–16).

The 1994 UNDP Human Development Report, for example, asserts that in the globalized world, the 'traditional North–South cleavage is no longer a useful basis for negotiations'. Not collective weakness of the South, but the individual country's domestic economic strength gives it its place in the international order. The Report concludes that

> now is the time to move on from the sterile confrontations of the past and to forge a new and productive economic partnership among the nations of the world – not on charity but on mutual interest, not on confrontation but on cooperation, not on protectionism but on an equitable sharing of market opportunities, not on stubborn nationalism but on farsighted internationalism. (UNDP, 1994: 61)

This far-sighted internationalism is translated into the idea of 'global public goods', which are defined as 'goods whose benefits reach across borders, generations and population groups' (Kaul, Grunberg and Stern, 1999).[26] However, UNDP reports also show how fragile the basis of these hopes is. With the exception of Japan, the countries ranked from 1 to 15 on the Human Development Index on key indicators such as life expectancy, adult literacy, schooling, GDP per capita, and the HDI itself are all in the North, and the lowest-ranked countries all in the Third World (UNDP, 1994: 129–31). In terms of security, military suppliers and buyers are also on different sides of the North–South divide (p. 55). In terms of the distribution of economic activity, the richest fifth made up exclusively of the Northern countries garner 84.7 per cent of the world GNP, 84.2 per cent of world trade, 85.5 per cent of domestic savings and 85 per cent of domestic investment. The figures for the poorest fifth of the global economy are 1.4, 0.9, 0.7 and 0.9 on these indicators. Upon its own figures, the UNDP Report shows global improvement, but growing inter-country disparity (p. 96).

In this context, the discourse of development cooperation can only be interpreted as another, less constrained, view of the 'trickle-down' theory – increased growth will eventually narrow the gap

---

26 The idea of a 'public good' and 'collective action' has been around for some time now. While a public good suggests non-rivalry and non-excludability, collective action is important to issues of governance, in this context across boundaries – political legal regimes to strengthen as well as to regulate markets, and some provision of 'equity and justice'. With globalization the externalities in the provision of public goods are borne by people in other countries, and therefore pose difficult dilemmas for governance institutions and discourses. The policy messages of Kaul, Grunberg and Stern (1999) are to urge the international political system to address three key weaknesses in the current provision of global public goods: the jurisdictional gap (the problem of state sovereignty), the participation gap (the civil society and private sector presence in international policy institutions) and the incentive gap (the compensation and benefit issue).

between the rich and the poor, men and women, if the global market is allowed to operate without undue restrictions, and where comparative advantage is allowed to determine the participatory levels of national economies in the international arena. This view dominates in the World Development Reports of the World Bank. The emphasis there is on efficient labour-intensive growth as a development strategy for poor countries, a growth based on market incentives, technological innovation, mechanization and extending of economic infrastructure. While poverty alleviation is made the focus of the 1990 Report,[27] for example, what we get is an 'a-historical approach to today's poverty, its neglect of the power relations leading to poverty and its top-down approach in dealing with the poor, perceiving them as patients in need of social services and safety nets' (Nijeholt, 1992: 17). Women in this context are treated as examples of the success and failures of various projects. Education, in the traditional liberal formulation, is seen as the key to women's development; however, even here the emphasis is on the utility of education in affecting women's traditional role of reproduction as the most effective population control strategy. In sum, there is a depoliticizing of the development agenda in the name of a consensus in the post-Cold War world in favour of a 'market-friendly' approach to development (World Bank, 1991: 1).

In parallel, in the report of the Commission on Global Governance (1995),[28] we see this development discourse stretched to cover the governing institutions too. The report speaks the language of 'global values' and 'common rights', and addresses the role and potential of a transformative politics of civil society organizations and NGOs (pp. 56–7). Its view of security is broader than the security of individual state borders, and encompasses people's human rights, and the need for de-militarization as part of the security agenda (pp. 71–4). It also points out that globalization of the market is confined to the movement of 'capital (but not labor) flows' but does not seek to make changes to the WTO in the light of this observation.[29]

---

27 See also the 2000/1 World Development Report, entitled *Attacking Poverty* (World Bank, 2000).
28 McGrew situates the approach of the Commission within the liberal-internationalist school, which is concerned primarily with illuminating the rational (efficiency) calculus of international cooperation while failing to acknowledge the inequalities of power that tend to make democracy the 'captive of powerful vested interests' (2000: 9).
29 For a feminist critique of the WTO, in particular the intellectual property rights regime, see Barwa and Rai (2002).

In his critique of the work of the Commission, Baxi comments on the discrepancy between its assumptions of globality, and the 'central facts of contemporary world disorder' (1996: 530). Violence and poverty, in particular, are growing apace, and both affect women in particular ways. The feminization of poverty and violence against women in creating and policing new and old inter-state borders have made the cooperative development envisioned by the Commission on Global Governance a fraught discourse for women. In this context Baxi rightly comments that '[i]f governance is to be conceived as a process, it is well to recall that process is permeated by structures-in-dominance, both in states and civil societies' (p. 532). The politics of cooperation as well as of confrontation and conflict need to be made visible here; the wishing away of confrontation is the confirmation of existing structures-in-dominance.

The Politics of Mainstreaming: Feminist Co-optations?

In this shifting pattern of governance debates and institutional initiatives, women have to address the issue of governance at different levels. The first is that of agenda-setting; the second is at the level of women's activism and its focus; and the third is at the level of institutional participation and mainstreaming of gender politics and programmes of development. I would argue that a disaggregation of these levels reveals a complex picture. First, there is a shift from addressing the problems of gendered development for women of the Third World to regarding these problems as shared between North and South. This has been made possible because of the dominance of neo-liberal economic policies in the western states themselves, as well as the imposition of structural adjustment policies on the countries of the Third World. The globalization of neo-liberal economic policy has allowed women of different countries to talk across borders, and to increase their associational activities globally. However, for feminists this poses a new dilemma. For years feminists have been struggling with the issue of difference. Third World feminists have taken issue with western feminisms' assumptions of commonality between the two. While neo-liberalism has faced women of the North and South with some similar issues arising out of the withdrawal of state welfare, can we disregard the wider historical and political contexts to view the effects of structural adjustment as common to the two? Can market-friendly development provide a new basis of 'global sisterhood'?

Second, globalization and structural adjustment have increased the engagement of women's civil society associations not only with the national state, but also with international organizations – the UN, but also the World Bank. Some feminists have advocated such a 'constructive engagement and "entry" into institutional processes and cognitive frameworks, rather than employing more overtly political tactics of capturing the resources and undermining the public image of such institutions . . . ' (O'Brien et al., 2000: 27). This could, of course, also mean providing legitimacy to the very organizations that are imposing conditionalities of various kinds – including withdrawal of state welfare – on nation-states. At the level of agenda-setting, the current activism of women's civil society organizations, particularly in the North, is thus focused on mainstreaming gender within international institutions. It also means a particular engagement with these economic institutions, which could lead to a charge of co-optive politics – that, together with other issue-based social movements, women's movements are also focused simply on gaining access to already established structures of power, rather than on challenging and, if possible, overthrowing these (J. A. Nelson, 1996; Burnham, 1999). While disputing such a blanket rejection of non-class-based politics, I would argue that in order to address the issue not simply of recognition of gender inequality but also of re-distribution of resources to overcome this inequality, women's activism has to invoke the politics of structural change – in terms both of patriarchy and of socio-economic structures of power. 'Mainstreaming gender' without attention to both remains a flawed project (Coole, 1997; Fraser, 1997; I. M. Young, 1997; Hoskyns and Rai, 1998; Rai, 2002b; and chapters 4 and 5).

In Conclusion

In laying out the various levels of governance that women have to negotiate with and struggle against, I have also sought to raise issues that these negotiations and struggles pose for them. Feminist movements as social movements have achieved a great deal in politicizing gender not only within the nation-state but also within the international system. That has been the success of the women's and feminist movements. In the new millennium, it is important to view this achievement with justifiable pride. When the World Bank begins to view gender as an important issue, when 'Women's Eyes on the Bank' make the Bank uncomfortable and want to engage in the gender debate, feminist movements can take heart (also see chapter 5). When gender inequality becomes one important issue for assessing human development, then women's social movements can be seen to have succeeded. However, as I argue in the next chapter, such engagements should also come with health warnings attached – changes in project funding and even perhaps some new policy initiatives, while important, do not make for the paradigmatical shifts in neo-liberal economic thinking that feminist economists have been demanding.

In discussing the character and role of social movements, Zirakzadeh suggests that contemporary social movements have the following characteristics: they comprise groups of people attempting to bring about a radical new social order; they involve people of a 'broad range of social backgrounds'; and they deploy confrontational and socially disruptive tactics as well as lobbying of power-holders (1997: 4–5). Social movements differ from state elites in that they do not have at their disposal means of coercion (legitimate or not); they differ from business interests in that they do not command sufficient capital to influence public policy through its movement; and they can be distinguished from interest groups in seeking large-scale social change – they are anti-systemic (O'Brien et al., 2000: 9). As such, social movements are also democratic (p. 10). There is, however, a more cautionary view that points to the integrative function that social movements perform: they can be safety valves of discontented popular movements (Scott, 1990: 15). The middle-class nature of women's movements' leaderships, for example, led many women activists in the Third World to keep distant from them. Feminists were labelled as western, educated and middle-class – an easy discourse for the local and state elites to use, but of no less concern to women who wanted to be seen to belong to the culture they were challenging. Finally, when we examine the rhetoric of many social movements, the critiques of the existing power relations are not always matched by a view of power that would allow them to move towards fundamentally redistributing resources. Increasingly, feminists are concerned that in succeeding in the battle for recognition of gender inequalities, feminist social movements are losing the struggle for redistribution of power relations (Fraser, 1997; Hoskyns and Rai, 1998). It has also been argued that the idea of a global civil society of which social movements (see Cohen and Rai, 2000a) are part is a 'liberal recasting of world politics in a period of globalization' – that via the agency of social movements within global civil society, 'the liberal dream of expanding freedom through voluntary association and the confidence in surmounting natural constrains reappears' (Kamal Pasha, 1996: 644). These concerns point to some difficult dilemmas for feminists working in the area of development. Questions of difference, of

elitism, of negotiations, engagements and oppositions to state structures that had faced them in the 1970s and 1980s have become more
complex still in the context of globalization. In the next chapter a
closer analysis of the economic fall-out of globalization in the shape
of structural adjustment policies reveals how contested and uneven
is the global economic and political space.

4 | Global Restructuring and Restructuring Gender Relations
The Politics of Structural Adjustment

Poverty has a woman's face; of the 1.3 billion poorest, only 30% are male. Poor women are often caught in a damaging cycle of malnutrition and disease. This plight stems directly from women's place in the home, and in society....

Gro Harlem Brundtland, Reith Lecture 2000 on Health and Population

...feminism is not simply a struggle to end male chauvinism or a movement to ensure that women will have equal rights with men; it is a commitment to eradicating the ideology of domination...so that the self-development of people can take precedence over imperialism, economic expansion, and material desires.

bell hooks, *Ain't I a Woman?*

Introduction

In the previous chapter we saw that globalization means many things to many theorists, and yet all seem to acknowledge that the expansion of markets is a crucial feature of globalization. I examined the embedded and gendered nature of the market to assess how women have experienced the liberalization of economies under globalization. Finally, I also argued for a perspective on globalization that is rooted in the processes of production, which would allow us to reflect upon the power relations obtaining between men and women, between North and South and among women in the context of global restructuring. In this chapter I examine the unfolding of regimes of global restructuring, and the impact this has had on the lives of women and men, and on the struggles that they are engaged in. I do this, first, by assessing structural adjustment policies (SAPs) and their gender-differentiated results. In the words of Owoh, a 'gendered critique of these policies goes beyond considerations of the impact of structural adjustment policies on women to a deeper discussion of gender, neo-liberal economics, and development' (1995: 181). Second, I examine the challenges that feminist economists have posed, at a theoretical level, to neo-liberal economics in analysing the impact of SAPs. And finally, through the examination of issues relating to the changing regimes of women's work, I raise tentative questions about this feminist critique itself. I conclude that global restructuring is affecting women's lives in complex ways. First, the social compact between states and citizens, however fragile in the first instance, is being further endangered, and women are suffering the effects of this breakdown disproportionately to men. Second, global restructuring is opening up new areas of paid work for women under particularly difficult conditions, which include lack of labour codes as well as increased levels of responsibility for care. This increased burden is widening the gap between resources of well-being available to women and men (DAW, 1999: xvii–xviii). Finally, global restructuring is also widening the gap among women along class lines, and between women of the North and South. Addressing this issue remains important for the legitimacy of feminist critiques of the mainstream economics that underlies the processes of global restructuring.

Stabilizing and Institutionalizing Structural Adjustment Policies (SAPs)

Globalization and SAPs

The current phase of globalization, I would argue, has witnessed progressive rejection of the three 'social models': Keynesian welfare states in the developed countries; the Soviet model, which challenged the welfare state system; and the attempts at 'national-capitalist development in the peripheral countries' that were made possible by the successful nationalist movements. Finance capital has become a predominant economic actor and has acted through a variety of means: '... floating exchange rates, high interest rates, privatization of formerly state-owned enterprises, huge deficits in the US balance of payments, and policies by international financial institutions forcing third world countries to put service of their foreign debt above all other considerations' (Amin, 1998: 22–3). Stein has identified three disturbing trends under globalization: (1) the growing volatility of currency flows, with consequent devaluations in currencies of the most adversely affected countries, as was evident in the East Asian crisis;[1] (2) the unevenness, reversal and even apparent marginalization of some regions, particularly Africa – and, I would argue, sections of populations – as a result of economic globalization;[2] (3) the growing hegemony of neo-classical economics as the only frame of reference for policies of stabilization, transformation and economic development (1999: 1–2). Introduction of SAPs was itself born out of a neo-liberal response to a crisis: the growing debt issue. However, it has been argued that 'crises and dislocations also are opportunities and can result in altered gender roles' (Monteón, 1995: 42).[3]

---

1 Singh and Zammit point out, 'at the macroeconomic level women lose more than men from slow and/or unstable economic growth, financial crises and meltdowns, and even more so the longer and deeper the economic downturn...' (2000: 1249).

2 According to UNCTAD, Africa's share of developing countries' foreign direct investment fell from 11 per cent during 1986–90 to 3.8 per cent in 1996. Sub-Saharan Africa receives only 0.6 per cent of the world's FDI. Under Adjustment, expenditure on education and therefore enrolment rates have plummeted. Girl child enrolment had risen from 30 per cent in 1965 to 69 per cent in 1980, and for male children from 52 per cent to 91 per cent. The figures were 64 per cent and 77 per cent in 1993 (Stein, 1999: 4, 7).

3 Monteón (1995) argues that with the Depression of the 1920s and 1930s there was a dislocation of labour and labour patterns for both men and women. This resulted in new labour and political mobilizations, including those of women. However, these mobilizations took place in particular patriarchal and cultural contexts, resulting in changes in some public areas of life but not focusing on shifting the 'patriarchal bargain' – the idea that women would be maintained in a decent life in the home. As economic recovery began, changes to gender relations formed part of the new balance of forces, and were reflected in the struggles for articulations of new social codes in reformed constitutions and new legal regimes. A similar argument has been made about the East Asian crisis and its impact on women's lives (DAW, 1999; Lim, 1990; Truong, 1999).

Reviewing SAPs

Much has been written about the origins of SAPs. The major reasons explored have ranged from the mismanagement of domestic economies in the aftermath of the oil boom and then the crash of prices, to the world financial system and its regulation (or lack of), and to the role played by western banks in overheating Third World economies, which resulted in the debt crisis. One major explanatory framework, world-system theory, posits the structuring of the world into a 'system' underpinned by the logic of capitalist relations. The potency of SAPs in refashioning economic and social relations is only now being acknowledged. From the admission of the President of the World Bank, James Wolfensohn, that 'if we do not have greater equity and social justice, there will be no political stability and without political stability no amount of money put together in financial packages will give us financial stability' (cited in Devetak and Higgott, 1999: 2) to the rather more predictable, but for that no less powerful, indictment by those opposed to the SAP regimes, we seem to be at a point when we can assess the consequences of this bundle of policies. Perhaps this is because of the length of time that has elapsed since SAPs were first introduced, so that a medium to long-term view is now possible. Perhaps too, with the collapse of the Soviet Union and the Eastern European states, SAPs are no longer policies directed simply at the Third World but have encompassed, what are now called 'transitional economies', providing us with insights into their functioning in new contexts.

As already discussed in chapter 3, the fall of the Soviet and Eastern European economies has also doubtless created a political space that allows for a critical examination of these policies without undermining the overall message that these embody: that of the efficient functioning of capitalism. Pieterse maintains, for example, that 'in the 1990s, unlike the 1970s, the big hiatus no longer runs between mainstream and alternative development, but between human development and structural adjustment, or, in other words, between two forms of mainstream development' (1998: 345). While one could argue that this change has occurred because of the strength of the alternative discourses and movements of development, it could equally be the case that these two 'mainstream' models can coexist while the socialist alternative that challenged the capitalist social order could not. The term 'alternative' has itself been incorporated into the mainstream. While one could argue, for example, that the United Nations voices concerns of many within the 'alternative' mainstream at international fora, its policy framework does not provide a paradigmatic shift. Rather, it speaks of a largely 'welfarist' agenda that arguably would allow poor countries to be more closely tied to the global, North-dominated economy.[4] The Copenhagen Declaration at the United Nations Social Summit in 1995 is reflective of this new managerial and welfarist approach to social inequality: '...globalization "opens new opportunities for sustained economic growth and development". The challenge, however, is to manage the rapid processes of change and adjustment which engender intensified poverty, unemployment and social disintegration, in order to enhance their benefits and mitigate their negative effects upon people' (*Mainstream*, 1995: 31). This view has synergy with the World Bank's approach to poverty in some key areas. The 'New Poverty Agenda' was first articulated by the World Bank in 1990 in its World Development Report, which emphasized a concern for the welfare of the poorest and most vulnerable sections of society, who were considered hardest hit by the implementation of SAPs during the 1980s. Poverty thus remains the central issue for development. What have not shifted, despite growing evidence regarding the growth of poverty, are the market-based assumptions of the macroeconomic framework that underpins many of the structural adjustment 'remedies' prescribed for countries in the South: market-led growth; the role of education and some safety-nets of welfare; and the responsibility of the individual as market agent (Whitehead and Lockwood, 1999).[5] Wider socio-economic issues are only marginally reflected upon, and always within the triadic framework sketched above. What has been focused on in terms of poverty reduction is,

> at the national level,...[reviewing] the impact of structural adjustment programmes on social development, including, where appropriate, by means of gender-sensitive social impact assessments.... At the international level...[ensuring] that multilateral development banks and other donors...strive to ensure that structural adjustment

---

4   For the tie-up between UNCTAD and the World Bank on debt management, see UNCTAD (2000).

5   Growth-led development, as espoused in the 1980s and 1990s is being increasingly questioned. There is also evidence, especially in the post-East Asian crisis period, that in countries where the national state retained capital controls and was able to resist pressures to restructure the economy from global financial institutions such as the IMF, growth has been more stable and the rise in poverty levels less acute (Stewart, 1998; Stiglitz, 2000). The UNDP poverty report (2000) also makes the point, which has been emphasized by feminist economists, that links between anti-poverty initiatives and gender issues are not generally made to the detriment of women, girls and children more generally.

programmes respond to the economic and social conditions, concerns and needs of each country... and enlist the support of... the Bretton Woods institutions, in the design, social management and assessment of structural adjustment policies.... (*Mainstream*, 1995: 31)

This approach poses fundamental problems not for a feminist analysis of female poverty and well-being, but for feminist activism and agency. (I will discuss this latter issue at length in chapter 5.)

In the following two sections I raise some questions arising from the discussions on the origins and implementation of SAPs, as well as from the more current debates about the consequences of their long-term institutionalization through global financial arrangements.

The Debt Crisis and SAPs

It has been argued that the debt crisis that led to the first phase of SAPs[6] arose not out of an oil slump, but more fundamentally from the contradictions arising out of the two 'cherished notions in US foreign policy: (1) that the Third World must naturally import capital; and (2) that private capital can, and should, handle the major part of capital flows to the Third World' (Payer, 1989: 7; see also Monteón, 1995). The rhetoric of modernization and the preferred strategies of achieving growth meant that most Third World countries that did not pursue import-substitution policies accepted these two 'notions'. Accompanying the rhetoric of modernization was the rhetoric of anti-communism. 'The "foreign aid" programmes of the US government began in the 1950s as a means of supporting anti-communist governments in the Middle East and in Asia. As developed countries began to 'tie' foreign aid disbursements to purchase from their own countries' businesses, the distinction between aid and export promotion became blurred' (Payer, 1989: 8).

---

6 Monteón (1995), in his study of Latin America, compares the Great Depression of the 1920s and 1930s and the 1980s debt crisis to make the point that this historical reading points to cyclical trends in Latin American development. These crises were ' "critical junctures", periods of massive dislocation'. We can see a similar dislocation resulting from the debt crisis and its aftermath, the structural adjustment that was enforced by banks and international financial institutions on Third World debtor nations in the 1980s and 1990s, and in the East Asian economic crisis. What is also interesting here is that the Great Depression in Latin America led to state intervention in economic policy-making and management. The result of the debt crisis has been deregulation of industry, the expansion of international trade and the strengthening of global governance mechanisms.

The blurring of the lines of aid and loans (from private banks and governments), of help and of financial deals, was furthered by a normalized discourse of 'foreign aid', which hid the reality of stringent repayment regimes.[7] Repayment posed several problems – a multiplicity of borrowings to repay old debts through seeking new ones. Export-led growth, which was the favoured strategy of the western donor nations (see chapter 2), was for most Third World countries a result of primary goods trading, never enough to generate the kind of surpluses needed to service growing debts. In the 1980s this was compounded by depleted international demand, and high US interest rates on short-term loans (Warburton, 1999: 165). Those countries that tried the domestic-led growth model fell foul of foreign exchange surpluses to service debts. By the mid-1960s debt service was 'eating up 87 per cent of new lending to Latin America, and 73 per cent of new lending to Africa' (Payer, 1989: 10). By the mid-1970s the levels of debt rose when the rise in prices of petrol increased costs of production, as well as foreign exchange deficits in oil-importing Third World countries. However, as Payer argues, 'The oil price crisis was simply fuel added to an already blazing fire' (1989: 12).

The crisis occurred at two different levels. As oil prices rose, private banks expanded business in the Third World. They did this, however, with much harder terms of loan-servicing (high interest rates and short maturities). Between 1981 and 1982, for example, the seven largest debtors in Latin America (Argentina, Brazil, Chile, Colombia, Mexico, Peru and Venezuela) experienced a collective rise in interest costs of 17 per cent, a fall in export earnings of 9 per cent, and a drop in new lending of 16 per cent. When Mexico and Brazil, the two largest Third World borrowers, defaulted on their debt payments in 1982, the world financial system was in crisis. While oil-importing countries suffered due to harsh lending rates, with the fall in oil prices during the early 1980s, oil-producing countries such as Nigeria were also caught up in the crisis. When the oil prices were high, the Nigerian government pursued a development strategy that depended entirely upon the maintenance of a high oil price rather than diversification of production. While this strategy led to an expansion of the public sector job market and benefited women as they joined the labour market as nurses, teachers and secretaries, it also led, in many cases, to very high levels of corruption (*IDS Bulletin*, 1996). Import agents increased their influence and the relations

---

7   For an analysis of how law – national and international – has been used in the managing of the debt crisis as well as making the argument for debt cancellation, see Adelman (1993).

between the state bureaucracy and those with economic and political power became more complex. Women gained and lost in this oil-feverish economy depending upon their class positioning. 'The "mythical" explanation of the manner in which women were incorporated into the ...Nigerian oil economy is that of the wife of the high-ranking army officer or civil servant who uses her husband's influence to obtain contracts with government departments... to supply them with imported goods' (Dennis, 1991: 92). The Nigerian development strategy during the oil boom, which involved large-scale borrowing to finance import-substitution industries and food imports to reduce urban living costs on the basis of an overvalued naira, contained the seeds of the economic crisis (p. 93).

In the wake of the debt crisis of the 1980s, the structural adjustment package took shape as part of the 'debt forgiveness' strategy, and was widely used in many Third World and later in 'transitional' economies. The Baker Plan of 1985 was introduced by the IMF and the World Bank to set out the conditions that qualified countries for debt-reduction packages, but this proved unsuccessful and soon gave way to the Brady Plan of 1989 (Warburton, 1999: 166). It included: (1) a drastic lowering of the trade barrier, exposing local producers to foreign competition; (2) reduction in subsidies and price controls to remove 'distortions' in the market-set prices at the local level; (3) a restructuring of financial systems by withdrawing controls on capital movements; (4) the privatization of state-owned enterprises; (5) attracting foreign investment and reducing capital flight by removing state controls;[8] and (6) minimizing state intervention in the management of the economy, and also in the provision of social services. SAPs thus combined two sets of policies: 'an initial IMF-led stabilization program concerned with demand-side adjustment (including devaluation, price liberalization, and fiscal austerity) and an accompanying expenditure-switching, World Bank-led structural program concerned with supply-side adjustment (removal of subsidies, introduction of user fees, and privatisation of social programs)' (Owoh, 1995: 182). A 'shock therapy' treatment of 'ailing' economies was recommended that would see the implementation of all these reforms in tandem and over a short period to avoid prolonged inefficiency and social dissent.

---

8 Seguino notes that 'gender inequality, which contributes to women's relatively lower wages, was a stimulus to growth via the effect on exports during 1975–1995. Empirical analysis shows that GDP growth is positively related to gender wage inequality, in contrast to recent work, which suggests that income inequality slows growth' (2000: 1211).

Market, individual choice sovereignty and a delegitimization of the state as an agent of development form the neo-liberal core of these sets of policies. The emphasis on markets meant an insistence on moving production from non-tradables that are largely produced and consumed within national boundaries, to production of tradable goods and services that are exchanged in international markets. As we shall see below, for many feminist critics this emphasis on the market and on choice is indicative not only of male-biased policies, but also of the discipline of economics in which these policies and policy assumptions are embedded. The role of the state, while reduced through the implementation of reforms, remained critical to introducing SAPs. It has also been noted that SAPs were not always introduced due to pressure from international financial institutions (IFIs). In Nigeria, for example, the Shagari government introduced its own package of stabilization policies under the Economic Stabilization Act of 1982 and opened up negotiations with the IMF (Dennis, 1991).[9] The nature of the state is important here, as is the context within which it functions. Thus since the 1980s there has been a renewal of interest in the processes of democratic development, including conditionalities for further aid that are not just economic but also political.

Amin has argued that the debt crisis arose out of the revising of North–South relations at a time when capitalism was unable to expand through encroaching upon and dominating fresh pre-capitalist areas, as it had done during the colonial period (1976: ch. 6; also Hoogvelt, 1997: ch. 3). Politically, McMichael (2000) argues, the debt crisis also heralded the demise of the Third World as a collective entity as the impact of structural adjustment and rates of growth diverged among countries. The debt crisis also increased the role of global institutions in the management of the world economy: the debt regime took shape as poor economies became increasingly dependent upon the resources available for disbursement through these institutions. Conditionalities were placed on and accepted by the poor countries, tying them more securely within the global economic market. For example, it was decided that the forty 'heavily indebted poor countries' (HIPCs) that pursued the structural reform of their economies demanded by the World Bank/IMF would be eligible for a large amount of aid on concessional terms. Of the forty, Uganda alone met the condition of completion of two enhanced structural adjustment facilities (ESAFs), that is, sustained adjustment

---

9 Stewart (1998) has argued that countries than 'adjusted' on their own initiative did significantly better in reducing poverty than did those who 'adjusted' under IMF or World Bank pressure.

for six years, which allowed a proportion of its debt to be converted into grants (Addison, 1998: 45; Warburton, 1999).[10] In 1999 a new 'facility', the Poverty Reduction and Growth Facility (PRGF), was introduced to replace the ESAF. The IMF claimed the 'PRGF-supported programs... differ from ESAF programs in significant ways'. First, 'key social and sectoral programs and structural reforms aimed at poverty reduction and growth are to be identified and prioritized during the participatory PRSP [Poverty Reduction Strategy Papers] process, and their budgetary impact costed taking into account the need for efficient, well-targeted spending', and, second, the 'primary focus is on improving the management of public resources, achieving greater transparency, active public scrutiny, and generally increased government accountability in fiscal management' (IMF, 2001). Seventy-seven low income countries are eligible for PRGF assistance instead of the earlier forty. However, Chossudovsky points out that the imposition of policy-based conditionalities on debt-ridden nation-states by the IMF and the World Bank leads to the 'enforcing the legitimacy of the debt-servicing relationship while maintaining debtor nations in a strait-jacket which prevents them from embarking upon an independent national economic policy' (1998: 51). Thus, for example, the Brady Plan worked through supporting the conversion of commercial bank loans into new bonds backed by the US Treasury with reduced principal or interest rates, and used for debt buy-backs. However, in 'comparison to the government bonds of developed countries, the potential for capital gains and losses is very much greater' (Warburton, 1999: 166). So, for example, while this system helped rescue the Mexican currency in 1994 through bailing out US investors in Mexican bonds, 'the impact on emerging debt markets was quite the opposite.... The clear message from the emerging debt markets is that prudent risk assessment will always be swept aside by tides of global capital' (p. 167), as was shown during the East Asian financial crisis in 1997 (see table 4.1).

---

10 After the Prague conference on debt relief in 2000 the World Bank and the IMF agreed to relax conditions for debt relief in order to enable twenty countries to benefit from the deal – still short of the figure of twenty-four promised at the conference. The Jubilee 2000 campaign against debt has argued that what is needed is 100 per cent cancellation of debt by all lenders, not just individual countries, as the bulk of debt is owed to IFIs such as the World Bank and the IMF. Crashing commodity prices in 2000 led some to speculate that some African countries will be paying more on debt servicing after the G7 debt deal than before (Denny, 2000).

Table 4.1 External debt of selected countries, 1990 and 1997

Economy	Net private capital flows (US$m)		Foreign direct investment (US$m)		External debt as % of GNP
	1990	1997	1990	1997	1997
Albania	31	47	0	48	22
Algeria	−424	−543	0	7	65
Angola	237	−24	−335	350	206
Brazil	562	43,377	989	19,652	23
Bulgaria	−42	569	4	498	96
China	8,107	60,828	3,487	44,236	15
Côte d'Ivoire	57	−91	48	327	141
Ecuador	183	829	126	577	72
Ethiopia	−45	28	12	5	131
Ghana	−5	203	15	130	57
India	1,872	8,307	162	3,351	18
Indonesia	3,235	10,863	1,093	4,677	62
Kenya	124	−87	57	20	49
Malaysia	769	9,312	2,333	5,106	48
Mozambique	35	37	9	35	135
Nicaragua	21	157	0	173	244
Nigeria	467	1,285	588	1,539	72
Panama	127	1,443	132	1,030	88
Philippines	639	4,164	530	1,222	51
Slovak Republic	278	1,074	0	165	48
Tanzania	5	143	0	158	77
Uganda	16	179	0	180	31
Vietnam	16	1,994	16	1,800	78
Zambia	194	79	203	70	136

Source: World Bank, 1999b: 270–1

Assessing SAPs

Elson (1989) and Moser (1989) have used four criteria to assess the impact of SAPs on women's lives: changes in incomes, in prices, in levels and composition of public expenditure, and in working conditions (Elson, 1989: 69).[11] Evidence in all categories is mixed

---

11 Elson makes the point that intra-household distribution of resources will vary from inter-household distribution, and that we need a class-differentiated analysis of SAPs based on empirical research on the 20 per cent richest and 20 per cent poorest households (1989: 69). Moser has made a similar point in that

depending upon the sectors, geographical areas and the depth of SAPs, implementation. However, Elson points out that there is sufficient evidence to suggest that women's labour is being stretched unbearably to accommodate cuts in public social spending and the expansion of women's work outside the home (see table 4.2). Moser points out that more poor women in SAPs-affected areas are working for longer hours than before (1989: 79). Cerrutti points out that '[i]n relative terms, more women now are compelled to work than ever before but they are also more frequently unemployed and with intermittent labour force trajectories' (2000: 889). Young children are being looked after by daughters while their mothers are out at work, and as a result the future of the daughters is being constrained as they forgo education to fill in the care-gap at home (Moser, 1989: 80). McAfee points out that the emphasis

Table 4.2 Women's work under globalization

HDI rank	Female unpaid family workers (as % of total), 1990	Female economic activity rate (as % of male rate), 1995	Labour force (as % of total population), 1995	Women's share of adult labour force (age 15 and above), 1970	Women's share of adult labour force (age 15 and above), 1995
High human development	48.5	57.2	44.7	27.8	37.2
Medium human development	–	26.1	52.0	38.2	42.9
Low human development	–	55.9	43.7	36.4	38.2
All developing countries	48.4	64.4	47.8	36.5	40.6
Least developed countries	41.4	76.2	46.9	43.2	47.7
Industrial countries	75.2	79.1	49.4	39.7	44.2
World	58.4	67.5	48.1	37.5	41.4

Source: UNDP, 2000

'the capacity of low-income women to cope with [SAPs-induced] change differs according to whether women are "coping", "burnt out" or "hanging on"' (1989: 75). While both points are important, I am not aware of the second insight having resulted in any systematic gender- and class-based data-gathering on the consequences of SAPs, which limits the analysis and also the policy recommendations of scholars such as Elson (1989) and Moser (1989).

on revenue generation has meant an expansion of tourism in the Caribbean, which is despoiling the environment, and has led to increase in prostitution (1989: 75). Elson, (1989) also suggests that while SAPs might be redirecting revenue from urban areas to rural areas in some cases (see Safa, 1995), the expenditure of rural populations on urban-produced goods is rising, with a net result of declining incomes resulting in widespread malnutrition and poor health of women. Also, land remains in the control of men, which consolidates the rights of men over women's labour, as well as re-enforcing prevalent social norms. In such a situation, market distortions on lines of gender continue to affect women's ability to take advantage of the product of their labour (Evers and Walters, 2000: 1343; also Agarwal, 1997; Patel, 1999). Moser detected nutritional problems among young children, mothers spending less time with them, and increased levels of domestic violence as total household incomes decrease together with the increased levels of women's work (1989: 80). Safa, on the other hand, in her research on the effects of export-led industrialization in Puerto Rico and the Dominican Republic, found that, though women seem to be enjoying greater autonomy with the expansion of work, levels of insecurity are also high due to the increased dependence of these countries on US capital, as a result of which there has been a considerable weakening of workers' bargaining power in the phase of 'feminization of labour' (Safa, 1995: 107–9). The trend towards expansion and casualization of the work of women, while contributing towards strategies of survival, is not conducive to 'sustained growth and development both on a personal and national level' (Elson, 1989: 72).

Here we come to the methodological problem of measuring poverty, which has been identified by many scholars in different contexts (Drèze and Sen, 1989; Blumberg et al, 1995; Kabeer, 1994). Traditionally poverty lines are drawn on the basis of per capita incomes and percentage of population. Another traditional measurement of poverty is to examine the levels of household incomes in particular areas. This perspective has been challenged, and the process of widening the definition of poverty is ongoing. As we saw in chapter 2, the gendered critique of households led to disaggregating the interests of women and men within the household, and therefore to distinguishing household income from individual well-being. The question of well-being has also focused on what constitute the qualitative indicators of poverty. Kabeer defines the matter simply: '... the poor are those who are deprived of basic human needs' (1994: 137; see also Blumberg et al., 1995). An 'ends' perspective in this case would focus on levels of deprivation of needs, and a means perspective on the adequacy of resources to avoid deprivation.[12] One area that cuts across this ends/means dichotomy is that of labour – it is an end in terms of accounting for levels of employment, and it is a means as it brings in wages as well as possible non-material resources such as autonomy to avoid deprivation. Are increasing levels of women's employment under globalization becoming part of the strategies for the individual and collective development of women?

The International Division of Labour

It has been argued that for many countries the globalization of production and exchange and the integration of world markets have reinforced the international division of labour. With it has emerged 'an enhanced separation between the site of *production* and the site where *value is added*, since local labour in producing countries represents only a cost of production and not a purchasing power value necessary for realization, the product being destined for external markets' (Campbell, 1989: 18). By the 1980s the international division of labour also reflected remarkably new characteristics: 'The Third World's exports included more manufactured goods than raw materials, and the First World was exporting 36 percent more primary commodities than the Third World' (McMichael, 2000: 56).[13] What also became rapidly clear was that women were central to this new international division of labour. As early as the mid-1980s, about 1.8 million workers were employed in a total of 173 EPZs around the world. By the late 1990s, more than 200 EPZs employed about 4 million workers, most of them women (p. 94), leading to claims of a global feminization of labour (Pearson, 1998, and below). This division of labour has created not only new labour hierarchies, but also a division between producers and consumers, both nationally and between the women of the South (mainly producers) and of the North (mainly consumers) (Mies, 1986: 116).

Another feature of this international division of labour has been that the national sites of production therefore remain secure within the geography of the poor nations, while global capital moves with

---

12 For a discussion of basic needs and entitlement approaches to poverty, see chapter 2. See Kabeer (1994: ch. 6) for a detailed analysis of needs- and entitlement-based gendered analysis of poverty.

13 Stein, however, points out that Africa's exports have not displayed this characteristic, remaining largely (92%) primary products between 1970 and 1991 (1999: 5).

minimal restraint. This discrepancy of power is increasingly evident when we compare the capital availability of transnational corporations (TNCs) as opposed to the poor nation-states, indeed at times whole regions. For example, the combined revenues of General Motors and Ford exceed the combined gross domestic product for all of sub-Saharan Africa. Overall, fifty-one of the largest one hundred economies in the world are corporations, and TNCs are involved in 70 per cent of world trade. More than 30 per cent of this trade is 'intra-firm', that is, it occurs between units of the same corporation (Corporate Watch, 1999).

To point to the playing out of unequal power relations between nations when examining SAPs is not, however to obscure the role that nation-state elites have played in their introduction. There were 'corruptly inflated contracts for kick-backs, unproductive investment in stadia, new capital cities and similar prestige projects, an anti-rural bias in government programmes, large and chronic budget deficits, official collusion with MNCs [multinational corporations] and large military spending' (Onimode, 1989: 3). This complicity has been read either in tandem with the systemic issues arising out of the expansion of capital (Amin, 1998) or as a means of demonstrating that the problem lay not with the socio-economic model of capitalism sold to Third World states, but with the lack of institutional capacities of these states (World Bank, 1994, 2000). Issues of governance (Hewson and Sinclair, 1999; Picciotto, 2000; and chapter 3, this volume), of democratization and accountability (Luckham and White, 1996) have an important place in analyses of relations of states and markets. It is not surprising that this interest in governance arose at the time of the collapse of the Soviet model. The collapse led to the fundamental shifting of economic (and in many cases nation-state) boundaries and the expansion of capitalist market relations. The result has been an expansion of the SAPs regime to include the former Soviet-bloc countries. The price paid by these countries for being incorporated into the world economy has been high – especially so for some (see table 4.1).

Institutionalizing Structural Adjustment

The package of SAPs put together by international financial institutions, and endorsed by the major western economies, forms an important part of the global restructuring of economy within the framework of neo-liberalism. While, at the start of the twenty-first century, this framework is being challenged and to some extent

modified, we are also encountering a process of long-range institutionalization of liberal economic policies through the power of discourse as well as the establishment of global economic regulatory
bodies. Thus accumulation of capital, as always, is being comple-
mented by an 'accumulation of power in other forms, e.g., knowledge, military capability, regulatory capacity' (Thomas, 1998: 162).
In the context of the changing role of the national state, these
regimes of power play a particularly important role of normalizing,
legitimizing and promoting the 'common-sense' discourse of free
enterprise and individual and corporate property rights, as opposed
to an envisioning of a collective good. Institutions such as the IMF
and World Bank, and increasingly the World Trade Organization
(WTO) are situated at the heart of this new phase of globalization
and its regulation (Chossudovsky, 1998: 42–3; Scholte with O'Brien
and Williams, 1998).

It has been argued that the relationship of international financial
institutions and national governments of the Third World has been
fundamentally redefined through the establishment of the WTO.
Mohan has outlined four key themes reflected in the debates on this
relationship: first, the argument that the state is no longer the defini-
tive policy unit; second, the question of responsibility in the context
of the state being decreasingly an originator of political action, while
IFIs exercise power without responsibility; third, the importance of
the normalizing power of the neo-liberal discourse, which enhances
the position of the IFIs; and, fourth, the focus on the 'local' or 'civil
society', which allows IFIs to bypass the state in the name of democratization through consultation with NGOs (1996: 289–91). The World
Bank's World Development Report, 2000, claims that '[a]n effective
WTO serves the interests of developing countries in four ways: It
facilitates trade reform; It provides a mechanism for settling disputes;
It strengthens the credibility of trade reforms; [and] It promotes transparent trade regimes that lower transactions costs', and that these
benefits 'explain the willingness of developing countries to join the
WTO in increasing numbers' (p. 53). Others, however, have taken a
different view. Chossudovsky, for example, argues that '[m]any of
the clauses of the structural adjustment programme (e.g. trade liberalization and the foreign investment regime) have become permanently
entrenched in the articles of agreement of the WTO. These articles
have laid the foundations for 'policing' countries (and enforcing 'conditionalities') according to international law', as opposed to the
earlier *ad hoc* loan arrangements as means of regulation (1998: 35).

One of the most important areas where these institutions are particularly interventionist is that of capital investment. As we have

seen, SAPs have opened up Third World economies to foreign investment, on the one hand, and to world trade, on the other. We have also seen an increase in the privatization of foreign direct investment as liberalization of Third World economies has progressed. While official capital investment in developing countries was around US$55 billion in 1998, down from US$58.5 in 1990, the comparative figures for private capital are US$150 billion, up from US$30 billion (World Bank, 2000: 7; also table 4.1 above). Thus, 'Over 70 per cent of resource flows to the developing countries in 1994 came from private market sources, another 22 per cent bilateral aid and only 6 per cent from IFIs.' At the same time, in line with the profitability criteria applied by private investors, 'four-fifths of private flows since 1990s have gone to only twelve developing countries, with the majority having no access to the market for finance' (ODI, cited in Thomas, 1998: 173).

The institutionalization of privatization is taking place at the global level through the regulation of trade, especially with the conclusion of the GATT negotiations in 1995, and the setting up of the WTO. Foreign direct investment has, for example, led to the establishment of EPZs across the Third World; to the introduction of labour regulation, which has been adverse to workers' interests in many cases; as well as to job creation in particular sectors of domestic economies, with consequences for the development patterns of Third World nations (see below). Another critical area of regulation is that of labour. While, increasingly, domestic prices of goods are being brought into line with international prices through the process that has been called 'dollarization', the labour market is not being unified at all. Indeed, what we are seeing is the fracturing of the labour market into two, characterized by a 'duality in the structure of wages and labour costs between rich and poor countries. Whereas prices are unified and brought up to world levels, wages (and labour costs) in the Third World and Eastern Europe are as much as 70 times lower than in the OECD countries' (Chossudovsky, 1998: 41). When these aggregate differentials are mapped onto labour markets with Third World economies, the disparities make the lower end of the labour market particularly deprived. As we shall see below, the consequences for women of this duality, in addition to the gendered duality of labour markets, are significant.

Accompanying the institutionalization of neo-liberal economic policy has been the institutionalization of the role of private capital within the framework of global governance. Further liberalization and the expanding role of the TNCs and the regulation of foreign investment were the subjects of the proposed Multilateral

Agreement on Investment (MAI) in the late 1990s, to which the majority of developing countries would not have belonged, but which would have involved dispute settlement among states. Such an exclusion of most Third World states has, of course, an historical parallel with the establishment and development of the Bretton Woods institutions themselves (see chapter 2). Khor argues that MAI would have had a critical impact on the lives of people as national states are unable to exert much control over their economies (1996: 21).[14] At the same time, the national states remain pivotal, in terms both of policy design and of implementation of SAPs, and thus their capacity in terms of bureaucratic functioning needs to be increased. The focus on governance (see World Bank, 1994, 2000; UNDP, 2000) thus becomes a significant part of the bundle of policies that are SAPs. All these features of the new global economic regimes have important consequences for the changing relations between men and women, and between nations, through their impact on how production is organized, marketed and regulated. In the next section I examine two examples of privatization: of knowledge and of natural resources. This will allow me to raise some issues both about local and global struggles of women to challenge these regimes, and regarding feminist critiques of global restructuring.

Commodification of Provisioning: Privatizing Natural Resources

One of the new areas in which we can detect the increase in the remit of international regulation through the WTO and other international financial institutions is the highly problematic one of intellectual property rights. Here, issues of capital investment, labour and conditionalities come together. When globalization is said to ride on the back of a 'knowledge-based economy', the definition of what is knowledge and what can count as property becomes crucial (Barwa and Rai, 2002). Feminists have examined these issues in different contexts (see chapter 2), but institutionalization of SAPs through international legal regimes is giving the issue an increased urgency.

---

14 However, under pressure from a growing movement against the MAI, 'the OECD states were forced first to suspend and then abandon the proposed... MAI, after 4 years of preparation and 3 years of intensive negotiations' (Picciotto, 2000: 1).

Privatizing 'the Natural', Commodifying the Social: The Neem Tree

'Monsanto Quit India' is a powerfully evocative slogan of the movement of a section of Indian farmers struggling against the promotion of genetically modified seeds. It has a resonance with the 1942 Quit India movement against continuing British rule. It also captures the idea of neo-colonialism by focusing on a TNC as the target for struggle. Nationalist discourse is thus used to harness the discontent felt by farmers as they face a threat to their livelihoods from 'corporate colonialism'. A second powerful discourse, linked to that of nationalism, is that of land. In a predominantly rural country like India, land signifies social status as well as wealth. Notions of purity as well as independence are intertwined in the ownership of land (see chapter 1). The commodification of land under the British led to a major economic upheaval in traditional Indian society leading to displacement of millions from rural communities, and a class/caste-based increased differential access to land. What is worrying small and medium landowners in India today is whether a new international economic regime is going to result in yet another wave of displacement and disempowerment. 'Where Europeans are concerned about the safety, environment and consumer implication of GM foods, the debate in India mostly centres on neo-colonialism – who owns and controls the technology – economic dependency and "food security"' (Vidal, 1999: 16). The worry is not without foundation. In the words of a Monsanto director, 'We are aiming to consolidate the whole food chain' (p. 16). One way this consolidation is occurring is through the power of regulation. Shiva and Holla-Bhar argue that 'the new GATT institutionalizes the international "harmonization" of property rights legislation and global monopoly ownership of life forms along the lines of US law' (1996: 148).

Two issues are interwoven here: the idea of property and the idea of knowledge. Patenting is not new; what is causing problems is the extension of patent laws to cover many areas previously not considered applicable. Underlying this extension is an idea of 'improvement' that allows patenting of existing natural products.[15] As Barwa

---

15 To qualify for patent right, the invention has to be novel, non-obvious and of practical use. Thereafter, the right confers on the holder a time-bound monopoly of the given product to enable the inventor to recoup the cost of development of the product and also to compensate for the risk undertaken. In addition, it is also claimed that such rewarding of invention encourages others to create new inventions and thus help in the extension of scientific and

and Rai (2002) point out, patents are secured for both *products or processes* in all fields of technology, provided that they are new, involve an inventive step and are *capable of industrial application*. Two developments stand out here. First, both product and processes have now been brought within the remit of exclusive marketing rights. As a result, for example, farmers will not be able to keep seeds from their crops. As women form an increasing number of small and poor farmers, this provision is affecting them particularly. Second, patents privilege particular forms of knowledge – 'stabilizing' historically developed processes of production would entitle modern industrial companies to patent products and processes and deny nature's and people's creativity at a time when TNCs already hold 90 per cent of all technology and product patents world-wide (Greer and Singh, 2001).

The case of the neem tree has become a critical one in the debates about the regulation of patents. The neem tree has been used by Indians for thousands of years as medicine, toiletries, contraception, timber, fuel, and in agriculture to improve the fertility of the soil and as an insecticide. In 1971 the neem tree was 'discovered' for the western market by a US timber importer; since 1985 over a dozen US patents have been taken out on the claim that the modernized extraction processes used by US companies constitute a 'genuine innovation over traditional extraction processes, used for millennia' (Shiva and Holla-Bhar, 1996: 152). Two separate issues are raised in this context. The first is a cultural one: while Indian scientists in the 1960s and 1970s had already extracted a stable essence of the neem tree, they did not go down the patenting route, 'in part...[because of] a recognition that the bulk of the work had already been accomplished by generations of anonymous experimenters' (p. 157). That the US Congressional Research Service calls such social experimentation and use-development of specific knowledges 'obvious' brings up the second issue: what counts as knowledge? The process of commodification of social knowledges developed over many years allowed through patent 'protection displaces farmers as competitors, transforms them into suppliers of free raw materials, and makes them totally dependent on industrial supplies for vital inputs such as seeds' (p. 157). This discourse of use value versus commodity

---

technical knowledge, which benefits society as a whole. It is argued that international protection of intellectual property rights has, therefore, been placed on the agenda of trade negotiations to safeguard the competitive position of some countries against intellectual piracy and has enabled the overly rapid diffusion of their comparative advantage (Barwa and Rai, 2002).

value is also, of course, gendered. As argued in chapter 3, in the global market systems hypermasculinized values recognize only certain forms of knowledges, work and competition. While women have been traditionally excluded from any recognition based on these values, the male populations of Third World countries also get 'feminized' through economic emasculation in the market place. This is evident in the case of the Warrangal farmers of India, 500 of whom took their lives in 1998–9 under a combination of local and global structural pressures (Vidal, 1999: 10; see also Shiva, 2000).

Under the pressure of the WTO and the liberalization of world economies, the Warrangal farmers saw two changes to earlier patterns of economic life. The first, in response to shifts in national economic policy in the late 1980s, was to move from a combination of non-tradable food production and cotton production to an overwhelming emphasis on cotton production for the market. Second, in lieu of aid, the state-subsidized seed-supply system was dismantled and the farmers had to buy patented seeds at the 'market value'. As world prices for cotton tumbled, and the farmers' cotton crops failed due to the unreliability of the new 'hybrid' seeds, the debts they had incurred to buy these seeds became too much to bear.[16] A spate of suicides in this relatively prosperous area shocked the country, and has fuelled the opposition to the increasing pressure for the adoption of genetically modified 'terminator' seeds. In this case, while men are visible in their tragedy, women themselves remain invisible. The prevalent denial of access to land to women makes their lives as widows and daughters of widows particularly problematic. So, from philosophical debates about the nature of knowledge to the lives of women left behind by men who could not withstand the pressures of structural change, new economic regimes take effect.

Water Privatization

Another area where commodification of natural resources is leading to new challenges for women is that of privatization of water resources. While the majority of those working on issues of water

---

16 The fragility of microeconomies is easily exposed by natural disasters. The drought that hit the state of Punjab, India's most fertile area, in 1999–2000, led to similar results. Shiva (2000) argues in her Reith Lecture on sustainable development that 'drought is not a "natural disaster". It is "man-made". It is the result of mining of scarce ground water . . . to grow thirsty cash crops for exports instead of water prudent food crops for local needs' (see also Lovejoy, 2000).

management 'share the unverified premise with irrigation analysts that women's uses of water mainly occur in the domestic or non-market sphere', Zwarteveen argues that 'the most important source of gender differences with respect to water lies not so much in the gender specificity of water uses, but in gender differences with respect to access to and control of water' (1997: 1335–6). She points out that women almost everywhere use water for domestic and productive use – mostly as co-farmers with their husbands, but also, in areas where single-headed households exist, as farmers in their own right.[17] So, while men and women both have a stake in the provision of and access to water for productive work, gender differences emerge in the nature of work and therefore of timing of use of water (p. 1337). In this context the privatization of water resources becomes an important structural issue for farmers, both men and women, who seek provision of this most important natural resource.

In the context of water provision the term 'privatization', can be said to include operation and management responsibilities and costs of irrigation systems to water-users' associations of various kinds; pricing of water on the basis of quantity of water used, establishing water markets for buying and selling water for both individual and productive sectors, in both rural and urban areas (Zwarteveen, 1997: 1343). The arguments being advanced in favour of privatization of water include cost savings for the public sector, increased irrigation efficiency through pricing, increased allocative efficiency through water markets, and improved management of irrigation systems (p. 1344). At the base, and in common to SAPs in general, is the shift from non-tradable use-based understanding of natural resources to a tradable commodification of water as natural resource. Two considerations come to mind immediately: first, 'not all benefits of water may be easily quantified or expressed in monetary terms, and therefore risk being undervalued by the market'; and, second, 'in most situations female farmers have less formal and direct possibilities of demanding improved services' (pp. 1344–5). This means that an increased privatization of water resources risks further marginalization of women within the agricultural sector. Further, privatization of water and irrigation systems cannot take place without the acquiring of land, posing serious issues of disempowerment

---

17 In the drought-prone desert state of Rajasthan, India, parents take into account the distance of the groom's house from the nearest source of water when arranging their daughter's marriage. Women are exclusively responsible for securing water for household consumption.

for poor or marginal farmers, who can be faced with cruel choices of debt-clearing through sale of land. And when TNCs are players in the acquisition of land for water, the lack of accountability for the welfare of the poor becomes a real problem.

The question of accountability poses difficult questions. Even under democratic regimes, it is only the national state that is the site of accountable government. It is up to national governments to deal with the terms of trade questions with the TNCs. The nature of the government and of the political system becomes very important in this context. Equally important, of course, is the nature of the global economic regimes. Thus, in the case of the neem tree we find that when the global regulatory pressures were less severe, the Indian government decided that 'the widespread common knowledge and common use of need was one of the primary reasons . . . for not registering neem products under the Insecticides Act of 1968' (Shiva and Holla-Bhar, 1996: 152). The situation is different with the tightening of the regulatory framework under the Trade-related Intellectual Property Rights (TRIPs) accord. While in June 1995 the Upper House of the Indian Parliament forced the government to defer indefinitely a bill that would have brought India into compliance with the WTO's new rules under TRIPS, this challenge was reversed under severe pressure in March 1999, when the Indian government signed up to the accord.

The challenges to global economic pressures have thus come at different levels: through challenges to the paradigms that underpin the discourses of privatization and the market; through global networking among activists; and through local-led movements in response to direct threat to people's lives and livelihoods. In the next section I explore one of these challenges: the feminist critiques of global restructuring.

Challenging 'Strategic Silences': Feminist Critiques of Global Restructuring

As we have seen above, most poor women have been worse off because of SAPs. The discourse of global restructuring 'recommends a fundamental reordering of the mode of regulation and a new definition of the public good, but is silent about the gendered underpinnings of this shift' (Brodie, 1994: 48).

Altogether, Bakker (1994a) identifies five paradoxes that are affecting women's lives under global restructuring. First is the changing nature of the state, which is at the same time minimizing its remit in the area of economy and becoming more invasive in the area of regulation of reproduction. For women this has meant increased awareness of the power of the state at a time when it is in retreat from its earlier social roles. The repressiveness of some population programmes, as well as their differential impact upon women of various groups, is causing women to organize, and at the same time to confront differences among themselves. Second is the paradox of austerity and consumerism. Austerity measures are resulting in increased insecurity, convergence of male/female employment patterns with decreasing male wages, and casualization of labour at a time when consumer-led economic recovery is being touted as a way out for Third World economies. In India, for example, this paradox has had tragic results, with a sharp increase in dowry murders in areas hitherto less influenced by the dowry culture. Third is the paradox of the privileging of women as producers as well as reproducers in the context of the withdrawal of state provision of welfare. Women are being increasingly mobilized into work, as austerity and insecurity means that the male income is no longer secure (see table 4.2). However, with the withdrawal of health and education provision by the state, and the privatization of these facilities, women's lives are being further stretched to cover the expanded time/space within which they have to operate. As carers, and increasingly as providers, women's labour is being considered infinitely elastic, leading many (for example, Elson, 1995) to suggest that this will result in the breakdown of women's health and reproductive capacity. At the same time, the displacement of male labour by a feminized workforce is leading to increased levels of violence against women, and not everywhere do women experience an enhanced social status for being the 'bread-winner' (see Stichter and Parpart, 1988; Cerrutti, 2000). Fourth is the paradox of sustainable development and the consumerist model of development, at odds with each other on counts of environmental degradation and the impact of consumerism on the rights of marginalized populations of today and of the future. Thus, both in Andhra Pradesh in India and in Chiapas in Mexico, peasant movements have originated from the commercialization of agriculture under the new WTO initiatives in the agrarian sector. Fifth, and finally, Bakker points to the paradox of the home being constructed at the same time as a haven and as a work site with the flexiblization of work.

As noted in the discussion above, SAPs were initially a response to the slowing down of many Third World, especially African, economies. However, over time they have emerged as 'a long-term development agenda undertaken by international financial institutions to ensure global financial stability' (Owoh, 1995: 182). This development resulted from the discursive dominance of the neo-liberal economic orthodoxy. Çagatay, Elson and Grown have argued that the discipline of economics needs to be weaned away from the study of choice under conditions of scarcity and towards the examination of the provisioning of human life. 'This concept [of the provisioning of human life] emphasizes those things human beings need in order to survive and flourish (such as food and health care) and their production through market work and other activities such as unpaid labor in the home and volunteer work in communities and social organizations' (1995: 1827). As Grown, Elson and Çagatay summarize, feminist analyses have offered several insights that challenge the traditional framework of macroeconomics: '... gender is a category of social and economic differentiation that influences the division of labor, and the distribution of work, income, wealth, productivity of inputs, and economic behavior of agents' (2000: 1148). First, by making unpaid household labour visible and treating labour as a produced input, feminist analysis challenges the notion that paid productive economy can function in isolation from the world of home-bound labour (see also Beneria, 1999). Second, feminist analysis has brought gender, 'as a category of social and economic differentiation (like class and race)', to bear upon our understandings of 'distribution of work, income and wealth, the productivity of work, and the behaviour of agents in the economy' (Grown, Elson and Çagatay, 2000: 1148). Finally, a gendered analysis of economic policies and legal regimes also allows us to understand the ways in which gender relations are disturbed and then reconstituted at different social levels within particular political economies. Elson and Pearson, for example, have argued that women's access to work in world factories (EPZs) leads to a 'dialectic of capital and gender' whereby we witness a 'tendency to intensify the existing forms of gender subordination; a tendency to decompose existing forms of gender subordination; and a tendency to recompose new forms of gender subordination'. They emphasize that 'there is evidence of all three at work in the case of women employed in world market factories' (Elson and Pearson, 1998: 199). Thus, 'feminist economic analysis points to the gender biases of micro and meso-level institutions, such as households, government agencies, firms and even markets, from which macroeconomic outcomes emerge' (Çagatay, Elson and Grown, 1995: 1829). When we apply these insights of feminist analysis to concrete empirical studies, the relevance and importance of these interventions becomes clear.

Gendered Regimes of Work and Survival

The opening up of markets has been at the heart of globalization. However, it has not been the same in all sectors and neither has it been played out on a power-neutral field among states. While the market has opened up – or, more accurately, in the case of most Third World countries, been 'encouraged' or forced to open up as part of the SAPs package – for capital to move more freely, it has not opened up in the area of labour mobility. While globalization of capital markets has contracted the space/time distanciation, labour markets continue to be much more structured by state boundaries. Further, capital market deregulation has gone hand in hand with increased constraints and controls upon labour organization and capacities to bargain. There has emerged a dual wage, which is increasingly consolidating a gendered North–South divide between labour markets. Finally, where opening up of markets has led to new opportunities for employment for women, this has largely been in very vulnerable sectors – EPZs, homeworking and migratory labour. All these sectors are clearly gendered – women comprising most of the labour mobilized in EPZs and homeworking, and increasing numbers of migratory populations.

Discussing women's work in the context of economic recession in Europe in the 1980s, Rubery points out that

> a continuation of the upward trend in women's employment could be the result either of progress towards the homogenization and equalization of the male and female employment roles, or be caused by the persistence of differences in sex roles on the labour market, with demand for female labour protected by rigid patterns of sex segregation or by the effects of employers' more intensive search to reduce costs under recessionary conditions. (1988a: ix)

For women in countries experiencing SAPs, this question poses important issues. In many countries, opening up has meant the creation of EPZs, which have seen the overwhelming mobilization of women's labour at the same time as the organized male labour force has been facing mass redundancy and unemployment. Flexibilization of labour, in part owing to technological change and in part because of the new international division of labour, has also led to increased employment for women – situated within the space of the home as homeworkers (Phizacklea and Wolkowitz, 1995), as well as outside it. Finally, the growth of the service sector has also pulled increasing numbers of women into the labour market. However, 'it is not simply changes in the economic structure which determines women's employment opportunities. These changes are conditioned by the system of state and institutional regulation of the labour market, and by the organization of social reproduction . . . ' (Rubery, 1988b: 8).

Women's labour outside the home, which had been part of the non-tradable economy of the family, is now, under pressure of structural changes, becoming tradable in the labour market. While in the urban economies 'domestic labor tends to concentrate on the transformation of market goods for household consumption', in agrarian economies, where a large part of women's labour in the household is subsistence work, the agricultural and household-related tasks is 'highly integrated in time and space, and productive and reproductive activities are highly intertwined' (Beneria, 1985: 132–3; 1999). The context of state regimes and SAPs is thus also mediated by the spatial economies within which women work. It has long been assumed by both liberal and Marxist feminists that paid work is important to women's empowerment within the family. In the context of SAPs we are witnessing a shift in women's work outside the home. More women are working outside the home to supplement family income. Interestingly, this shift has been described by some as 'feminization' of labour, where economists have pointed to the narrowing of gender differentials in paid work, while others have termed it 'masculinization' of labour, referring to increased risks that women are becoming vulnerable to – risks that in the past were characteristic of men's work in the labour market (see Elson, 1999: 613). And this increase of women's employment could also be read as evidence of 'harmonising down' of conditions of work (Safa, 1995) – a question of survival, and not of empowerment through control over resources generated through waged work.

Export Industries and Women's Work

It is now well established that women form the majority of the workforce in the sites of globalized production: the EPZs (see table 4.3). For example, women constitute 71 per cent of the EPZ labour force in South Korea, 80 per cent in Mexico, 83 per cent in Malaysia, 87 per cent in the Philippines and 88 per cent in Sri Lanka. However, as Truong (1999) points out, in Taiwan, women's representation in the administration in this sector is only 2 per cent of the total employees. In the 1970s,

> EPZs appeared to many as the ideal solution. Segregated as they were
> from the rest of the local economy, they were unlikely to have the

economically and socially damaging consequences which a sudden transition from high protection to open international competition would probably have entailed. Oriented as they were to export, they would create far more jobs than would ever be possible through simple import substitution. And the presence of sophisticated foreign enterprises was viewed, rightly or wrongly, as one of the most effective means of acquiring sorely needed foreign technology. (ILO in Adelman, 1993: 196–7)

In order for this strategy to work, foreign direct invesment was attracted by many means which included tax holidays to investing companies and 'above all... the provision of "favourable" industrial

Table 4.3 Women's share of jobs in major export industries, selected countries, 1977–1990 (per cent)

Country	Textiles (a)	Clothing (b)	Electronics (c)	Total (a)–(c)
Colombia				
1977	33.0	80.0	NA	49.9
1984	34.3	79.8	NA	55.9
1990	–	–	NA	–
Cyprus				
1977	–	–	–	–
1984	66.5	83.2	45.8	78.8
1990	72.3	86.5	33.5	81.8
Korea (South)				
1977	69.0	73.0	55.3	66.9
1984	65.7	76.7	52.0	64.3
1990	57.3	72.0	48.7	56.9
Malaysia				
1977	–	–	–	–
1984	63.7	89.4	73.7	75.2
1990	57.8	85.3	75.3	75.3
Sri Lanka				
1977	52.6	82.8	56.0	56.0
1984	57.5	89.1	72.8	72.8
1990	50.8	89.4	76.3	76.3
Thailand				
1977	–	–	NA	–
1984	75.0	93.0	NA	81.3
1990	75.6	81.9	NA	92.4

Source: Seguino, 2000: 1217

relations systems which inevitably rebound to the disadvantage of workers' (p. 198; Fernandez-Kelly, 1997). We have already noted in our discussion of globalization and the nation-state that a combination of nationalism, international competition, global pressures to liberalize economies, and a general ideology of 'developmentalism' have become predominant factors affecting state policies.[18] Workers' rights – and, in particular, women's workers' rights – in export-led industries have been adversely affected by these conditions. Women workers in unionized industries in the Dominican Republic, for example, earn on average 23 per cent more than their counterparts in the non-unionized EPZs. State dependency on foreign direct investments means that workers have no redress in state law: 'The government has said we can't bring Free Zone problems to them because what goes on in there is the owners' business. The Free Zone is a state unto itself' (McAfee, 1989: 82).

We find an overrepresentation of young women in this sector – in Taiwan, according to Truong (1999), '20–24 and 30–39 [per cent] constitute the highest figures of female workers'. As women's labour becomes valuable to the family/household income, the need for controlling becomes more important, and gendered regimes of social regulation become more fierce. While work in EPZs, for example, might provide women workers with a material base for escaping the increased pressure from the natal family, the social networks within which they exist might not allow the choices to be varied, and might lead in many cases to an exchange of patriarchal authority of the father for one of the husband. The recomposition of gender subordination might result in instability of employment, gender assumption about women's skills and even personality types. As shown by studies of women's conditions of work in EPZs (Fernandez-Kelly, 1997; Lim, 1990), such a recomposition leads to the normalization of social regimes of power within the workplace. As Fernandez-Kelly points out in her study of the Mexican *maquiladoras* (export processing production zones/sites), 'Workers complain that superintendents and managers are prone to demand "special services", like overtime, in exchange for granting personal "favours" such as a loan or time off

---

18   The Malaysian government argued, for example, that 'the concept of freedom and rights held by developed countries, especially European countries, is different from the one held by developing countries...they are not practical to their political systems and the security of their countries...' (in Adelman, 1993: 203). For a discussion of International Labour Codes and the currently debated Codes of Conduct for TNCs, see Barrientos (2002) and Barrientos, McClenaghan and Orton (2000).

from work to care for children. Yet workers acknowledge a personal debt to the person who hired them' (1997: 205). Thus there are limits to women's liberation through waged work (Elson and Pearson, 1997).

The Electronics Industry: A Case Study

As table 4.3 shows, women comprise a major share of the labour force in the clothing, textile and electronic sectors. The question of options that women have in a globalizing economy is further complicated when we examine the nature of recent expansion of women's work in this sector. First, the costs attached to working in this sector are significant. International and national subcontracting of work has resulted in the spatial fragmentation of the work site. Small production sites make for insecure and non-unionized workplaces for women. The regulation of these sites is not so easy, as some of them are even clandestine units in order to avoid tax. Small production units are also less sensitive to the new health hazards associated with new technologies, such as repetitive strain injury, and as existing legislation is not equipped to deal with this, the lack of trade union support becomes critical here. Further, as Rohini Hensman writes, 'It is true that new technologies create new jobs for women.... But firstly we should note that these are not the same women who have lost their jobs; typically they are young, single and sometimes more highly educated or qualified' (cited in Mitter, 1999: 8).[19] Mitter concludes from this that '[t]he outcome of this complex restructuring is that the groups that have less access to requisite education and training miss opportunities for formal sector employment, even when the economy is expanding' (p. 5). For example, the need for state provision of education is self-evident here, but sits uneasily with the pressures on the state to withdraw from service provision. Especially in countries where there has not been a strong history of state provision of education and health, this issue of declining welfare is militating against the interests of poor women. 'In the absence of an enabling state and family, the increased opportunities of paid work alone will not guarantee sustainability and quality of women's work' (p. 11).[20] However, as I have argued in chapter 3, states themselves are gendered terrains. For national states, capital formation also takes place through gendered patterns of migration. The Philippines state,

---

19   For a comparative analysis of age-based segregation of women's work in rural China, see Rai and Zhang (1994) and Jacka (1996).

20   Scholars such as Lim (1990) have argued that women's work in EPZs does, despite issues of working conditions, provide women with access to much

for example, has actively encouraged migration to relieve internal poverty: by 'law migrant workers must remit between 30 and 70 per cent of their earnings and in 1992 the Government collected $9.6 million in passport fees alone' (Phizacklea, 1999: 30).

Migration and Gendered Vulnerability

Between 2 and 3 million people migrate each year. This accounts for 2.3 per cent of the world population (World Bank, 2000: 37–8). It has also been noted that migratory flows are increasingly feminized. Such gendered and high levels of migration are also testing the limits of globalization. As Sassen has noted, 'when it comes to immigrants and refugees,... the national state claims all its old splendor in asserting its sovereign right to control its borders', despite the denationalized economies of these states (1995: 59). Where migration is concerned, the vulnerability scales for women are also very high – most migration that takes place for both men and women is distress migration across either rural–urban boundaries or regional and national boundaries. In many cases, where migration is difficult and women resort to 'illegal' means for gaining access to other countries, this vulnerability is further increased in the face of the wrath of the 'host' nation-state and the often racialized hostility of the 'local' populations. Leaving behind the spaces occupied by families marked by histories and configured by communities in the context of a struggle for survival is an extremely layered but painful process.[21] Because of their greater vulnerability to sexual and physical abuse, because of the emotional stress of leaving behind families, and because of the terms of their migratory patterns as domestic menial workers, prostitutes or low-paid professionals such as nurses, women are particularly affected by this differentiated opening up of markets (Chang and Ling, 2000). Women, argues Phizacklea, 'may have very different reasons for migrating from those of men' (1999: 30). These reasons might have to do with an active choice by women to escape social relations that are oppressive, or because of structural reasons of household poverty and available

---

needed resources and therefore alleviates gender subordination. For a thoughtful discussion of the issues raised by this analysis, see Jackson and Pearson (1998).

21 Immigration as a process not only reconfigures the lives of migrants but also plays a 'crucial role in the new urban regime with its polarized social structures and plentiful cheap labor' (see Kofman, 2000: 129). Global cities are increasingly dependent upon this vulnerable migrant population.

opportunities for employment in certain sectors of employment dominated by women, such as the entertainment industry or domestic service (see also Enloe, 1989).

However, Phizacklea argues, neo-liberal economic analyses of migration that emphasize 'push–pull' factors – low–high wages – and the rational choices that individuals make do not account for the differences between the nature of choices that women and men can and do make. Indeed, this version of migratory patterns 'may well have influenced the policies on migration adopted by a number of developing countries, the Philippines being a prime example' (1999: 30) . At the international level, the neo-classical explanation does not take into account the histories of migratory flows, nor the way that racism and structural disadvantage interact to exclude migrants from benefiting from the 'pull' factors in terms of appropriate use of skills, much less any enhancement of their skills base (p. 30). As Radcliffe points out in the case of Peruvian Andean families, 'it is not the potentially higher wage-earning labour which leaves the peasant unit, but the members whose labour is of minimal value, owing to its gender and peasant origins', in the context of a sexual division of labour that does not allow unmarried daughters to participate in extra-household exchanges of labour (in Phizacklea, 1999: 34). One of the ways in which the recomposition of gender oppression takes place at the local, national and international level in the context of migration is through the immigration law of both the home and the 'host' nation-states. Since 1974, Phizacklea observes, it has been difficult for non-professional migrants to find a host country, except for reasons of family reunion. 'The vast majority of migrants entering in this way are women ... women's experience of migration is mediated by immigration policies and rules which ... continue to treat women as confined to a male-regulated private sphere' (p. 41). For example, as del Rosario (1994) has shown in the case of Filipina sex workers in the Netherlands, it is the sex worker, and not the procurer of her services, who pays the price, through deportation, for seeking to bypass the gendered regimes of immigration law (also Pettman, 1996). However, once women are able to leave behind the locales of their domestic oppression, new, if circumscribed, opportunities do open up. Women do act as agents in making difficult choices when they migrate – whether it is from the rural to the urban production locale, or from the national to the international (see Gardiner-Barber, 2002).

Pellerin reminds us that the basis for migration need not be internally coherent and may span the 'world order', which includes 'economic, political and ideological levels of social practice'. She also sees migrants as participants in the restructuring of the 'world order' as they are affected by it, both individually and collectively (1998: 83). What Phizacklea's work emphasizes, however, is that the agency of women – whether as workers or worker-migrants – is not that of a free wage worker in the classical Marxist sense. The female worker cannot dispose of her labour power simply as her own commodity; she is enmeshed in social, economic and legal gendered networks that allow her some choices and deny her others. She is not free of social constraints that prevent the realization of her labour power – her role as reproducer of labour makes her less free than men in this regard. As long as this role of reproduction of labour is assumed by, falls to and is normalized (through law, for example) as falling to the woman, the agency she has for making life-choices remains limited. If markets are gendered spaces, as I argued in the previous chapter, then this cautionary view seems an appropriate one.

Elson (1999) points out that, overall, women in the labour force typically endure a longer working day than do their male counterparts. This is, first, because of the differentially high levels of employment of women in EPZs, where labour regulation is relatively weaker, and, second, because, in addition, women continued to carry the primary responsibility of work in the home. Also, a woman's entry into paid labour might be offset by the withdrawal of male income in supporting family needs. Further, there is also evidence of women's income being controlled by male members of the family. Finally, operating in the labour market also exposes women to greater risks – a destabilization of the earlier arrangements for a work situation contingent upon external factors outside her control, especially in the context of the withdrawal of state services, and the constant threat of capital flight by TNCs. Such an analysis of women's work has led feminist economists to emphasize market-based exclusions experienced by women enmeshed in social relations that continue to be normalized through discourses of law and citizenship.

Economic Theory, Feminist Critiques and the Citizenship Debate

As we have seen above, the market efficiency model is based on a dogma of neo-liberal economics: demand-side restraint and supply-side flexibility, that is, stabilization and structural adjustment.

Stabilization policies depend upon cutting down aggregate demand – cuts in government spending on services, salaries and investments are part of this package. In this monetized economy, '[m]oney mobilizes human effort, via prices and wages.... But money's mobilizing power is incomplete.... The ability of money to mobilize labour power for "productive work" depends on the operation of some non-monetary set of social relations to mobilize labour power for "reproductive work".' However, these social relations are also 'reshaped in response to the power of money. Nevertheless, neither can the monetary economy sustain itself without an input of unpaid labour, and input shaped by the structure of gender relations' (Elson, 1994: 40). This imbrication of monetized and non-monetized economies is not reflected in the economic theory underpinning stabilization and restructuring policies. It is the insistence of feminist economists that this 'strategic silence' is addressed (Bakker, 1994b).

Taking Polanyi's concept of embeddedness further, and expanding it to cover 'non-market relations which surround and structure all markets', feminist economists have argued that 'market goods and services are allocated through the political structure and social relations of markets, which may promote dominance and subordinancy between parties to an exchange' (Bakker, 1994a: 4). Further, though, as argued in chapter 3, markets do enable those previously excluded to access the economy, markets are also 'likely to reflect and reify existing resource allocations and socially constructed gender divisions of labour that influence endowments' (p. 4). This is the clear challenge that feminists pose to the neoclassical conceptions of perfect competition guiding markets. As Palmer (1991) has argued, gender relations based on unequal terms of exchange between men and women lead to resource misallocations. These can be viewed as a tax on women and lead to systematic 'market distortions' of a so-called 'neutral' field, which are not recognized as such, and therefore continue to be obscured in the market-competition/efficiency rhetoric. Folbre et al. (1992) in the context of Latin America, and Gordon (1990), in the context of OECD countries, take up this analysis in the context of the citizenship deficit that women experience as a result of this unacknowledged structural tax. The argument is that market-based inequalities reinforce a masculinized economic and political citizenship, which does not recognize the unequal division of unpaid work, and consequently the unequal time allocations that men and women can make between the private and public worlds. The limitation of welfare states, the restructuring of state expenditure on public provision, the delegitimization of Keyensian interventions – however contested and partial – in the market economy – all reinforce this growing gap between men and women in the exercise of their citizenship rights.[22]

The Keynesian interlude, though precarious and rhetorical in most state–capital relations (see Magdoff, 1998), did emphasize social citizenship rights. Feminist debates on citizenship recognized the different possibilities afforded to women to challenge their confinement within the private sphere as the welfare state expanded the public space (Fraser, 1989). As we saw in chapter 1, for women in the Third World, these debates were carried out during the period of nationalism and decolonization when many nationalist elites insisted upon the expanded public space in order to reconfigure social relations to conform to modern capitalist or socialist norms. For women both in the North and in the South, the expanded public sphere in its gendered manifestation constituted both a public patriarchy to be struggled against, and a sphere of increased possibilities of social citizenship. However, the discourse of citizenship is changing in the context of global restructuring. The individual 'sovereign citizen' of early liberalism, who, for feminists, has always been a male figure policing the boundaries of the private and the public (Pateman, 1985), casts his long shadow over this process. As 'Davos Man' (see chapter 3), he is an individualist cut loose even from the ties of nationalism, of cultural and historical situatedness, and is driven only by the profit motive. In this reading, the market is a stage for the individual economic actor able to compete with other individual actors. In Janine Brodie's words, 'It is clear that the current moment of restructuring can be viewed as a concerted discursive and political struggle around the very meaning of the public–private. The proponents of globalization seek radically to shrink the public – the realm of political negotiation – and at the same time, expand and reassert the autonomy of the private sector and the private sphere' (1994: 55). In terms of citizenship, this discourse of privatization has spawned a new definition of 'the good citizen' as 'one who recognizes the limits and liabilities of state intervention and, instead, works longer and harder in order to become self-reliant' (Drache, in

---

22 In drawing up a 'decalogue of citizen rights in combating structural poverty,' Friedman includes the following: professionally assisted birth; a safe and secure life-space; an adequate diet; affordable health care; a good, practical education; political participation; an economically productive life; protection against unemployment; a dignified old age; and a decent burial (1996: 169). A feminist analysis of this 'decalogue' would show that the concerns of women, and of Southern women in particular, are only partially reflected in it.

Brodie, 1994: 57). In this reconstituting of the private and the public, women get placed 'simultaneously in the workforce and in the home. This provides a formula for a crisis in social reproduction' (Brodie, 1994: 58), but it also might provide the context wherein women's movements can mount political claims to a new social citizenship.

Linking the macro-analysis with the micro through a gendered critique of neo-classical economic theory is thus an important method developed by feminists to challenge the gender-neutral rhetoric of legitimization of SAPs (Elson, 1994). This has been done by examining the impact of SAPs on women's role within the family (Afshar and Dennis, 1991; Elson, 1995), work (Beneria and Feldman, 1992), education (Staudt, 1998b), health (Owoh, 1995; UNRISD, 1995) and organizations (Wieringa, 1995). However, as Elson's analysis points out, 'the very ability of a person to function as an economic individual – that is, an individual able to enter into voluntary contracts to exchange goods and services – is constituted by the state .... The ability of women to enter into economic contracts is constrained by the way that state legislation typically construes women as less than full citizens' (1994: 35). It is this meso-level economic analysis that needs to be further theorized if we are to evaluate the full range of structural constraints upon men and women in the context of stabilization and adjustment policies. This is important if we are to go beyond the politics of changing the hearts and minds of abstract policy-makers, where the state is outside the restructuring processes, in order to examine the structural constraints upon women in different contexts of global restructuring.

Here it is important to confront the tension between the feasibility argument – engender macroeconomics regardless of politics, because policy outcomes might change for women, making real difference to real lives – and the question of the redistribution of resources needed to challenge the increasing economic pressure on the poor – men and women. In their introduction to the special issue of *World Development* on 'Gender and Structural Adjustment', the editors write: 'The papers in this issue suggest that it is possible to incorporate gender in most macroeconomic models, whether they are neo-classical or structuralist. Some models, however, may be more conducive than others to furthering our critique of macroeconomic processes as structured by gender inequality, and for seeing possibilities for feminist transformation of the economy' (Çagatay, Elson and Grown, 1995: 1829; see also Grown, Elson and Çagatay, 2000). The way in which the difference of approaches is cast reflects a hesitancy to acknowledge the political incompatibility of different standpoints, and that a choice between models means making a choice *against* another model. Such an acknowledgement is quite different from suggesting that a critical engagement with dominant economic models, institutions and discourses is necessary if we are to have regard for practical as well as strategic interests of marginalized women.

In Conclusion: The Social Compact under SAPs

The rolling back of the state in the face of expanding markets is a motif of global restructuring policies and politics. The discourse of market efficiency goes hand in hand with the delegitimization of the state's role in the economy. Welfare states are under considerable pressure to reduce social expenditure as gendered languages are used to cast women as the receivers of welfare and men as the producers of value. In this context, it is important to note how state policies are addressing separately but in parallel the dual expectations of women: as workers and as providers of social goods within the household. This is happening in tandem with significant strains upon budgets supporting human capital formation, such as education and health.

Globalization is putting under pressure the idea of a stable social compact based within the boundaries of the nation-state, between citizens and national governments (see Kothari, 1995; Lasch, 1995; Figueroa, 1996; Devetak and Higgott, 1999; chapter 6, this volume). While one can contend that the social compact in many Third World states has been at best rhetorical, and at worst very unstable, if not, at times of crises, absent, the pressures of global restructuring are, one could argue, fundamentally changing the ways in which we think about this compact in the first place. The language of privatization, the market, reliance on individual striving rather than the social fabric, the rethinking of the idea of the welfare state – all are part of this destabilized notion of the social compact. The social compact of the nation-state is indeed gendered, and is related to the underpinnings of nationalist thought and discourses. Brenner (1993) has argued that gendered aspects of global restructuring and retrenchment of the welfare state in the US, for example, have placed disproportionate pressures on women, especially working-class women.

In emphasizing the gendered nature of global restructuring, Brenner also poses questions for 'second wave feminism'. She argues that '[i]n the face of the severe constraints on the reforms that can be won under the current political balance of forces, the survivors of the second wave...have conceded to intense conservatizing pressures' (p. 155). Here, I would like to return briefly to the point made earlier about the tension between feasible politics – politics of the possible – and the politics of transformation. When one sees the proliferation of materials being produced by feminists urging policy shifts by national states, by international financial as well as social institutions, one begins to wonder about the shifts in feminist thinking itself. Here the differences among women and feminists become paramount. While, for some, an engagement with the institutions of global power – the World Bank, for example (Scholte with O'Brien and Williams, 1998) – is critical in the face of the national states' eroded power, others, like the ecofeminists, take an oppositional stand against globalization that translates into an anti-industrial rather than an anti-capitalist stance (Shiva, 2000). From a socialist feminist standpoint, Brenner argues that the pressures of global conservatism 'will only be reversed when feminists can challenge in *practice* the now dominant interests in the state.... [This] requires a broad and militant mobilization from below incorporating movements for democratic rights that are far more inclusive, new, more social and political forms of trade-union struggle, and national political organization(s)...' (1993: 155).[23] Is such a broad coalition possible given the differences among the various streams of oppositional politics? I shall return to this question in the next chapter.

---

23   In November 1998, '182 women from 22 countries representing 104 organizations met in Kuala Lumpur to Resist Globalization and Assert Our Rights'. These women asserted that Third World women have suffered most from globalization in Asia, where economic crisis has brought large-scale unemployment and displacement, deepening poverty, and creating food insecurity due to increasing loss of biodiversity and the appropriation of land and water resources by large TNCs and the elite (Just Act, 1978). They argued that the Asian Crisis had shown that while 'G7 governments have bailed out their Wall Street cronies...workers who have contributed to the economic growth are retrenched and migrant workers forcefully deported....Our defence budgets continue to swell and the military is used to repress dissent of workers, indigenous communities, ethnic minorities, democracy movements, peasants and students.' They declared that 'privatization of health care is a violation of women's basic human rights to total well-being', and concluded, 'our governments, local elites and local businesses are the collaborators and implementers of this agenda.'

5 | Gender and Multi-level Governance
Feasible and Transformative Politics?

Why...should the women's movement, or at least sections of it, feel that they can short-circuit the usual painful and slow processes of reaching out to women by trying to get to the largest number of women in the shortest possible time? Are the costs of 'collaboration' [with the state] not important?

Uma Chakravarty, 'Rhetoric and Substance of Empowerment'

Introduction

In chapter 3 I discussed how governance is being globalized and as a consequence the nation-state is being repositioned as well as re-positioning itself. In the previous chapter I raised some questions about the tensions between feasible politics – politics of the possible – and transformative politics. Given the changing nature of govern-ance and the changing nodes of power, how are women's move-ments responding in terms of strategizing for change? In this chapter I will explore some of these issues and the resulting ten-sions. I will do this by making a multi-level analysis of political strategies at the global, national and local levels. Such an analysis will allow me to reflect upon the issues of feasibility and redistri-bution raised in the previous chapter, as well as on how globalized processes of production are producing particular forms of challenges to globalization, and organizations to mobilize these challenges. I will also highlight the differences that are emerging among women as a result of these mobilizations, as well as the terms of solidarity among them. I examine the concept of power and suggest that, for the discourse of empowerment to be valuable to feminist practice, we need to be aware of the structural constraints that inhibit women's agency in general, as well as to frame differences among women. I argue that a recognition both of women's interests and differences among them as well as of the need for a redistribution of socio-economic resources is needed to strengthen the concept of empowerment.

Women's movements, women's activism and feminist discourses have transformed the language of development. However, like the discipline of Economics, development policy-making has remained focused on a modernist agenda of growth. As Agarwal argues, 'gender continues to be viewed as an issue of "special interest", whose incorporation into development analysis and program interventions has been at best piecemeal. Most discussions among development economists and policy makers (both in governmental and non-governmental forums) remain ungendered...' (1997: 1373). The growth agenda is itself being spoken about in a language that earlier development 'experts' would find radical; gender-sensitive, people-centred, sustainable, empowering, are all words familiar in the reports of development agencies and the vocabularies of today's development experts. However, the institutions that exert so much influence over the economic policy of nation-states remain largely unaccountable, especially to Third World interests. International financial institutions are being held to account not so much by nation-states, it could be argued, as by what might broadly be termed 'civil society organizations' or 'non-state actors'. This shift is posing important and difficult issues for these organizations and actors.

Reflecting some of these concerns arising from the spread of global governance, Development Alternatives with Women for a New Era (DAWN) have pointed out that '[t]here must be diverse sites of change in all sectors and at all levels of human society' (1995: 10). These sites of change may be located in three major sectors at three major levels (see table 5.1). While such a multi-level analysis is useful, it is also important to see these levels not as discrete, but as overlaid and overlapping. So, for example, local NGOs are often dependent upon state funding and/or external finance. Similarly, discourses of governance generated at the global level – through UN conferences, for example – create a framework for institutional initiatives at the state level. And, finally, social movements continue to be imbricated at all levels. They contribute to levels of universalized discourses, and to some state-level initiatives or mobilizations against state policies. They challenge TNCs and particular

Table 5.1 Sites of change

Sites of change	Market	State	Civil society
Macro	The global economy, including international financial institutions and transnational corporations	Global governance, including inter-governmental organizations such as the UN and regional groupings	International non-governmental organizations and networks
Meso	National economies	National governments	National citizenry, including nationally-based NGOs and civic organizations
Micro	Local markets and community-based economies	Local governance, including informal political structures based on kinship, religion or ethnicity	Local communities, both urban and rural

Source: DAWN, 1995: 10

states on particular issues but also create norms of socio-economic and political behaviour that become difficult to ignore at any level. Women's environmental human rights movements would be some of the examples here.

Keeping this imbricated nature of different levels of governance in mind, in this chapter I will examine the different strategies that women are developing in challenging the pressures of globalization, on the one hand, and making use of new opportunities, on the other. In doing this I will be focusing on *the politics* of gender and development. As Molyneux points out, 'The identification of different kinds of interests raises...issues which are rarely considered in the development literature, namely, what are the *politics* (not just the power relations) involved in the articulation of women's diverse interests?' (1998: 236). The issue of political analysis is crucial at a time when the transition to neo-liberal development under SAPs is being normalized as *the* discourse on development.[1] The nature of the

---

1 See, for example, the 2000 UK Government White Paper on *Eliminating World Poverty: Making Globalisation Work for the Poor*, which entails the UK government committing itself to supporting 'continuing reductions in barriers to trade, both in developed and developing countries, and work to improve the capacity of developing countries to take advantage of new trade opportunities'

challenge that women's movements can pose to these conditionalities – which are daily presented to us as common sense and inevitable – is dependent upon such a political analysis.

I begin with the vexed question of the women's interests that women's movements articulate and represent. What are these interests? How do we make sense of these in the context of differences among women? I will then go on to examine case studies at three levels of governance, taking into account the different levels mentioned above, but in the overlapping ways that I have discussed. The first is an examination of the role that women's NGOs and groups are playing in holding multilateral organizations such as the World Bank to account on the issue of gender sensitivity in policy-making and implementation. The second is the example of UN-promoted 'mainstreaming of gender' through 'National Machineries for the Advancement of Women'. Finally, I examine an initiative by the Indian government in the province of Rajasthan: the Women's Development Programme. Building on these examples, I will address the question of the opportunities and constraints that women's movements face in dealing with multilateral governance in the context of global economic pressures. I conclude by examining the discourse of empowerment and suggest that both structural constraints and women's agency in articulating and pursuing their interests need to be considered together if we are to understand the possibilities and the limits of engagements with institutions of power.

Women's Interests, Women's Movements and Women's NGOs

I concluded chapter 4 by suggesting that women's movements need to examine critically their participation in the normalizing of certain discourses of power, and to think through the strategic consequences of not doing so. Here I begin with an analysis of women's interests, which form the basis of women's activism, in order to pursue the theme of women's empowerment under globalization. In this context the question of what interests women's movements seek to represent in particular contexts becomes important, especially as under globalization women's movements are increasingly being regarded by states as well as international economic organizations as objects of 'policy concern, as their potential as vehicles for the

and to working 'with others to manage globalization so that poverty is systematically reduced' (DFID, 2000: 11–12; see also chapter 4, pp. 122–6).

delivery of goods and services to those in need [is] realized' (Molyneux, 1998: 221).

Women's Interests: Theory and Praxis

Much has been written on the concept of women's interests (Molyneux, 1985, 1998; Jonasdottir, 1988; Moser, 1989; Alvarez, 1990; Young, 1990). Issue has been taken with the concept itself in two different ways. First, there is the claim that women's interests are often equated with identity politics and particularistic demands.[2] Refuting this criticism, Jonasdottir (1988) has argued that women are not just another 'interest group' because they exist in an historically determined conflictual and subordinate relationship to men. Young has argued for a politics that is able to reflect the 'togetherness' as well as 'difference' of those involved: '... both a unified working-class based politics and a group differentiated politics are necessary in mobilizations and programmes to undermine oppression and promote social justice in group differentiated societies' (1995: 156). Young sees difference as a relational and not a 'substantial' logic, where difference can be seen as overlapping and shifting in different contexts, and not fixed and immutable. Difference as 'otherness', where the norms and values, experience and culture of the dominant group is normalized to measure the 'other' and find them lacking, can only generate unhelpful dichotomies, argues Young. Such an understanding of difference is mutually exclusive and categorically opposed, and based on a 'logic of identity' that projects identity as mutually exclusive rather than as interdependent. This 'robs the definition of a group's attributes of its own specificity' and denies 'the heterogeneity of social difference', without which an understanding of interests becomes problematic. First, it leads to calls for assimilation of the 'other' as a process of inclusion, which in fact tends to perpetuate inequality. Second, at times in response to the first, it leads to calls of separatism, which, while understandable, also lead to closure of group identity within particular boundaries,

---

2 In the Soviet Union early feminist activists such as Inessa Armand had to struggle against the Communist Party establishment to set up separate women's organizations. The argument for disparate, particular interests proving divisive to class politics was put forward by Marx (1977) in 'On the Jewish Question' and became the basis for the scepticism with which women's interests were considered (see Lapidus, 1978; Rai, Pilkington and Phizacklea, 1992). For the same argument but in the context of race, see Wilson (1987).

making an impossibility of the overlapping identity argued for above (pp. 158–64).[3]

There has also been some debate on women's interests and gender interests – the latter being interests addressing relations between women and men; the former concentrating on women's lives. Women's interests have been articulated both in terms of ensuring minimal conditions of well-being (Nelson and Chowdhury, 1994) – health, shelter and protection from violence within and outside the home – and as in terms of empowering capacities – making choices and being able to actualize the choices made (Kabeer, 1999). Some feminists have argued that framing women's interests – both practical and strategic – in terms of general interests of a just society can be an effective way of giving them greater salience in wider political debates and policies (Dietz, 1992; Mouffe, 1992). This would be an effective way of mainstreaming – as opposed to adding gendered analysis to existing paradigms of power. The current climate of global restructuring can be a good starting point for such reformulations of policy. For example, government portfolios, which were traditionally considered 'soft' – welfare, health and education – are now where fundamental arguments about resources allocation are taking place.

Interests have also been theorized in terms of praxis. Molyneux (1985) makes an analytical distinction between women's 'practical' and 'strategic' needs. Practical interests reflect women's immediate and contained demands – for better conditions of work, equal opportunities, child-care, housing, water, and so on. These interests do not challenge the wider framework of patriarchal structures of power. Strategic interests reflect the need to shift the paradigms of power: 'In the formulation of practical interests there is the assumption that there is compliance with the existing gender order, while in the case of strategic interests there is an explicit questioning of that order and of the compliance of some women with it' (Molyneux, 1998: 235). Molyneux has been taken to task by some for reading off women's interests from their general subordination and thus obscuring the differences among women (Marchand, 1995; Wieringa, 1995), and by others for making too rigid a distinction between the two sets of interests (Kabeer, 1992). However, Molyneux argues that the 'pursuit of particularistic interests... is of course not necessarily at variance with strategies that pursue broader goals and interests and may be framed in terms of general principles...' (1998: 239). The distinction also allows political strategizing to take place. As

---

3 For a discussion of a politics based on such an understanding of difference, see chapter 6.

Molyneux points out, 'The political *links* between practical and strategic interests are ones which can only emerge through dialogue,
praxis and discussion' (p. 236).

Jonasdottir (1988), addressing the issue of structure and agency,
has argued that both agency and subjectivity must be recognized in
any definition of interests. It is because of this that she has made a
distinction between needs and interests, which have tended to be
conflated in the gender and development literature (see Moser,
1989). Needs, upon this critical reading, are assumed to exist, while
interests have to be articulated and are therefore 'willed'. Fraser
(1989), however, uses the term 'the politics of needs interpretation',
which would point to a continued overlapping of the two concepts.
It is important to emphasize that both needs and interests are formu-
lated within particular contexts that frame the processes of making
choices (Jonasdottir, 1988; Kabeer, 1999). Because of this situatedness
of interests, we also cannot take 'women's interests' as an acceptable
convergence, except in a minimalist sense. Issues of class (Hoskyns
and Rai, 1998), religion (Ali, 2000; Lubeck, 2000) and ethnicity
(Yuval-Davis and Werbner, 1999) all impinge upon and disturb this
category. Further, given the evidence presented in chapter 4, we
have to assess whether globalization and economic restructuring are
having any impact on debates and mobilizations around women's
and gender interests. Could one argue that most women's activism
today is addressing practical interests of women rather than their
strategic interests? That the paradigmatical shifts that Molyneux
writes of are not the focus of feminist engagements?[4]

If the question of women's interests is a difficult one to answer,
the question of representing these through civil society and institutional politics is an equally vexed one for women. Further, there is
also the question of who can represent women's interests and at
what level. Overlaying these, as we saw in chapter 3, is the broader
political issue of whether or not to engage with or 'collaborate' with
state institutions, and other structures of power at all (see Rai, 1995,

---

4 Clark (forthcoming) for example, suggests that for all NGOs engaging with
global financial institutions, 'it is good campaigning strategy to have clear institutional targets, specific events to make the inherently complex and amorphous
issues more tangible, and winnable battles to keep their troops motivated for
the long haul. Long-term campaigns – for a goal as elusive as an improved
international economic order – need to be broken into "bite-size pieces".' It is
clear that Clark is referring not to a transformative agenda but to a reformist
one, or practical interests, even as he refers to 'an improved international economic order' in terms of a long-term agenda of the NGOs.

1996b; chapter 6, this volume). This question can be asked in the context of women's engagement with institutions of power that are not only local or national but also international or multilateral.

Representing Interests: Women's Movements

Social movements have been defined as 'organized efforts at the grass roots to represent interests excluded from or poorly represented in formal arenas of authoritative negotiation and value allocation' (Tétreault and Teske, 2000: 9).[5] However, increasingly, even well-established interest groups with existing institutional access also 'use the social movement form to reach new constituencies and advance their claims' (Meyer, 2000: 52). Arguably, 'new' social movements – of which feminism and women's movements are part – emerged in the 1970s and 1980s at a time when economic and fiscal crises led to the emergence of a consensus around policies that we now recognize as global restructuring (Boggs, 1995; Lynch, 1998). 'New' social movements were critical not of these emerging convergences but of the ossification of the bureaucratic state, on the one hand, and the 'old' class-based movements, on the other (Giddens, 1990). However, as Cohen and Rai have argued, 'a review of the history, complexity and subsequent evolution of other social movements eludes any simple bisection into "new" and "old"' (2000b: 6). Both labour movements and human rights movements, for example, show how old and new have elided and mutated such that to make a clear distinction between them is to deny the organic nature of the development of these movements (Baxi, 2000; Munck, 2000). Lynch, however, concludes that 'theorizing about social movements in the 1970s and 1980s made a double move – from a critique of capitalism to an interest in the "higher goals" of rights, peace, and democracy, and from a focus on "particularistic" movements ... to movements motivated by "universalistic" values and objectives' (1998: 162).[6] For the women's

---

5 Vargas and Olea, for example, describe the Peruvian feminist movement thus: 'It locates itself historically within the broad spectrum of the left.... It is basically, but not exclusively, an urban movement, largely middle-class, having strong links to grassroots women's movements forged at a time when both were strong and visible ... It has also been a pluralistic movement, with differences, ... but with no great conflicts, ruptures or substantial changes in orientation' (1999: 249).
6 Such a characterization does not take into account the distinctive nature of different social movements. Wilson (1973), for example, outlined four types of movements: transformative, reformative, redemptive and alternative (see Cohen and Rai, 2000b, for a fuller discussion).

movements this double move created new opportunities and solidarities. It also raised difficult issues when the slogan of 'sisterhood is global' was challenged on counts of class, colour and sexuality (Stienstra, 2000).[7]

Another issue for social movement theorization is how globalization is affecting social mobilization. Cohen and Rai point out that '[e]ven if their discourse has been deficient, in practice the mobilization of capital on a increasingly global scale has forced a number of social movements to move rapidly away from the national, let alone local, scale of opposition and confrontation' (2000b: 7).[8] Global social movements are now predominating – both in providing normative frameworks for challenging globalization as well as in mobilizing and coordinating political praxis in order to do so. Several factors have contributed to this shift from the national to the global. First, globalization of economic and political institutions of governance is making it imperative to engage at the appropriate levels.[9] Second, the development of communication networks has facilitated organization at a global scale, as well as being facilitative of high levels of access to documentation and information for the NGOs (Tinker, 2000; Youngs, 2002). Third, in part owing to the trajectory of the development of these movements, in part owing to the spread of global capitalism, there is evidence of a growing convergence in values around which social movements can mobilize across borders. These include democratization, human rights, and a growing concern with the environment (Cohen and Rai, 2000b: 10–11).

What does the rise of these global social movements signify? Does it suggest that a global public sphere is now emerging under

---

7   It is also interesting to note that the challenges for the women's movements on grounds of difference that remained prominent in the 1980s were those based on 'identity' issues rather than on issues of economic and social positionings (see Fraser, 1997; Hoskyns and Rai, 1998).

8   Rob Walker has suggested that '[s]ocial movements and world politics are supposed to be understood as expressions of two distinct ontological realms, the inner and outer', while it is precisely the multiplicity of social movements and the multiple sites of their functioning that give them their power (cited in Marchand and Runyan, 2000: 58).

9   Some social movements have emerged as globalization has led to a perceived threat to national cultures – fundamentalism, for example, can be considered such a response to globalization (Lubeck, 2000). Thus social movements are not necessarily liberating or democratic. Just as civil societies are fractured spaces for women, so are social movements (Fine and Rai, 1997; Teske and Tétreault, 2000).

globalization of the economy, which requires that political actors become global too? Where does this leave activism at the national and the local levels? I have discussed some of these issues in chapters 3 and 4. Here I will concentrate on reviewing the changing roles of non-governmental organizations as political actors on these three levels.

Non-governmental Organizations:[10] Civil Society in Action?

The expansion in the number of NGOs working world-wide has been exponential. For example, in Kenya alone there are 23,000 registered women's groups, and the number of cross-border civic groups increased more than tenfold from the 1960s to a total of 16,000 in 1997 (Scholte with O'Brien and Williams, 1998: 4). This increase has led to talk of an 'associational revolution' and also to a slippage between the community of NGOs and the concept of civil society. NGOs, for example, came to be seen as representative bodies of 'people's interests' who needed to be consulted by the state at the national and international levels (the European Commission, for example) in order to maintain the moral equilibrium so important to the stability of capitalism (Giddens, 1991; Cohen, 2000). More critical voices, however, have challenged this slippage. In the words of an Eastern European feminist, 'We were hoping for a civil society, and all we have got is NGOs' (cited in Einhorn, 2000: 117).[11]

There are several reasons for this slippage between civil society and the NGO sector. In terms of politics, at the time of the collapse of the Soviet Union and its satellite states, the forces seeking to build democracy were handicapped by the lack of a civic space in these societies. The building of civil society was therefore central to liberal concerns regarding the transitions from authoritarian to democratic states. The role of civil society groups, not NGOs, was critical in these transitions, and brought into relief the importance of groups of citizens confronting institutions of power by insisting upon their

---

10 There is no standard definition for NGOs (see Willetts, 1995). NGOs can be defined in the narrower sense as organizations outside the state, though they might in part be funded by the state, engaged in advocacy rather than governance activities on specific issues of concern to them. In the wider sense they are seen as coterminous with grassroots organizations, community-based organizations and civil society organizations, or indeed with civil society itself. I use the term in its narrower sense, and definitely not interchangeably with civil society.
11 Fine and Rai argue that 'it is necessary to hold together the constituent elements of civil society – including the system of needs (the market), the system of rights (the law) and non-statal associations – rather than highlight one of these aspects of civil society-state relations' (1997: 2).

rights to participate in the politics of the nation. However, these groups were amorphous, spontaneous and necessarily unstable over time. Once the transitions had occurred, these groups, in many cases, either melted away, marked time, transformed themselves organizationally into what we would recognize as NGOs or founded new political parties. In the context of the resources that were poured into these transitional societies to institutionalize change, it became possible for funders to do business with identifiable and organized groups rather than amorphous movements.

This period of transition in Eastern Europe also led to increased attention being paid to the processes of democratization in countries in other parts of the world. In some countries development NGOs were already in existence, but the whole sector was given a new fillip as a result of the changing global political context. For example, 1,500 NGOs have consultative status with the United Nations Economic and Social Council (Tinker, 2000: 221), and there has also been an increasing interaction between NGOs and the World Bank. This growth of 'privatized governance' (Scholte, 2000: 151) outside national political boundaries by NGOs and other organized groups could be regarded as part of the process of democratization. These groups could be seen as representatives of civil society, as well as groups that could hold governments accountable for their constituencies, and also as service-providers for their constituencies. As the strength of the various social movements gathered pace, and international organizations such as the UN and the World Bank came under scrutiny for their lack of transparency, it also became expedient for these institutions to make links with NGOs as part of their reformist response. For NGOs, the change in the global political climate allowed them access to policy-making bodies at both international and national levels (Tinker, 2000). Sometimes, it allowed them to by-pass the constraints imposed by the nation-state by taking their case to international organizations and fora – new political spaces within which to function. An engagement with these institutions also brought with it differential levels of funding for the NGOs that allowed them to plan ahead, strategize and link up with other groups. NGOs could also begin to see themselves as providing tangible resources and results for their constituencies (see Baden and Goetz, 1997; Mayoux, 1998; Miller, 1998; O'Brien et al., 2000: ch. 1). Further, one could argue that the NGOs could see themselves as working towards an internationalization of citizenship – national political boundaries do not get in the way of their concerns and their activism. Global governance provides not only the context, but, increasingly, also the mechanisms with which to operationalize this international citizenship – through the WTO, the International Court of Human Rights, and through UN-sponsored conferences on social development, the environment, and women.

In order to understand the benefits and the pitfalls of the growing relationship between the NGOs and institutions of power at different levels, it is perhaps useful to differentiate the NGO sector. The NGOs have been seen to be integrationist or agenda-setting (Jahan, 1995: 1; Scholte with O'Brien and Williams, 1998).[12] Here we need to disaggregate between the politics of agenda-setting NGOs – right-wing fundamentalists and Marxist or socialist NGOs make for radicals with a difference (Baden and Goetz, 1997). So when we speak of an engagement between women's groups and NGOs it is important to keep these distinctions in mind. All these sets of NGOs could be quite legitimately representing interests of sections of civil society. The legitimacy that they provide to economic and social institutions at the international, national and local levels must, then, have different weight depending upon the relevant political contexts. At the international level this question of legitimacy that different groups provide becomes a vexed one. In the national context it is more possible to situate particular NGOs and groups politically. Fundamentalist groups, for example, could be regarded as just that. In international fora, however, the question of 'cultural sensitivity' when linked to particular issues can at times make it difficult for fundamentalist groups to be challenged. How have women's NGOs approached the increased avenues of participation and influence? Have they, as Sue Cohen has suggested, 'committed [themselves] to an ideology that was hardly debated – in theory, action or in process'? (2000: 12).[13] How accountable have they been to those whose interests they seek to represent?

---

12   Scholte distinguishes between three sets of civic organizations as they engage with international organizations: the conformists, the reformers and the radicals (2000: 8). While the conformers accept the dominant discourses of global economic and social regimes, the reformers seek changes in policies and operating procedures – micro-credit for women or greater transparency, for example – while not disputing the framework within which these changes are insisted upon. The radicals, on the other hand, challenge the paradigm within which global economic and social institutions function.

13   Cohen argues in the context of the Delors's period of the European Union that while women's NGOs did participate in consultations on poverty with DG V of the European Commission, these were generally 'undertaken as part of the Commission's own agenda..., whilst the nature of the underlying ideology which prompted these measures, or the rationale for them, was barely addressed' (2000: 13; also see below).

Strategies for Change: Macro, Meso, Micro

In this section I examine women's NGOs' and feminist scholars' engagements with development agencies at three different levels: global, national and local. What has been the rationale for this? What have been the benefits and the pitfalls? Bangura has pointed out that '[p]erhaps the greatest barrier to the institutionalization of gendered development is the inflexible nature of the dominant neo-liberal discourse... wide gaps exist between the fundamental premises, values and goals of neo-liberalism and the broad gender discourse' (cited in O'Brien et al., 2000: 47). In chapter 3 I argued that the engagements of social movements, such as those organized around discourses of anti-poverty and the environment, have been unable to shift this core feature of global economic institutions such as the World Bank. In chapter 4 we saw that the challenge of feminist economists to neo-classical economics has been thorough, but that the engagement of mainstream economics with feminist economics has been at best partial. Given these factors, should women's movements be engaging with global economic institutions? Does even a small shift in the politics of the dominant institutions 'provide emancipatory movements with space for manoeuvre' (Cohen, 2000: 34)? What does the experience so far show?

The Bank, the Manager and the Women's Movements

The World Bank, as we have seen (chapters 2 and 4), has been pivotal to the normalizing of particular discourses of development and policy-making. Its role has changed significantly since the 1990s. From funding specific development projects, it has now become involved in policy-based lending, that is, imposing not only economic but also political conditions on its clients. It has therefore become the target of NGO activity on both counts – development projects are important, but more critical is economic policy-making. As Miller points out, ' "disengagement" – proposed by some feminists – is untenable as long as multilateral development institutions continue to exercise influence over the development policy process' (1998: 139).

The NGOs that decide to engage with the World Bank have to negotiate an organizational map in order to be successful advocates.[14] The Bank is not a monolithic institution. 'It has always been

---

14 According to Clark (forthcoming) the following reasons contributed to the NGO engagements with the Bank and international financial institutions more

somewhat torn between two competing identities...[as a] bank, an institution driven by a "disbursement imperative for capital-driven growth-oriented lending"...[and as a] development organization with a stated objective of poverty reduction through economic growth' (O'Brien et al., 1997: 26). There are three sets of actors who make an engagement with the Bank possible: the Bank's President, who is its public face and can therefore signal changes in its policies as well as initiate new ones; the Executive Board, with funding-based power relations between countries of the North and the South; and the feminist bureaucrats (femocrats), as internal critics seeking to influence policy.

NGO engagement with the Bank has become possible, first, as it has asserted the 'comparative advantage' that NGOs have over state bureaucracies in delivering development resources to the poor, and, second, because of the impact of NGO lobbying on public opinion on specific issues (O'Brien et al., 1997: 29). NGO involvement with the Bank's projects increased from an average of 15 a year in the 1980s to 89 out of 156 by 1991/2 (p. 31). The NGOs have built upon this recognition, but they have also been engaged with feminist critiques of neo-liberal economics. How do these two aspects of NGO and feminist work with the Bank overlap, contradict and translate into Bank policy? Is the distinction suggested above between 'strategic' and 'practical' interests of women relevant here?

The World Bank President, James Wolfensohn, was the first President of the organization to attend a UN Conference on Women, in Beijing in 1995. His presence signalled a change in the Bank's approach to the questions of gender. Responding to this, 900 women activists presented him with a petition titled 'Women's Eyes on the Bank', which advocated a gender-sensitive transformation of the Bank's policies and practices, and the need to hold the Bank accountable to the Beijing Platform for Action (Miller, 1998: 141–2). There were four specific demands: (a) to increase the participation of grassroots women in economic policy-making; (b) to institutionalize gender in the design and implementation of the Bank's policies;

---

generally: debate was brought within target institutions, such as the G7, regional bodies such as the European Commission, national parliaments; the North experienced a creeping conservatism, including the perceived failure of aid and loan regimes; building on some victories for other battles – success in one area led to greater confidence of successful advocacy and campaigns in another; comparative perspectives of Southern partners made Northern economic actors appear more reasonable; the debt crisis made economic justice an important issue to mobilize on.

(c) to increase the Bank's investments that reach women; and (d) to increase the number and diversity of senior women at the Bank (O'Brien et al., 1997: 43). These demands thus sought to mainstream gender in the Bank's policy framework, its organizational structures and its implementational bureaucracy.[15] However, the Bank's femocrats, while a resource for women's NGOs, do not have much contact with women's groups and are also constrained by the organizational culture of the Bank.[16] So, while women's NGOs have expected much from them, the feminist bureaucrats themselves have felt isolated and unsupported by both internal and external groups (O'Brien et al., 2000).

Assessing mainstreaming of issues in governance agendas, Jahan (1995) has pointed out that the need is not simply for organizational change, but also for a transformatory approach that would lead to a fundamental change in the mainstream itself. If we are to assess the engagement of women's NGOs with the Bank, we need to ascertain the range and limits of possibilities that the NGOs have been able to explore and influence. Despite several gender-sensitive initiatives, the Bank's fundamental approach to economic growth and its endorsement of the neo-liberal market-based economic framework have not shifted. The instrumentalist argument pervades its policy-making – women's education and health in particular are linked to the programmes on population control, for example. In a comparative study of six World Bank poverty assessments in four countries – Ghana, Zambia, Tanzania and Uganda – for example, Whitehead and Lockwood find that '[t]here is a tendency to locate WID/gender concerns in the soft areas – such as human resources – in an organization giving strong analytical and policy priority to economics' (1999: 528). As a result of treating gender as discrete, and as a cultural issue related to women's 'social status' in some cases and to 'gender division of labour' in others, there appears to be a somewhat 'accidental' diversity in the way in which these assessments address the issue of the gendered nature of poverty (pp. 528–30).

Similarly, the argument of women's empowerment is cast in terms of securing women with trade and credit regimes rather than raising

---

15 Mainstreaming has been defined as 'a strategy for making women's as well as men's concerns and experiences an integral dimension in the design, implementation, monitoring and evaluation of policies and programmes in all political, economic and societal spheres so that women and men benefit equally and inequality is not perpetuated' (ECOSOC, cited in Staudt, 2002).

16 I argued similarly in the context of Indian parliamentary elections (Rai, 1997).

questions about the persistence of gendered inequalities that deny them the rights of controlling the fruits of their own labour. So, for example, the Operational Directive on Poverty Reduction (World Bank, 1991) provided the following recipe for reducing poverty: '...broad-based growth brought about by the removal of price distortions and the provision of credit and infrastructure, basic social services, and safety nets' (Whitehead and Lockwood, 1999: 532). Thus out of thirty-four micro-credit programmes with large numbers of poor clients, the Microcredit Summit Campaign found that, on average, '76 per cent of the borrowers were women' (Van Staveren, forthcoming). This strategy for 'empowering' women was provided with an institutional basis with the establishment of World Women Banking in 1995, which now operates in forty countries and currently supplies credit to 10 million women (p. 24).

Such an understanding of poverty reduction results in a subordination of gender equality to that of increasing welfare (Jackson, 1996). What can also be detected since the late 1990s is that as the Bank's interest in poverty measurement and reduction has increased, efforts to mainstream gender, however fragile, have stalled (Whitehead and Lockwood, 1999: 528). The 'Women's Eyes on the Bank' campaign has also necessarily been set back.[17]

However, has the engagement of women's groups with the Bank achieved nothing? Clark (forthcoming) points to three areas where, together with many other NGOs, women's engagement with the Bank has been successful. First, debt reduction is now being seen as beneficial to the global economy and not an encouragement to state-led financial mismanagement and profligacy. An efficiency argument has been successfully normalized. Second, structural adjustment is being tempered by social priorities such as poverty

---

17   Indeed, Clark (forthcoming) has argued that the Bank should not now be a focus of NGO agitation at all as it is now not the

> volume player in global finance that it is often assumed to be....Secondly, the Bank's policy influence is dwarfed by that of others – in particular the US government and Congress, EU, Japan, and consortia of bankers and MNC leaders....Thirdly,...the reforms which the Bank has undergone in the 90s [make it a much more transparent organization]....Fourthly, since the appointment of James Wolfensohn as President...the Bank...seeks to modulate the established order.

Does this mean that, among others, 'Women's Eyes on the Bank' has been successful and therefore come to the end of its natural life, and that the focus should now shift to lobbying the US government, the IMF or the EU?

reduction. The evidence of particular pressures under which women have experienced structural adjustment has been important in this tempering of economic policy with concerns for social welfare. Third, credit to the poor (women) is now considered to be both an important means for empowering them and an economically viable policy.

However, it is important to remain cautious even in these limited shifts in governance that an engagement with the Bank has brought about. In her assessment of micro-credit schemes in Kenya and Cameroon, for example, Josephine Lairop-Fonderson (2002) reflects upon the disciplinary power of credit schemes. She concludes that while these do make some difference to individual women's lives and the lives of their families, they also perform an integrative function in that they make women increasingly dependent upon the rules of the market. Goetz and Gupta (1996) found in their study of the Grameen Bank in Bangladesh that only 37 per cent of women borrowers retained control over their loans.[18] As we saw in chapter 3, markets are embedded in dominant social relations and poor women and men do not have the resources to influence the outcome of market regulatory discipline. In many cases, micro-credit increases the workloads of women without changing the power relations within the family, and the language of empowerment of women through participation in market relations can further erode subsidies that are extremely important to women's coping and survival strategies (Goetz and Gupta, 1996; Lairop-Fonderson, 2002; Weber, 2002).

The engagement of women's NGOs and activists with the World Bank raises some difficult questions. Lobbying the World Bank means dealing with economists who are not necessarily convinced of the agendas of the women's NGOs, and who speak a language that is inaccessible to the activist women; it therefore means making time and expending energy to learn this language. Time and energy are at a premium for most women activists. The process of 'consultation' with Bank (or other major economic institutions') representatives is not without its power imbalances, and can therefore be alienating (Cohen, 2000). The gathering of information required to challenge the economic indicators that the Bank officials bring to bear upon these discussions also requires resources and training that

---

18 For a critique of this reading of women's continued subordination, see Kabeer (1999). She points to alternative research in Bangladesh, which claims that access to credit is associated with an increase in women's asset holdings, in their purchasing power, and even in their political participation (p. 455). The gathering and measuring of empowerment is thus a difficult process.

many Third World NGOs cannot provide. Consequently, many Southern NGOs have in fact looked to the Bank as an option for funding. As Chiriboga (forthcoming) has pointed out, however, this 'has the risk of creating a clientelistic [sic] relation, where favorable comments are exchanged for funding possibility', and of losing international and Northern allies. The differential resourcing of NGOs and questions of access thus become important issues of difference among the NGOs: '...the evolution of the campaign [Women's Eyes on the Bank] to date is illustrative of the power differences between women's movements North and South, of the importance of geographical location, and also of delays in the spread of communication technologies to marginalized social movements' (O'Brien et al., 2000: 65).[19] Moreover, the costs of engaging with multilateral organizations – especially those associated with the enforcing of SAPs – are differentially felt by women's NGOs. Women in the South are often faced with abuse for engaging with 'foreign' organizations. There are also questions of NGOs' accountability for the terms of their engagement with multilateral organizations (see Rai, 2002b). Attempts to leap-frog the nation-state by approaching multilateral organizations can also result in the undermining of democratic politics or struggles towards a democratic politics on the ground.

None the less the increased levels of NGO activity, especially the forum of UN-organized conferences on women, have led multilateral institutions to address the question of gender equity and prompted many nation-states to do the same. One of the important strategies adopted by these states, and supported by the UN, is that of gender mainstreaming. In the next section I assess this meso-level example of governance through an examination of national machineries for the advancement of women.

State Feminism: a Vehicle for Change?

State-centred strategies are becoming increasingly important in addressing women's interests. This shift is occurring at a time when

---

19 For a thoughtful analysis of the way in which engagements with international financial institutions led to differences between NGOs of the North and the South, see Chiriboga (forthcoming). The World Bank has also made much of these differences (see Clark, forthcoming). Can these differences, no doubt real and quite evident in, say, the Seattle protests of 1999, be exploited by IFIs to 'divide and rule'? Have women's NGOs confronted the political fall-out of these differences? More research is needed in this area.

we are also acknowledging the change in the position of nation-states under globalization. One could argue that states, as managers of globalization at the meso-level, are currently in no position to be agents of change for women. It could also be argued that it is precisely when global economic forces are becoming predominant that women need to engage with nation-states in order to encourage the mediating role of the state *vis-à-vis* global forces or, depending upon the political conditions obtaining within a country, to insist upon the nation-state acting in accordance with its international obligations.

National machineries can be defined as 'the central policy coordinating unit inside the government'. The fact that this strategy is being sponsored by the UN and was part of the Beijing Platform for Action (UN, 1995) has given it a level of political visibility that has resulted in many states establishing ministries for women. Thus, while national machineries for women have been around for more than two decades, it is only since the 1990s that they have taken on the status of a global strategy for the improvement of women's status. The main task of a national machinery is to 'support government-wide mainstreaming of a gender-equality perspective in all policy areas' (UN, 1995: para. 201). National machineries are thus 'catalysts' for promoting gender equality and justice (DAW, 2000a: 10).[20] There has also been a discursive shift that has marked the organization and work of these machineries. While earlier machineries focused largely on women's welfare, especially on the state's population and health programmes, the current emphasis is on these machineries being vehicles for engendering state policy across the board. The language of the promotion of women's rights has become important to these institutions (McBride Stetson and Mazur, 1995).

For the nation-states, there have been several reasons for attempting to mainstream gender through the establishment of these institutional mechanisms. In some countries, such as India, the strength of the women's movements and their participation in the various UN Conferences on women have ensured that the strategy

---

20 The All-India Democratic Women's Association – a long-established women's organization affiliated to the Communist Party of India – noted that the draft of section H of the Platform for Action dealing with national machineries does not mention the following but should: '1) Establishment of *autonomous* bodies to monitor Government policies and make recommendations *binding* for the Government which if it does not accept, it will have to submit explanations to elected legislatures; 2) The crucial question of political will. 3) Affirmative action to narrow the gender gap in all important spheres' (1995: 12).

of mainstreaming through the institutionalization of WID/GAD units in government has found visibility and converts. For example, the momentum of the women's movements and the Commissions (1975 and 1985) set up to assess the role of women in Indian public life led to the establishment of the National Commission for Women in 1990. Third World states – for example, Bangladesh, Jamaica and Morocco (Goetz, 1998: 55) – are also under pressure from donor agencies to institutionalize mechanisms and procedures for mainstreaming gender. There has also been the realization by the nation-states that implementation of SAPs has led to massive changes in the labour market, with women joining it in large numbers. The provision of welfare services has also become a contentious issue with direct implications for the division of labour within the family. Consequently there have been changes in the family and gender relations that states need to map out and to influence and regulate. An engagement with issues of gender is therefore important, as is engagement with women's NGOs, which are seen to represent the women's movements and interests.

The report of the UN Experts' Group Meeting on National Machineries for Gender Equality suggested that the mandate of the national machineries should include development of policies, policy advocacy, co-ordinating and monitoring policy, reviewing legislative and policy proposals, initiating reform for gender-sensitive legal systems, co-ordinating gender audits of implementation of policies and ensuring that constitutional debates include a gender perspective (UN, 1999: 10–11). National machineries were thus envisaged as nodes for acknowledging, listening to, recognizing and integrating different dialogic communities within 'changing preference sets'. They were to transmit these changing preference sets to policy-makers at the national, regional and international levels. They were also to be conduits between civil society and states, and to represent states at international bodies. Representing women's interest to governance circuits at different levels was one of the important tasks of national machineries. The mandate of these machineries, thus, places a great deal of stress on their agenda-setting role. They are to translate civil society debates on changing women's interests for the policy programmes of governments. Here it is important to emphasize, as Staudt does, that, '[m]ainstreaming women is an activity that is embedded in bureaucratic and political contexts. Development paradigms differ from country, as does the foreign policy agenda that rationalizes a development paradigm. *Context matters*' (1998b: 177–8). Thus, while Australia, Canada and the Nordic states of Europe have had a strong and fairly successful movement of feminist engagements with the state (Hernes 1987; Watson, 1990; Johnson, 1999b; Sawer, 1998), my own study of the machinery in India (1998b), or other studies, such as on Uganda (Kwesiga, 2002), present a rather mixed and pessimistic picture. The typology in table 5.2 provides an overview of the levels, norms and functions by which national machineries can be characterized.

Table 5.2 National machineries: a typology

Type of legitimacy	Instrumental norms	Major functions
High formal-substantive level The location of the machinery is at the highest level of the government, and there is regular interaction between the machinery and state bureaucracies producing a high level of commitment to the agendas of the machinery. This is reflected in the substantive monitoring role of the machinery. The Swedish machinery would be an example of this type.	• Constitutional mandate, constitutional law, executive order or act of parliament • Own budget or % of budget of body it is affiliated to • Administrative staff of 51 people or more	Monitoring Co-ordination Regulatory Executive Promotional
High formal level The machinery is located at the highest level of government though on a less secure basis, reflected in the reduced function of the machinery, especially in the context of monitoring state bureaucracies. The Ecuadorian, and Ugandan machineries would be examples of this type.	• Presidential or supreme executive order or act of parliament • Budget allocated annually by the government, or dependent upon international aid to the extent of 50% or more • Administrative staff of less than 50	Co-ordination Regulatory Promotional
Intermediate formal level The machinery is not situated at the highest level	• Executive order, government resolution or Cabinet mandate	Co-ordination Regulatory Executive

Table 5.2   (*cont.*)

Type of legitimacy	Instrumental norms	Major functions
of government, though it has access to the top levels of government. The Indian and UK machineries would be examples of this type.	• Budget allocated annually by the government, or dependent upon international aid to the extent of 50% or more • Administrative staff of less than 50	Promotional
Low formal level The status of the machinery is low, with very few allocated resources and irregular contact with the policy-making bureaucracies. Several Eastern European countries would be examples of this type.	• Executive order, government resolution or Cabinet mandate • Budget allocated annually by the government, or dependent upon international aid to the extent of 50% or more • Administrative staff of less than 5	Co-ordination Regulatory Promotional Advisory
Individual focal point Where a well-known individual is responsible for raising the profile of gender issues within government and policy-making bureaucracies.	• Focal point designated by the government • No resources allocated • Activities carried out by a single person	Promotional

Source: Adapted from ECLAC, 1998: 19

As structural adjustment policies have taken hold, and state institutions are slimmed down, we find very often that women's machineries, as mechanisms for advancing women's interests, face considerable constraints. They are shunted from one part of government (sometimes even within government buildings) to another, financial resources – never adequate – are reduced further, and pressure is increased to use these machineries to legitimize governmental withdrawal of health and social welfare budgets (Goetz, 1998; Kwesiga, 2002). In my study of women's political participation in village-level institutions in India and China, I have argued that examinations of policy outcomes and framing discourses of development 'fail to make explanatory space for structures of inequality that impinge upon the daily lives of women in particular configurations' (1999: 247). As part of governmental structures, national machineries can be effective in bringing to light some issues, but not others. Further, different political spaces accruing to them frame their effectiveness as critics of governmental policy. 'Reasonableness' in government can undermine the oppositional/challenge politics that might be required to shift the status quo. In India, for example, over a period of six years of its functioning, women's groups on the left have in large part created a distance from the National Commission of Women. It is being cast as an elitist, bureaucratic organization; a pawn in the hands of various governments. Global strategies of change can thus be rather blunt instruments, insensitive to the *politics* of governance, which can legitimize or delegitimize these initiatives (Rai, 2002b).

The differences in the political contexts within which women live their lives point to the problems of globalizing governance strategies. Reviewing the various initiatives that national machineries have been able to make in different political contexts (see UN, 1999), I would conclude that national machineries have been able to build more stable alliances with women's civil society groups in western political economies (including Australia). Here, the combination of welfare state regimes, consolidated democracies and strong women's movements has been able to secure a commitment from governments to mainstream gender into government policies. This has not been easy, not without political reverses, and is definitely not yet embedded in the structures of governance of these countries. However, as the issues of redistribution have been subsumed under the debates on welfare, it has been possible for national machineries to make important interventions (Sawer, 1998; Johnson, 2000).

In most Third World countries, however, the situation is variable, and more pessimistic. The lack of any real welfare state structures, the increasing pressures on women under the SAPs-induced withdrawal of the state's infrastructure, the increasing disparity in people's economic conditions in the context of generalized scarcity and mass poverty, and, in many cases, fragile democracies – all make the role of the national machineries more problematic (Kardam and Acuner, 2002; Kwesiga, 2002). The dangers of co-optation into the state of women's groups working with/in national machineries, and consequent delegitimization or increased distance from the civil society organizations, become more real. In the context of Ecuador, Silvia Vega (2002) argues that '[e]xperience demonstrates that there is greater mobilization, greater public visibility, greater impact on public opinion, a greater degree of participation by women when such an initiative arises from below, from civil society . . .'. However, research in many countries shows that the relations between civil society groups and national machineries are rather tenuous, especially under economically difficult conditions (Goetz, 1995, 2002).

Staudt (2002) identifies three obstacles that face national machineries. The first is the lack of good governance, which would include a non-corrupt state, transparent budgetary processes and an evaluative process that has at its centre the interests of civil society rather than the funders. The second is poor resourcing in terms of both budgetary allocation and political clout as well as appropriate training of staff at all levels. And the final obstacle is a compliance of most states with the hegemonic neo-liberal economic model, which does not take into account the care economy in which women predominate. While, as with micro-credit in the economic sphere, national machineries for women are an important resource for keeping gender issues in the political arena, their embeddedness in dominant social relations poses difficult questions for their viability as catalysts for the advancement of women. I agree with the conclusion of Devaki Jain, a founder member of DAWN, that largely 'the national machineries, embedded in hierarchical and patriarchal bureaucracies, are unable to generate the impulse for change that women's empowerment and gender equity demand. . . . National machinery for women's advancement is necessary but needs to emerge from struggle, politics and legal and political history, which allows for resistance, rebellion and affirmative action' (1995: 31).

The Sathins, the State and Social Change

If translating the global message of mainstreaming gender at the national level is dependent upon the political and socio-economic contexts of each nation-state, then the problems faced by women's groups as they engage with a fractured but embedded state at the local level are severe indeed.

Most of the women in the world still live rural lives. These, as we saw in chapter 4, are being transformed in different ways under globalization. The major issue remains control over land. Here the struggle of women is, on the one hand, the struggle of the dispossessed 'people', and, on the other, about the rights of women to own land (see Agarwal, 1994). In chapter 1 I argued for taking the rhetoric of nationalism seriously, when we consider issues of development. In many post-colonial countries the dominant cultural regimes have either denied women access to the land outright, or have denied this right in the (non-)implementation of modernist equal rights legislation. Indeed, as Agarwal points out, 'government land distribution programs have widened the gender gap in command over arable land' (1997: 1375). For women, this question of land rights remains critical. However, there is also a growing urgency about not only land but also, as we saw in chapter 4, the privatization of natural resources, which affects women deeply. Gender relations are being transformed under these pressures of globalization, and so are other social relations. Alliance-making in the rural context has emerged between women's groups and environmental groups, as well as human rights groups opposing the displacement of peoples in the face of big dam-building projects. Another approach to alliance-making has been to link up with state institutions and initiatives. As the example of the *sathin* movement, discussed below, reveals, however, such alliance-building also leaves women's groups with issues regarding the nature of opposition that they wish to mount. I shall now illustrate this using the example of women in a development programme in Rajasthan, India.

Chakravarty's careful study of the Women's Development Programme (WDP) elaborates the tension among the women's movements, NGOs and feminist bureaucrats and academics extremely well (Chakravarty, 1999). It also points to the differences among women's groups in the 'South', which undermine the monolithic construction of Third World women in dialogue with various groups of women in the North. The divisions, in both political spaces are about issues that are similar, however different the contexts.

The WDP was launched in 1984 in six districts of Rajasthan, with the assistance of UNICEF. The Indian state decided on this initiative after the 1975 Report on the Status of Women, the phenomenal growth of the women's movements in the 1970s and 1980s, and the launch of the UN Decade of Women. The aims included creating 'a new sense of worth among poor rural women and facilitating their awareness to develop strategies regarding social and development issues' (Chakravarty, 1999: 1–2). This was to be done through mechanisms that were both flexible and diverse. These mechanisms were to focus on improving women's participation in development schemes, 'especially [that of women] from disadvantaged communities' (p. 2). The agents of change in this scheme were the *sathins* (the feminine form of the word 'friend') at the village level, and the *pracheta* (secular preacher) at the district level. The following agencies participated in the training, communication and monitoring

required by the programme: the district-level Women's Development Agency, headed by the District Collector, representing the governmental authority; the State Information Development Agency (a
voluntary organization); and the Institute of Development Studies,
an autonomous research institute in Jaipur, Rajasthan. The 'structure
was an attempt to balance power between the government and non-
governmental segments' of the programme, and reflected the concern of a wide range of women's groups that had been consulted in
the process of setting up the WDP. While most women's groups had
supported the programme, many had been sceptical 'about the possibility of a fruitful collaboration between the state and the women's
movement in any form' (p. 3).

> The sathin was envisaged as a worker with a difference: a catalyst of
> women's empowerment at the grassroots. She was to be instrumental
> in the growth of women's collective strength, to increase women's
> bargaining capacity, and help them to articulate collective inter-
> ests.... But the effectiveness of the sathin was predicated upon a
> transformation within the sathin herself so that she could become,
> through this process, a woman leader. (pp. 3–4)

Training of the *sathins* was thus an important element of the programme. At the heart of their work was a commitment to 'collective
processes, working upwards through first evolving village level plat-
forms for articulating women's points of view and then moving
outwards to other groups of women engaged in similar processes'
(p. 3). Both practical and strategic interests were identified through
this process: from 'famine relief measures, to combating gross forms
of patriarchal and social oppressions'; minimum wages; recovery of
land from encroachers; issues of widows' claim to land; employment
opportunities for women; safe drinking water; and health care. The
articulation of these interests and mobilizations resulting therefrom
inevitably brought the *sathins* into conflict with the village social and
political hierarchies. As 'long as the sathins received support from
the district agencies, from the voluntary organizations, and through
them the government authorities, the sathins were not alone in their
activities.... The support of the district agencies was a crucial element in women's confrontations with caste and class oppressions
within rural society' (p. 5). However, this edifice based on cooperation between multi-level agencies and actors revealed tremendous strains as the government moved to prioritize the 'family planning' programme at a time of drought and crop failure in Rajasthan
between 1985 and 1988.

On the one hand, government-run famine relief programmes were the major means of survival for the rural poor; on the other, these programmes were used by local government officials to fulfil their quotas for the sterilization of women as part of the family planning programme. Women were caught between these twin pressures. The *sathins* mobilized opposition to this double oppression with the support of the non-governmental organizations involved in WDP. The district governmental sector, however, refused to discuss the issue, (p. 7). In a parallel move, the *sathins* from various villages and districts met in 1986 and identified land and health as the two areas that most needed to be addressed by WDP. As Chakravarty comments, 'The only aspect of women's health the state was interested in was that they should stop "breeding". The women who participated in the health camps held in Ajmer District, on the other hand, were concerned with a whole host of issues around their bodies' (p. 8). As this dispute on the question of linking family planning and famine relief showed, the alliance between various sectors of governance was a fragile one when competing interests clashed. The state institutions had a powerful position in this dispute.

This clash of interests became even more pronounced when the *sathins* tried to mobilize their resources by organizing themselves into a union, and by demanding the 'regularizing' of their status within the state structure as government employees enjoying security of employment and an adequate wage for their work. In 1990 *sathins* went on strike on this issue. The government agencies refused their demands, stating that the *sathins* were volunteers, not employees; that they were uneducated and illiterate and therefore could not *be* government employees. The fact that the WDP had envisioned the participation of poor, low-caste women as central to the success of the programme, and that these women could not be educated and literate, did not enter into their consciousnesses. Local government officials, such as the Block Development Officer, even sent letters to the husbands of the *sathins* instructing them to 'bring their wives to their senses' or accept the consequences. Chakravarty comments, 'From the movement of the sathin around wages and other related issues it is clear that while the sathins had been transformed from being "passive recipients" of development policies, the "upper" levels of the WDP had remained class bound and instrumentalist in their approach to the program' (p. 11). The tensions resulting from this fracturing of the WDP came to a head with the gruesome gang rape of one *sathin* – Bhanwari Devi – in 1992, and the acquittal of the rapists by the Supreme Court on the grounds that 'an upper caste man would not disregard caste ... differences to rape a low caste woman' (p. 16).

In the last few years, the *sathin* programme has been bureaucratized, as well as starved of funds. Chakravarty concludes from this that '[t]he government wants empowerment without breaking into the power of those, including themselves, who have power over the disempowered....[W]hile the sathins struggle...for the statutory minimum wage of workers and the survival and expansion of the scheme, the government claims credit for the "success" of the sathin programme in Beijing, Vienna and Geneva' (p. 18).

This story raises many questions. For the women's movements, there is the danger of providing legitimacy to programmes that are not under their control. For international organizations such as UNICEF there is the question regarding the nature and focus of training provision – by focusing on the training of the *sathin* and not on the upper echelons of the government hierarchy and the village-level political actors, the clash of political cultures becomes inevitable. For the non-governmental organizations and academic institutes there is the question of providing legitimacy to state-led programmes, but also of delivering appropriate levels of support for the *sathins* when and where these were needed. And for the *sathins* there is the real question of levels of risk involved in doing their work without adequate support, as well as of how to translate consciousness raising into practical results when the structures of power are supported by political hierarchies at every level. I will return to these issues in the concluding chapter.

The *sathin* initiative has now slowed down, and become more closely integrated into governmental programmes. The radical edge of the movement has been worn away, though many courageous women continue to participate in it.

Assessing the Politics of Engagement

What does our survey of multi-layered engagements of women's movements and NGOs with institutions of power tell us? At each of the three levels discussed above, women's groups are engaging with institutions of power. This is not an uncontested strategy – many women's NGOs find such engagements too problematic and politically flawed.

Analysing the case studies presented in this chapter, I would argue that NGOs and women's movements working with institutions of power at any level are constrained by the dominant paradigms of power. Most of the initiatives taken by these institutions under pressure from women's groups are 'integrating' rather than 'agenda-setting' (Jahan, 1995). The question that Chakravarty raises

– of short-circuiting change – is important here. The 'cultural' and 'socio-economic' structures that embed the local political institutions are significant constraints upon women activists. These constraints not only impose limits to change, they also raise the issue of co-option of women's groups into the hierarchies of power and influence. Second, in each case the issue of differences among women is crucial. The differences that have emerged among women have been many: between NGOs of the North and those of the South; between activists and femocrats; between those who decide to engage with multilateral and state institutions and those who don't; between those who are funded by multilateral agencies and those who are less well funded or not funded at all. These divisions are also about who gets heard and who doesn't, and therefore about the implicated nature of engagement that normalizes critiques through mainstreaming them. Third, and linked to this, there has been a recognition that the terms of women's engagements with multilateral bodies or state institutions do not generally favour women. All three cases discussed above show that there are marginal shifts in the paradigms within which various institutions of power function. The World Bank has, for example, shown a minimal shift in its approach to economics and policy-making; the national machineries of various countries are embedded in and constrained by the political economy of their contexts; and at the local level, state institutions work with women's groups within very narrow boundaries, reluctant to challenge the dominant social mores. Fourth, there are disagreements about the costs attached to the engagement of women's movements with institutions of power – and these are differentially borne by women in the North and South, and by women of different socio-economic strata. All three case studies presented above allow us to reflect upon the fact that that while a strategy of disengagement with multilateral and national institutions of power might be untenable, it is important to have cognizance of the costs of such engagements in terms of the fragmentation of women's movements, and in terms of the fracturing of dialogue among different NGOs and among groups within countries, and also between North and South. These costs, as we have seen, are not inconsiderable and are unevenly distributed. Most poignantly, for *sathins* like Bhanwari Devi, for instance, the cost is personally very high. Women's engagement with state institutions does not protect women like Bhanwari Devi, because the institutions of the state are too implicated in maintaining the status quo, while women's groups working within the parameters of state politics are unable sufficiently to challenge the dominant power relations. Finally, these examples also raise the question of the legitimacy not only of the machineries for mainstreaming gender, but also of women's NGOs speaking for women at international and national fora. Who can speak of the pain and confusion of activists on the ground, who feel betrayed by the system that they thought was going to be their ally for change?

In Conclusion

If the politics of engagement is an untidy process, it is also important to consider the consequences of non-engagement. I have argued elsewhere that while there are attendant costs of engaging with the state, the consequences of not engaging with it would also be very high (Rai, 1995). Examining the judicial activism of the Indian Supreme Court in the context of state violence and the development deficit in India, I have argued that while the law has considerable power to constrain demands upon the state, it also provides women with an important (if implicated) resource that they can mobilize against the more repressive institutions of the state (Rai, 1999). For most women in India, for example, state institutions figure only marginally in their lives. They loom large, in many instances in a brutal and violent way, only when women transgress the boundaries set by these institutions in various areas of public and private life. In that context, can one argue that 'to be "protected" by the very power whose violation one fears perpetuates the specific modality of dependence and powerlessness marking much of women's experience across widely diverse cultures and epochs' (Brown, 1992: 9; see also Smart, 1989, 1992)? In the face of the exercise of violent state power, the 'protection' given by a court order prohibiting that violence can make the difference between life and death to individual women (Williams, 1991). As Baxi has pointed out in the Indian context, the attempts at the structural adjustment of the Indian judiciary have gone hand in hand with the implementation of economic liberalization. 'The crucial question before peoples' movements' in India, he argues, 'is how the most people-friendly of governance apparatus (namely, the judiciary) can be both enabled and empowered, in confrontation with the forces, managers and agendas of Indian globalization, to serve the constitutionally envisioned paradigm of Indian development' (1997: 359).

The argument thus is not about whether or not to engage with institutions of power. It needs to be about how far the process of engagement is necessarily part of the outcome. In short, it needs to be about taking politics seriously in order to challenge the dominant paradigms, but with cognizance of structural power, which can be a powerful obstacle to attaining gender justice. Three political concepts are important to an understanding of such a politics: citizenship rights and entitlements; deliberative politics; and empowerment. I discuss these briefly in this concluding section.

Citizenship and Entitlements

Constitutional change and debates on citizenships are perhaps the one area where the activism of the women's movements at both the global and national levels, international pressure through the various UN conferences, and the establishment of national machineries for women *have* been able to open up new territory for gender equality. Legal and constitutional reforms promoted in many countries have resonated with the theoretical and strategic debates on women's interests and with feminist scholarship in the area of citizenship. It is in the operationalizing of particular citizenships that we can view the contexts within which new claims to citizenship rights might be made, and others extended (chapters 1 and 4).

Citizenship is a dynamic and unfolding concept. The struggles over what it means to be a citizen; the terms upon which citizenship can be crafted; the need to acknowledge differences among populations, and also an insistence upon equal citizenship rights; as well as the reopening of settled arrangements in the context of economic and social changes in the polity – all form part of this unfolding process. T.H. Marshall (1950) differentiated three stages of citizenship, which are now broadly associated with the three generations of human rights: rights of individuals; rights to political participation; and rights to social and economic security. One could argue that women's movements have reflected this unfolding nature of citizenship: from the early twentieth-century demands for universal political rights (which continue to be made), to the current insistence upon mainstreaming a gendered perspective in political institutions and economic policy-making; from the debates on the importance of entitlements to citizenship, which include socio-economic justice, to a discursive shift from national citizenship rights to the demands for universal human rights and even for a conception of global citizenship (Peterson and Parisi, 1998; Ali, 2000; Blacklock and MacDonald, 2000).

Feminist scholars have written extensively on citizenship, arguing that it is an important as well as a contested concept (Lister, 1997: 3). It has been argued that 'modern citizenship is inserted into a social field, . . . [where] freedom, autonomy and the right to be different . . . are pitched against the regulating forces of modernity and the state, and subverted by discourses of "culture and tradition" – of nationalism, religiosity and the family' (Werbner and Yuval-Davis, 1999: 1). Citizenship is thus embedded in the dominant social relations in particular contexts, while at the same time appearing as a universal discourse of rights. Feminist scholars have felt this ambiguity acutely and pointed out that although the term has as often been used in struggles to secure greater standing within the national political arena, it has also 'often simultaneously functioned to justify the exclusion of other members of the national community' (Narayan, 1997: 49). Citizenship can be exclusionary in two different ways. First, by denying national citizenship to individuals, it can be used to reject the 'human' claims of those who are thus denied. Second, by individualizing citizenship, it limits the political space to acknowledge collective rights to citizenship, and therefore an historically embedded understanding of citizenship (Kymlicka, 1995).[21]

Citizenship has also been important to the discussions on gender and democratization. Perhaps, here more than anywhere else, we are conscious of the changed international political climate. We also become aware of the political context of the old and new democracies, and of transitional or fragile democracies within which women have to negotiate their citizenships. In transitional societies the terms of women's inclusion in political life have been important (Blacklock and MacDonald, 2000; Zulu, 2000). However, these debates on citizenship are taking different forms, depending upon the nature of transitions. So in South Africa, given the history of systematic exclusion of black people from the polity, the focus of political debate has been on constitutional provisions for an engendered citizenship. In Guatemala and Mexico, the experience of military dictatorships has seen the women's movements shifting the debate from a citizenship-based to a human rights-based discourse. This shift is visible also in other states, where liberalization is creating tensions around the en-

---

21 Kymlicka, while assessing the importance of collective rights, makes two separate but equally important points. He suggests that collective rights address two different relationships. First, the relationship between the minority and majority populations or groups where 'the claim is that justice between minority and majority cultures requires certain "collective rights" which reduce the minority's vulnerability to the decisions of the majority' (1995: 14). The second is the relation between individual members of the group and the collectivity of the group. The claim here is that 'collective rights' should be able to limit individual rights to revise or reject group traditions in order to preserve these. Feminists have been ambivalent with regard to both these bases of citizenship rights (Young, 1990; Phillips, 1995).

vironment, or displacement of peoples, or conditions of employment. In countries where the transition has included a dismantling
of economic state structures, such as in Eastern Europe, citizenship
debates have necessarily had to take on board the new economic
realities (Zareska, 1998; Einhorn, 2000). The question of entitlements
to citizenship has, then, become important.

As economic restructuring of national economies under pressures
from international economic institutions takes effect along lines of
class, gender and race, issues of socio-economic entitlements to citizenship are increasing in importance. In her study of resource and
community management, Agarwal makes the important point that
'membership rather than citizenship has become the defining criter-
ion for access to these [land] resources' (1997: 1374). In her examination of Joint Forest Management schemes in India, she discovers
that there is 'a more formalized system of rights dependent on membership in the emergent institutions' (p. 1374). Usufruct rights of all
villages, in this case, are being replaced by those who can secure
membership of formal organizations set up to manage forests. The
terms of membership-based rights, ownership or access to land use,
for example, are different from citizenship-based rights, which include usufruct and inclusion in the community. The nature of citizenship that we envision can therefore be radically different, with
varied outcomes for women and men. Thus, feminist theorists and
policy analysts are pointing out the importance of distinguishing
between socio-economic and political bases of citizenships (Lister,
1997; Yuval-Davis, 1997). An emphasis on this distinction between
economic and political participation has led some feminists to examine the concept of entitlements.

Arguing for a rights-based framework that focuses on political
equality as enablement is one approach to citizenship.[22] Another
might be to insist upon social entitlements, which might lead to a
redistribution of economic and political resources. As we saw in chapter 2, Amartya Sen argues that 'in a private ownership economy, the
two basic parameters of entitlement analysis are "endowment"
(roughly, what is initially owned) and "exchange entitlement
mapping" (reflecting the exchange possibilities that exist through

---

22 For an excellent discussion about the 'rights question' for feminist scholars
and activists, see Kiss (1995). Addressing the question, 'are rights alchemy or
fool's gold?', Kiss concludes that those feminist theorists who reject a rights-
based discourse display a conceptual confusion and naïveté and do not take
into account the importance of rights to 'empower women and to create and
maintain social conditions of gender justice' (p. 18).

production and trade)'. He also points out that 'for the most of humanity, virtually the only significant endowment is labour power', so that 'the conditions governing the exchange of labour power (e.g. employment, wages and prices, and social security, if any)' are central to such an analysis (1990?: 140–1).[23] Following from this, Sen argues that 'a greater economic role for women definitely improves their status within the family' (p. 144; Einhorn, 2000).[24] As Einhorn notes,

> The notion of entitlements also enables us to think about the interaction of legal and political rights with property rights, economic rights and social rights. In other words, it allows us to oppose the delinking of states and markets suggested by the neo-liberal paradigm which constitutes the market as the sole regulator of society, and to map instead the combined impact of the operations of both market and state (through political legislation and social/welfare policies) on the social rights and opportunities of individual citizens and families. (2000: 119)

She concludes that '[t]his combination of . . . links between, state and grassroots, national and local, levels of politics and between states, markets and households is a necessary prerequisite for overcoming gender inequality and facilitating active citizenship for women' (p. 120; see also Einhorn, 1992; Randall, 1998: 202).

Globalization has created its own challenges to and strains on the concept of citizenship. Historically embedded within the boundaries of the nation-state, globalization is challenging this narrower conception and suggesting a global dimension to activism. While feminist movements have long emphasized the global nature of 'sisterhood', we have seen how this has fractured along lines of class

---

23 For a discussion of citizenship rights and 'the opportunity to earn', see Shklar (1991), who argues that the value of citizenship was derived primarily from its denial to those who could not earn a living, and therefore a 'vision of economic independence, or self-directed "earning" as the ethical basis of democratic citizenship has retained its powerful appeal' in Anglo-American political theory (p. 17).

24 For a challenge to this argument, see Narayan (1997), where she argues that such an emphasis on waged work helps to reinforce the 'relative unimportance of *unwaged* work, of the domestic labor and the care of dependents predominantly performed by women' (p. 51). Narayan sees this focus on waged work as a middle-class feminist concern, and suggests that this explains the importance of 'issues such as affirmative action, comparable work, and harassment at the workplace' in recent feminist agendas. As we saw in chapter 4, these agendas are not just the concern of middle-class women, but very important to millions of women working in terrible conditions across the world's factories.

and ethnicity, sexuality and (dis)ability, making it difficult to retain much optimism concerning this transcendence of national contexts. However, is the current phase of global restructuring providing women with a more tethered sense of global activism that we might call global citizenship? 'Women's Eyes on the Bank' provides an example of such global activism, whatever the outcome. We also noted in chapter 4 how global restructuring is posing difficult issues for women's work, within and outside the home, as even minimal welfare provisions come under threat. As Pettman (1996) suggests, this has directly caused the exponential growth in female migration, which has posed questions about the nature of a citizenship no longer rooted in particular nation-states. These increasing pressures have led to a growth of women's activism through a proliferation of NGO activities and acceptance of these by major multilateral organizations. Is a participation-focused definition of citizenship better able to address the questions of women's lives in a global world?

This discussion of citizenship in different contexts raises diverse and not always reconcilable issues for women's activism. However, if citizenship is to form the basis of communication and activism, of the definition of individual as well as group concerns, of rights as well as claims and duties, then, it seems to me, it must entail a deliberative process of 'rooting and shifting', that is cognizant of structural limits and possibilities of change.

Presence and Deliberation

Arguably, the case for a rights-based citizenship is premised on both a recognition of the importance of a 'politics of presence' (Phillips, 1995) and a 'deliberative democratic' argument. The argument about presence, as Anna Jonasdottir (1988) has pointed out, concerns both the *form* of politics and its *content*. The question of form includes the demand to be among the decision-makers, the demand for participation and a share in control over public affairs. In terms of content, it includes being able to articulate the needs, wishes and demands of various groups of women (p. 40). Phillips argues that the shift from the politics of 'ideas' (by which she means ideas organized within the structures of political parties) to the politics of presence (by which she means representation of identities in politics) is problematic. It is, she argues, 'in the relationship between ideas and presence that we can best hope to find a fairer system of representation, not in a false opposition between one or the other' (p. 25).

The advocates of deliberative democracy focus on the claim that political engagement can change initial political positions on

preference and interests.[25] Elster argues that deliberative democracy
involves three elements: process, outcome and context. Its starting
point seems to be that 'democracy revolves around the transformation rather than simply the aggregation of preferences' (1997: 1;
Knight and Johnson, 1997).[26] Feminists have argued for a similar
process/outcome-based politics when they have spoken of 'rooting
and shifting' or 'transversal politics', of situated deliberation leading
to democratic outcomes as particularly suited to the way women do
(or are predisposed to do) politics (see Yuval-Davis, 1997; Cockburn,
2000). The deliberative position, then, is that if different interests and
interest groups meet in democratic organizational contexts, 'common
good' can prevail over sectional interest. From this it argues for a
transformative politics that extends the range of potential solutions
on offer, as well as for a feasible politics of accommodation to take
shape (Phillips, 1995; Rai, 2000b; also chapter 6, this volume).[27] Open
deliberation and communication is possible only when different
groups are able to participate in a dialogue. Here we need to give
regard to capacity-building,[28] which includes both the 'means of

---

25 Critics have seen deliberative democracy as a procedural process for the
legitimizing of outcomes, and have suggested that it is silent 'about how intract-
able conflicts of interests or values can be resolved deliberatively' (McGrew,
2000: 18–19). As we shall see below, this seems to be a rather misguided criticism, even though there are caveats that one needs to place when dealing with
the structure/agency problem within the deliberative framework.
26 Squires (2002), however, makes the useful point that deliberative democracy is not really a model of democracy because in effect it augments aggrega-
tive democracy with deliberation and in doing so assumes the current
institutions of representative democracy as given. She also urges the advocates
of deliberative democracy to engage with issues not only of deliberation but
also of institutional decision-making and the operation of the rule of law. In
doing so, I would suggest, she makes a powerful demand. However, she also
falls into the trap of dichotomizing institutional and deliberative politics. I
would argue for a useful parallel exploration of the practical/strategic interests
debate discussed above where the pursuit of one is necessarily (but located in
specific political contexts) linked to the other, especially if the decisional
moment is to translate into the 'implementational moment'.
27 I have tried to untangle some of the issues raised in this section in the
context of *Panchayati* Raj Institutions in India. Originally these were deliberative,
non-party political bodies. Over a period of time their influence receded. A
quota for women on resurrected *panchayats* opens up the question of deliberative politics (Rai, 2000b).
28 The relevant capacities would be: (a) capacity to formulate authentic preferences where authenticity denotes the interpretative freedom of representatives;

freedom' and the 'extent of freedom', both of which affect the ways individuals engage in the deliberative process and even use the political goods available to them most effectively in their interests (Sen, 1992: 8). An attention to 'substantive equality' will ensure that individual citizens will have the appropriate personal resources to participate effectively in that process without risking threats, and through ensuring the enhancement of the capacities of political actors (Knight and Johnson, 1997: 293).

In juxtaposition to the liberal position, I would argue that this emphasis on capacity-building can allow us to focus not only on the relevant capacities needed to deliberate, but also on the redistribution of resources needed to enhance the capacities of the marginalized and the excluded, and hence on the structural change required for deliberative processes of politics to work (Rai, 2000b: 13). In doing so, we also become aware of the limits of this political strategy, which primarily focuses on the agency of deliberators rather than on the structural constraints that inhibit the 'extent' of their freedom and 'substantive equality'. What worries some critics – that legitimization of outcomes takes place in the name of the processes of deliberation (Stokes, 1998) – cannot, then, be taken as read. The process itself uncovers power relations that underlie political processes. This could then open up space within which to mobilize to extend political boundaries. Thus the two – the need for presence of different groups in politics and the possibility of communicative dialogue leading to the transformation of political agendas – can, upon this argument, go hand in hand.

Empowerment of Women

An active citizenship, substantive equality, and deliberative politics can thus be the pillars of women's empowerment. Participation in the processes of production of wealth as well as in discourses of politics can be an important resource for women's empowerment. However, as we have seen above, participation itself raises difficult questions for women and women's groups. This is especially so when the outcome of participation does not appear to empower women.

Empowerment has become a motherhood term within the development literature and practice, accepted and promoted by most

---

(b) effective use of cultural resources; and (c) cognitive capacities that require acquiring the information necessary to diminish uncertainty (Sen, 1992: 148–9).

major multilateral agencies (Parpart et al., 2001).[29] Feminists have been attracted to the term 'empowerment' for many reasons, including: its focus on the oppressed rather than the oppressors; its emphasis on 'power to' rather than 'power over'; and its insistence upon power as enabling, as competence, rather than as dominance (Bystydzienski, 1992: 3). The feminist literature on politics has also re-emphasized empowerment as development. Bystydzienski, for example, defines empowerment as a 'process by which oppressed persons gain some control over their lives by taking part with others in development of activities and structures that allow people increased involvement in matters which affect them directly' (p. 3). It has been seen as a process as well as an outcome. While outcomes are essential for accountability of those engaged in strategies for enhancement of empowerment, it is also important, however, to be cautious of not confusing the achievement of stated goals with empowerment of the group as a whole (Kabeer, 1999).

In the late 1980s, as a direct response to the specific problems facing men and women of the South, DAWN produced a vision of empowerment rooted in a commitment to collective action through 'political mobilization, legal changes, consciousness raising, and popular education' (Sen and Grown, 1985: 87). In the 1990s the concept of empowerment expanded to replace terms such as 'poverty alleviation', 'welfare' and 'community participation' (Batliwala, 1993; Moser, 1993) and to include institutional strategies for empowerment by most development agencies (see above, and UN, 1995; CIDA, 1999; Blair, 2000). Reflecting upon the three case studies presented in this chapter, I would argue that often strategies for 'empowerment of women' are a means for improving productivity within the status quo, rather than for challenging and transforming established structures and practices. Empowerment cannot thus transcend power relations; it is enmeshed in relations of power at all levels of society (Parpart et al., 2001). However, our discussion of citizenship rights, entitlements and deliberative democratic politics also shows the potential of realizing women's empowerment through a serious and sophisticated engagement with institutions of power. Thus we need to focus on the 'relationship between structures and agency, of challenge and transformation which transcend

---

29 Chandhoke expresses the same worry about the universal acceptance of the term 'civil society': 'It is time to worry for if groups who should otherwise be disagreeing on the concept come to agree on it, it means that the concept has been *flattened* out to such an alarming extent, that it has lost its credibility' (2001: 1).

the bounds of "discursive normality"...It also allows us to incorporate notions of power that recognize the importance of individual
consciousness/understanding (*power within*), and its importance for
collective action (*power with*) that can organize and exert *power to*
challenge gender hierarchies and improve women's lives' (Parpart
et al., 2001).

These debates about women's engagement with processes of
democratic change and the insights they produce are crucial for
those working with institutions of power that reflect and are part of
dominant structures, and for the construction of a politics of solidarity among women's groups. While the cautionary tales discussed in
this chapter force us to consider more carefully the costs for
women's groups (in time, energy, angst, increased vulnerability, as
well as legitimacy, with contention among women resulting in increased differences), the debates on citizenships underscore the importance of political engagement. In the next, and concluding,
chapter I examine more fully the implications of the rise of global
governance and women's engagement with political institutions.

6 | Critical Engagements
From Nationalism to
Globalization

If you have come to help me you can go home again. But if you see
my struggle as part of your own survival then perhaps we can work
together.
Australian Aborigine woman, cited in *The Manila Declaration on
People's Participation and Sustainable Development*

Globalization is posing many challenges to women. The increasing
complexity of the global economy and the nature of global governance are fundamentally reshaping the ways in which we think of the
world and our place in it. The end of the Cold War has made new
opportunities visible and viable; the binaries of that war are no
longer pre-eminent in framing our public political life. However,
for many of us, these changed traditions and economies do not
seem to improve our condition.[1] On the contrary, we can witness
increasing inequalities, violence and insecurities resulting from the
changes in the world economy. There have been varied responses to
these (un)changing circumstances on the contested intellectual
terrains of globalization and modernity. As we saw in chapter 3,
there has been a celebration of individualism, of hypermasculinities,
of individual agency, but also, because of the huge leaps in
communications technology, of opportunities for organizing across
borders, of disseminating information, of sharing strategies (see

---

1   'The number of poor people has risen world-wide, and in some regions the
proportion of poor has also increased,' notes the World Development Report,
2000 (World Bank, 2000: 25).

also chapter 5). While some have seen nothing new in globalization except its scale, others have linked it to a new era of postmodernity, and even post-postmodernity (chapter 3). The idea of the nation-state as the major actor in the economic and political worlds that we inhabit is also being challenged. This book began with an analysis of the nationalist discourses and their imbrication with the idea of development in the period of decolonization (chapters 1 and 2). Today, despite a proliferation of nationalist movements and the fracturing of old states under pressure from nationalisms, those ideas seem dated. New nations emerging out of the old, are still coming to life, but in a changed world. Further, while the nation-state seems to be retreating somewhat from our imaginations, the local space of our lives is looming large. Constant references to the local and the global, and their simultaneous coexistence in the idea of the 'glocal' (Robertson, 1992), imply that the nation-state is an irritating intermediary between these other two spaces, not knowing when to leave alone the growing relationship of mutual respect. Little surprise, then, that this celebration is also evoking more pessimistic responses.

In this concluding chapter I caution against nostalgia for the centralized nation-state among critics of globalization. As I argued in chapter 3, the nation-state continues to be a critically important actor in the international political economy, and as such it is not simply a victim of globalizing forces, but a participant in the refashioning of itself and of the world that we live in. Nostalgia, I argue, comes at a price. However, on the other hand, I also caution against the celebration of the local. It seems to me that at times, the level of theorizing of this space is marked by a naïve but politically dangerous disregard of the power structures that frame it. The local is of course a crucially important space for our daily lives, but, precisely because it *is* so immediate, we need to map it more carefully than many of those celebrating it uncritically are able to do.

Feminists have responded to these new pressures of globalization. New agendas for gender-sensitive development are taking shape. As we saw in chapter 5, one of the notable developments since the 1990s – especially leading towards and resulting from the 1995 Beijing Conference on Women – has been an increasing engagement by women's groups with social and economic institutions at macro, meso and micro levels. Here, I briefly discuss the ways in which the reconfiguring of the national state, and the changing local/global space are presenting women's movements with difficult issues, as well as increased opportunities for moving forward the struggles for greater equality and justice. In Pettman's words, I ask, 'Within the globalized political economy and its characteristic "forced march" of women..., what are the possibilities of a more internationalised and multilayered feminist politics, all the stronger for the criss-crossing of ideas, networks, and moving women themselves?' (1996: 212). I suggest that the continuing engagements with economic and political institutions are important, despite their limitations, as these allow us to take politics seriously and to build solidarity while at the same time underscoring the issue of difference among women. This productive tension, I would suggest, allows women to organize among women, and also to look to other emancipatory movements for support in their struggles for justice.

Nostalgic Critics of Globalization

The Nation-State as a Victim

The debate about the nature of the nation-state in the context of globalization has not only focused attention on the protean nature of power relations, but has also provoked another, more sentimental response. There is a growing literature on the nation-state in the 'nostalgic mode', which obscures as much as it reveals in its analysis of the nation-state under globalization. For women this debate is relevant because it uses some of the iconography of nationalisms that we saw evoked by nationalist movements in chapter 1, and also poses difficult questions about feasible politics.

In the post-war period the nation-state became both the embodiment of national aspirations for development and the site of social engagement. While the state was configured differently in various countries of the Third World, the role of the state in development was seen to be central in all contexts. Despite the failure of the state to deliver on its promises of political stability and economic growth with some attention to social justice, the nation-state remained central both to the theoretical critiques of development and equally to international organizations that sought to change national development trajectories through political pressure. Cold War politics provided a curious stability, which meant that the role of non-governmental organizations was minimal and regulated and generally confined to immediate relief needs in times of crises. Multinational corporations operated with impunity in some Third World states, but in others with much more caution, and within much less space. The 'spheres of influence' of the superpowers dictated some curtailment of state power, but also limited the challenges to it within its boundaries. It is with this context in mind that we must read the burgeoning nostalgia for the nation-state as the rhetoric of globalization gathers momentum.

Kothari has pointed out with concern that there is 'evidence of growing marginalization of the state in the face of a variety of glob-alizing intrusions – in fact a growing disempowerment of the state and of the national elite...in [their] power to enforce national prior-ities...'. He arraigns the protagonists of globalization for 'conver-ging on the need to reduce the role of the state in the affairs of the country and hand over things to market mechanisms and to increase integration into the "world market"'. For them, he laments, 'pres-sures and demands from within, emanating from one's own people, are more dangerous than the pressures and demands coming from foreign corporations....' For a long time, he reminds us, 'the nation-building exercise was conceived to be one that simultaneously led to greater unity of the nation and greater involvement and participa-tion for the citizen in the institutions of the state.' But now 'the retreat of the state and the erosion of the nation are going hand in hand, one being hijacked by the global "order" and "market" and the other facing serious challenges from within....' He warns that as the nation-state becomes more and more unable to cope, the national elites will 'turn away from the basic political challenge of nation-building and the related economic challenge of "development"'. He prophesies that '[a]s this happens, the autonomy of civil society too will decline and with it may also go down the modern search for a democratic order' (1995: 1593–1603). Lasch (1995), in the context of North America, makes a similar point about the diminishing nation-state and its consequences for democracy. He argues that the 'de-nationalization of business enterprise tends to produce a class of cosmopolitans who set themselves as "world citizens", but without accepting...any of the obligations that citizenship in a polity implies...'(p. 47). He bemoans the global decline of the middle class that has accompanied the diminishing of the nation-state: 'Whatever its faults, middle-class nationalism provided a common ground, common standards, a common form of reference', and warns that without such a bedrock of stability, 'society dissolves into nothing more than contending factions, as the Founding Fathers of America understood so well – a war of all against all' (p. 49).

A close reading of the literature in the nostalgic mode raises inter-esting questions for feminists and for women's movements. One could argue that this nostalgia for the nation-state also reflects male-dominated national elites' growing fear of powerlessness, which they had only just recently escaped through the processes of decolonization.[2] In chapter 1 I explored the ways in which the colonial discourses 'emasculated' the traditional nationalist elites; the process of regaining their masculinity had involved confrontation with colonial power, and creating an alternative hegemonic discourse that attempted to fix feminine identity, and feminize the 'other' within the nation. This process, Kandiyoti argues, led to a nationalizing of patriarchy: 'Whereas the traditional exercise of patriarchal authority tended to rest with particular men – fathers, husbands and other male kin – the communalization of politics, particularly when backed by state sponsored religious fundamentalism, shifts the right of control to all men' (1991a: 14). In the context of this public patriarchy, national bureaucracies of the nation-state regained their masculinity by setting themselves up as the opposition to the traditional forms of patriarchy. Within the dominant discourses, largely based on equality, they created spaces for women's emancipation from the 'pre-modern' conditions of the colonial society (chapter 1). Control over national development agendas enhanced the sense of power flowing back to the indigenous male elites, invoking the images of rational protectors, and planners for future national development. These agendas, as we saw in chapter 2, remained tied to the ideas of modernization, mechanization and industrialization – arenas where women's presence was minimally visible. As ecofeminists like Shiva (1989) have pointed out, the discursive framework of science and rationality employed by these modernizing elites also contributed to the marginalization of women within the processes of development.

One could argue that the operations of the global market threaten to emasculate the national bureaucracies' reconfigured sense of self. In assessing gender relations within Malaysia's Muda region, for example, Hart comments that 'not only are men incorporated into political patronage relations, from which women are largely excluded: in addition, they are confronted with a principle that defines them as superior and responsible for women, simultaneously with an incapacity to put this principle into material practice in the domestic sphere' (1991: 115). The national patriarchies find themselves in similar positions *vis-à-vis* global economic forces and their domestic populations. This is not to suggest that the concerns outlined by Kothari and Lasch do not have any merit. As shown by the examples from even more consolidated democracies, such as India (discussed in chapter 4), national elites are under tremendous pressure to

---

2 I have come across no such nostalgia among feminist scholars writing on nationalism or the nation-state.

conform to the demands of global capitalism. Even where there is, in the name of nationalism, certain resistance to these pressures, the room for manoeuvre is shrinking, creating greater distance between the elites and the citizens, increasing social tensions and even resulting in political instability. It is also becoming clear that the threat of capital flight is a powerful motif in the relations between states and investors, dominating the agenda-setting processes within nation-states. However, my argument is that the growing pressures under which national elites find themselves do not constitute an entirely new stage in their development, and that the recollection of the glory days of the nation-state is not only nostalgic but also disingenuous.

The disempowered state is presented as a hapless victim of global market forces, as if it is not implicated in any way – through mismanagement, greed, incompetence and policy changes – in the 'opening up' of its markets to these forces. Further, the defenders of the nation-state paint a picture of the nation-state and its elites as largely benign, struggling under historical burdens of racial, communal, and religious hatred, trying to bring order to disordered societies, promoting enlightenment to bear upon traditional prejudices that had not until then allowed a sense of national purpose: 'The relationship of the new nation to pre-existing identities was in part to be one of transcendence, though it was far more to be one of encompassing them and in some ways even "representing" them all in a composite manner' (Kothari, 1995: 1594). The costs of the building of composite national entities and identities were, however, borne in large part by the marginalized, subaltern, non-hegemonic groups of which women were a significant part. Also, this benign picture of transformative nationalist elites is based upon a very narrow base. There are a few countries, like India, Tanzania, and Egypt, that experienced sustained periods of political stability in the aftermath of successful nationalist struggles, and where the nationalist state enjoyed some sustained legitimacy. In these countries, the state elites did seek to change the existing power relationships. However, even here, levels of social inequality and economic poverty remained significant. In many other states, as dependency theorists have pointed out, the economy remained dependent upon global capitalist market forces, and the state elites remained cut off from the needs and aspirations of their citizens. The current enthusiasm of many national elites for adjusting to the demands of global economic institutions shows how implicated the national states are in the whole process of marketization and globalization.

In and Against the State

As we saw in chapter 5, for feminists, the nation-state has always presented serious intellectual and strategic challenges. For some, any engagement with the state has been questionable on the grounds that 'the state... produces state subjects *inter alia*, bureaucratized, dependent, disciplined and gendered...' (Brown, 1992: 9; also see Allen, 1990). There has been an ongoing debate within the feminist movement about the expropriatory power of institutions (see Ehren-reich and Piven, 1983; Brown, 1992; Pringle and Watson, 1992; Rai, 1995). The various positions have covered the entire spectrum from rejecting 'dealing' with state institutions entirely, to suggest-ing an 'in and against' the state approach, to examining the benefits of working with/through state institutions. I have argued elsewhere that for women, as for other marginalized groups, the state and civil society are both complex terrains – fractured, oppressive, threatening and also providing spaces for struggles and negotiations. These struggles and negotiations are grounded in the positionings of vari-ous groups of women articulating their short- and long-term interests in the context of the multiplicity of power relations that form the state in any country. In its turn, the state and its institutions are also 'shaped' by the forms and outcomes of these struggles. While deny-ing any intentionality to the state, or a necessary coherence to the alliances formed and engaged in struggles against states, there are, however, particular characteristics of Third World states that need to be examined to form a judgement about the various possible spaces for mobilization by women in their interests.

My study of women's struggles against and engagement with the state in India, for example, showed that while state institutions and dominant political parties have taken up the cause of women's representation as part of the generalized discourse of modernity to which they subscribe, this discourse is not unified. As such, it allows sections of the state to take initiatives to respond to the struggles of women for equality as well as empowerment. This results in contra-diction between different fractions of the state, which allows further possibilities for negotiation and struggle by and in the interests of women. Further, the capacity of the state to implement its policies and enforce its laws is undermined by the weakness of the economy and of the political infrastructure, and by widespread corruption, which leads to the delegitimization of government and the political system. This lack of capacity further enhances intra-state conflict (Rai, 1995). The state thus cannot be regarded as and engaged with as a unified entity. It remains a fractured terrain that women's groups and struggles need to respond to in complex ways.

Thus, in my earlier work (1995, 1996b, 1999) I have suggested that women's movements need to work 'in and against' the state. An engagement with the state should not be considered simply as one option to be weighed against others; it is a necessity. I have argued that a recognition of the particular splintered complexity of the state and of the multiplicity of the strategies of struggle is needed by women to confront and/or use state fractions in their own interests. An understanding of a relative autonomy of state fractions from the existing social relations and infrastructural capacity, on the one hand, and of state embeddedness in social relations and the consequences of such embeddedness for women, on the other, is necessary for engaging with institutions of power in a critical and thoughtful way. Such an approach, derived from analysis of particular struggles, also points to the potential for a strategy that holds in tension the engagement with, and the mobilization against, structures of power, be they at the local, national or global level. In the context of 'the neoliberal frame' under globalization (Runyan, 1999), I would suggest that strategizing for change in this way has become ever more critical. As the global reach of social and political movements increases through technological and information networks, and as the pressures of international trade and markets begin to impinge significantly on national economies, leading to a fragmentation and repositioning of nation-states, the relationship between local struggles, social movements and the national state is being constantly reshaped (Cohen and Rai, 2000a; Stienstra, 2000).

I would suggest further that for a critical engagement with structures of power, the terms of engagement need to be clearly thought out. As we saw in chapter 5, not all, or even most, of these terms can be determined by the women's movements, but a sensitivity to the issues at stake is still important if we are realistically to assess the extent to which agendas of institutions and structures of power may be shifted. Finally, I would argue that an engagement with power structures need not rule out – indeed, needs to build upon – a strong movement of opposition to these structures. Without such a double move, early feminist concerns about co-optation within dominant discourses and by structural regimes of power become very real. Such an analysis of 'in and against' organized power structures needs to reflect upon 'the shifting distinctions between representation within the state and political economy, on the one hand, and within the theory of the Subject, on the other...' (Spivak,

1988: 275–6).[3] In doing so, we can begin to address the tensions between feasible and transformative politics.

However, political institutions cannot be the sole focus of these struggles. Civil society itself needs to be democratized at both national and global levels. While providing a space for mobilization, it also constrains the construction and organization of interests that challenge the dominant discourses of gendered power. The relationship between political institutions and civil society thus becomes an important arena for negotiations and struggles. Where political institutions are deeply 'embedded' in civil society and its 'peak interest groups', these institutions are constrained not to propose policies that would be opposed by these groups.[4] However, the modernist project to which they subscribe means they cannot be entirely neglectful of issues arising from women's struggles, and this forces them to take issue with some of the dominant interest groups. The result is a policy framework and its implementation that are at best patchy, allowing for another set of possibilities for struggles around expanding the domain of reform as well as improving the capacity of state fractions to implement existing policies effectively (Rai, 1995).

While some analysts have bemoaned the marginalization of the nation-state and of state elites in the debates on global governance, others have emphasized the emancipatory potential of 'the local' in the political economy of globalization. Many feminists have participated in this celebration of 'the local'. Where are women most able to participate in struggles to improve their lives, they ask? Participation, a key concept in feminist politics, has been assumed to be most effective at the local level. So much so that in some countries there have been struggles to institutionalize local-level political participation through legislation on the premise that development policy outcomes are sub-optimal when not supported by broad-based participation from the social groups targeted by the policy (Robinson and White, 1998; Blair, 2000). In Bolivia, for example, a Law of Popular Participation became effective in 1994, and in India, under the 73rd and 74th Amendments, the village-level governance institutions

---

3 Using Marx's discussion of the 'working class' in the *Eighteenth Brumaire of Louis Bonaparte*, Spivak makes the important point that a Subject is necessarily divided and dislocated and its 'parts are not continuous or coherent with each other', even while 'in so far as millions of families live under economic conditions of existence that cut off their mode of life...from those of the other classes...they form a class' (1988: 276).
4 The 'opt-out' clauses of most human and civil rights international conventions, for example, are symptomatic of such compromises.

(*panchayats*) were given greater powers and resources, and a quota of 33 per cent was secured for women's representation on these reinvigorated institutions. In the debates on political participation of women, usually the first agencies held up for scrutiny are at the village level. In the context of globalization, the emphasis on NGO activity has also brought this political space into focus; the most effective NGOs work at the local levels (see chapter 5). The nation-state thus seems at times to be being replaced by the expansion of the local in political discourse. In the following section I examine this concept of the local – not as a missing link between the nation-state and global governance, but as a problematic terrain on which women have to function, and which affects the ways in which they are able to access the local economy and beyond. It is important to do this in order to see how the debates on post-development and the changing/contracting role of the state are affecting the lives of men and women.

The Local as Refuge?

If women's work challenges the divisions between the public and the private, their lives also raise questions about the importance of the local spaces that they occupy. 'The local' has found a privileged place in the vocabulary of different groups concerned with issues of development and democracy: basic needs theorists, environmental-ists, sustainability groups, feminists and those intervening in the human rights debate. There are several reasons for this. First, the emphasis on the local allows a critique of nationalist agendas of political elites focused on major industrialization projects. As Pearson (1998) has commented, these projects assumed the man as worker, and in countries such as Brazil and India, we see rapid industrialization in the 1960s and 1970s resulting in falling levels of women's employment in the public sphere. Second, a focus on the local challenges the universalism of scientific discourses upon which the framework of modernization was built, by pointing to the sali-ence of local knowledges and paradigms: 'It is *local* knowledge that informs the birthing skills of the *sages-femmes* studied by Bohme.... And it is *local* knowledge produced by workers that is the object of appropriation and control in both Taylorist and "postindustrial" strategies of industrial management' (Kloppenburn, 1991: 14; see also Berry, 1991; Esteva and Prakash, 1997). The idea of the local is sensitive to the context of people's lives. 'Related to the theme of context or locale is the idea of distance, which also has social,

emotional or geographical dimensions...between authors and subject...[between] First Nation or Diaspora women' (Marchand and
Parpart, 1995: 7). Third, a focus on the local allows people to participate in the economic and political life of their community: 'Thousands of small grassroots groups are realizing that there is no need
to "think big" in order to begin releasing themselves from the
clutches of the monopolistic...economy; that they can free themselves in the same voluntary ways as they entered it' (Esteva and
Prakash, 1997: 280). Finally, a focus on the local also challenges
authoritarianism by promoting decentralization and autonomy.
The local, upon this view, is democratic, inclusive and the site for
feasible politics of resistance to both global and national nodes of
power.

The recent emphasis on the 'grassroots' in the development
funding agencies and their agendas is proof of the importance now
being attached to the concept. NGOs as part of civil society also find
favour within this discourse. The argument there is that the local is
not only closer to the lives of people, it also allows for greater sensitivity to local ecology; it is more accountable and more participatory
(World Bank, 1994). Finally, a focus on the local also challenges the
possessive individualism of the liberal rights discourse by arguing
that the universal language of rights cannot capture the complexities
of historically rooted cultural practices that empower people at the
local level in their communities: 'In most Latin American, Asian or
African villages, collective or communal rights have clear priority
over *personal* or *individual* rights; legitimate hierarchies (of the elders,
for example) have primacy over equality...; and concrete customs,
rather than abstract universalizable laws, support communal bonds
and organize social support' (Esteva and Prakash, 1997: 282; see also
Sachs, 1997: 290).

The focus on the local has been a powerful challenge to many of
the fundamental reference points of development theory and practice. By advocating a decentralization of power, it has tried to make
nation-states more accountable, people's – especially women's – participation more feasible, the contexts of people's lives more visible,
and the universalisms of science less monolithic. However, we need
to sound a cautionary note here. This caution is dictated by various
concerns. The first is that the privileging of the local space is very
often linked to issues of the capacity of the national state. It is interesting that the World Bank and the IMF are emphasizing the local
space at the same time as the economic and political conditionalities
they are imposing upon the national state are increasing (chapter 4).
The forcing open of national market boundaries is resulting in the

reconfiguration of demographic and geographic spaces within countries. This opening up has led many Third World countries to experience huge migratory flows of populations for the first time. These flows have been inevitably from the countryside to the urban centres. With the establishment of Free Economic Zones, these flows have also seen the huge increase of women migrants (chapter 4). The local space in the countryside has changed enormously, as has the urban landscape. The concept of the local in this context is itself being stretched. What is the locale for the migrant woman? Her home that she has left behind, or her present location, which is not home? This displacement is also resulting in increased vulnerabilities for women (chapter 4). Sexual violence and economic exploitation are increasing in many liberalizing countries. This is happening in tandem with the whittling away of state-based support infrastructure: hospitals, schools, refuges and other social services are being closed, cut back or privatized.[5] In this context the question of decentralization becomes difficult. While economic policies are being crafted in international arenas, the consequences are being felt and lived at the local level. The role of the nation-state becomes vital in this context: at times it is complicit in the 'glocalization' of society (Robertson, 1992); at others it is a mediator between the local and the global. A shift of focus away from the nation-state means a neglect of the crucial mapping of the nation-state's role and influence.

Second, my caution stems from the discourse of the local itself. I would suggest that for women the village is not necessarily a space of freedom or security. Indeed, as we saw in the discussion of the Women's Development Programme in Rajasthan, the levels of culturally validated oppressions, exclusions, violations and surveillance that women experience in villages are extremely high (chapter 5). Marxist materialists have argued that urbanization resulting from industrialization will lead to the breaking down of the ascriptive roles in society, which affect women in particularly restrictive ways (Desai, 1989). I would argue that urbanization, while presenting its own problems and struggles, does afford women a relative freedom of action often denied them in the locales of their villages. I suggest further that 'empowerment through localization' could also be seen to be a westernized discourse, where, because of comprehensive industrialization and urbanization, the local and urban have gone hand in hand since the advent of second wave

---

5 This is not to suggest, of course, that the local space was less oppressive to women before the increased pressures of globalization. It was perhaps more stable and for some women more secure.

feminism.[6] When this discourse is transposed to the rural local of the majority of Third World women, different cultural contexts make the valorization of the concept more problematic. This is not to take away from the importance of the local in the lives of women, but to query the privileging of it as a freer, less distant, more empowering space. It is with such querying that we restore the politics in the local, rather than treating it as a homogeneous, co-operative and democratic space.[7] The local is as fractured a space as the national or the global. It has its own hierarchy of power in operation, with the resources to defend existing relations of power, and to suppress dissent. It is also therefore the space where democratic struggles need to be organized; it is not in itself a means of democratizing life.

As we saw in chapter 5, a growing literature on empowerment points to local spaces as arenas of participatory politics.[8] However, within development discourse and practice, participation, as well as the local, has been depoliticized; participation, as well as the 'decentralized space', has become the panacea for accountable development. Blair notes that by the 'mid-1990s USAID was supporting about 60 [democratic local government] activities... [and the UNDP] assisted over 250 decentralization activities in various countries...' (2000: 22). As an example of local and decentralized development practice, let us review Robert Chambers' Participatory Rural Appraisal (PRA) technique, which is particularly popular with development agencies.

The starting point of this methodology is also dissatisfaction with the top-down approach of state-led development. 'This approach is highly critical of Western experts, emphasizes the need for less top-down approaches to development and assumes the knowledge and analytical skills of the poor, no matter their education, can be brought to light and strengthened through participatory methods which will lead to true empowerment and development' (Parpart,

---

6   I am grateful to Catherine Hoskyns for bringing this point to my attention. The local in the industrialized West is a more diverse, anonymous and mobile space for women to work upon. Even on this more hospitable terrain, however, feminists have worried about the differential costs of participation in local politics along the lines of class and ethnicity (Phillips, 1993).

7   Such unproblematized views of civil society also abound (see Fine and Rai, 1997: Preface; Chandhoke, 2001).

8   Blair concludes his study of legislation to increase women's participation in local political institutions in six countries by noting that '[t]here is no indication that women acting consciously as a group have had much effect on local public affairs...' (2000: 24).

1999: 260). Experiential innovation rather than theoretical abstractions is emphasized in this approach. Inclusiveness of the least privileged is one of its pillars. In a gendered critique of this methodology, Parpart, however, points to the deeply embedded patriarchal norms that PRA practitioners carry with them, and emphasizes that '[p]ower structures exist at the local level as well' (p. 264; see also Kabeer, 1995; Tiessen, 1997). She further states that '[c]ontrol over knowledge is often an essential element of local power structures, thus not something local elites are willing to discuss' (p. 265). Thus, giving voice to the marginalized as part of the PRA programme might be both disempowering and threatening for different groups and individuals, especially for women. Gender-specific training is not generally part of the PRA programmes and formalized skill-share programmes are often not suited to women's work patterns (pp. 266–7). Finally, an understanding of structural economic power is largely absent from this methodology, as are the identity-based politics that so influence the choices that men and women make, as well the options that they feel are open to them (pp. 269–71). As such, '[p]articipation as project methodology [can become for states and international institutions] the most tractable of the NGO approaches to participation...' (P.J. Nelson, 1996: 624). PRA thus becomes a technique for the efficient policy implementation, part of the 'new managerialism', rather than a politically challenging process of local empowerment. It is widely used by national as well as multilateral institutions in the name of participative development (P.J. Nelson, 1996; McMichael, 2000).

I would argue that such a leaking out of politics from concepts serves only to maintain the status quo through instrumental confusion between ends and means. As we saw in chapter 5, NGO activity has proliferated in recent years. It has been seen as indicative of the lack of capacity of nation-states, on the one hand, and of the privatization of social welfare, on the other (Arrellano-Lopez and Petras, 1994; Craske, 1998). While the unaccountability of states is targeted, that of the NGO sector is largely ignored. Kabeer (1995) has suggested that even when NGOs promote gender sensitivity within their programmes, they often fail to have much impact on local institutional structures. The work of the NGOs, while extremely important under conditions of globalization, can also be seen as instrumental in the de-politicization of popular protest (Craske, 1998). The bridging of the global–local divide by international NGOs creates a new range of problems. As Goetz (1996) has argued, state-funded and -managed local organizations are sometimes more sensitive to local customs and social relations and therefore better able to move gender agendas forward, than are the international NGOs, who are seen as alien to the local milieu. The local thus presents as many challenges to women in negotiating their gender position as do the national and the global. Making use of each spatial and political level requires complex negotiations in furthering the advancement of women's position.

Spivak has suggested that 'the possibility of collectivity itself is persistently foreclosed through the manipulation of female agency' (1988: 283). In chapter 1 we saw this closure taking place through the ideology of nationalism, in chapters 4 and 5 through the normalization of globalized discourses of production and politics. Spivak notes also that despite the complicity of western intellectuals in participating in maintaining these closures,

> [b]elief in the plausibility of global alliance politics is prevalent among women of dominant social groups interested in 'international feminism' in the comprador countries. . . . [On] the other side of the international division of labor, the subject of exploitation cannot know and speak the text of female exploitation, even if the absurdity of the non-representing intellectual making space for her to speak is achieved. The woman is doubly in the shadow. (p. 288; see also Liddle and Rai, 1998)

So, can we regard the international conferences, the politics of national machineries, and the individual/collective struggles of the *sathins* in rural India, discussed in chapter 5, as spaces where the subaltern woman can be created but cannot speak? What Spivak is contesting is a 'solution' to the problem of activism whereby 'a monolithic collectivity of "women"' are included in the list of the oppressed 'whose unfractured subjectivity allows them to speak for themselves against an equally monolithic "same system"' (p. 278). Many feminist and women activists are seeking to address this tension through debating deliberative democracy as a means to achieving solidarity (chapter 5).

Critical Engagements: Deliberation and Solidarity

Yeatman argues that for a politics of solidarity to become possible there has to be a 'readiness on the part of any one emancipatory movement to show how its particular interest in contesting oppression links into and supports the interests of other movements in contesting different kinds of oppression' (1993: 231). Such a readiness to engage with other political movements needs, in turn, to build upon a recognition of differences. A recognition of difference has been made the basis of theoretical explorations on representing interests (Young, 1990; Phillips, 1995). There is some pragmatic merit in this approach. For example, it allows for strategies of affirmative action to be reconsidered as a means of increasing women's visibility in policy-making arenas (Rai and Sharma, 2000; Åseskog, 2002). However, this approach has also been criticized. The critics point to the problems arising from a focus on difference: of essentializing and freezing identities; of privileging certain group-based identities and not others; and of the impossibility of achieving accountability (Phillips, 1993; Shadmi, 2000).

Lister identifies three elements of a 'politics of solidarity in difference', which one might call the basis of a deliberative or dialogic democratic politics, as a way of moving forward from these debates. The first, she asserts following Mouffe (1992), is 'some kind of *"framework agreement"* of political values or *"grammar of political conduct"* in order to provide the foundations for citizen engagement' (1998: 77). Such an agreement does not mark any understanding of consensual politics; it reflects more a process rather than an outcome. In terms of development such a framework agreement could be the acknowledgement of women's exclusion, on the one hand, and the process of dialogue that might allow a possibility of representation of 'women's interests', however defined, on the other. A second element of this politics of solidarity that Lister identifies is *'a commitment to valuing difference'*, which she describes as 'a non-essentialist conceptualization of the political subject as made up of manifold, fluid, identities that mirror the multiple differentiation of groups' (p. 77). Such a valuing of difference allows women's movements to recognize differences among their own ranks, as well as to communicate with other emancipatory movements through multiple memberships as well as the creation of channels of dialogic communication. The third and final element of this politics of solidarity is dialogue, or a deliberative, communicative ethic. Extending Habermas's concept, feminists emphasize that 'such public dialogue becomes a space for the articulation of diverse voices, especially those not normally not heard' (Lister, 1998: 78; also Benhabib, 1992; chapter 5). Yuval-Davis (1997), following the work of Italian feminists, has called this communicative ethic the politics of 'rooting and shifting'. The idea is that 'each participant in the dialogue brings with her the rooting in her own membership and identity, but at the same time tries to shift in order to put herself in a situate of exchange with women who have different membership and identity' (Cockburn, 1998: 8–9). The result is a 'transversal politics', 'which give recognition to the specific position-ings of those who participate in them as well as to the "unfinished knowledge" that each such situated positioning can offer.... The boundaries of a transversal dialogue are determined by the message rather than the messenger' (Yuval-Davis, 1997: 130–1).

The imagining of such politics opens up exciting possibilities. It allows us to reflect upon a new form of *politics*, which has long been a preoccupation of feminists, without essentializing women them-selves (see Goetz, 1991; Benhabib, 1992; Tripp, 2000). It also allows us to underscore the importance of representative politics. Represen-tative politics requires a level of autonomy of representatives that might allow some 'shifting' to occur in debates on policy-making and in accountability to constituencies. This needs to be balanced, however, by the 'rooting' in communities that have elected women to represent them. It then becomes important within representative political systems to insist upon the expansion of the sphere of equal-ity between the sexes, and on grounds of other markers of identity, enhancing the presence of those excluded from formal politics through policy initiatives such as affirmative action, or quotas. Finally, meta-norms, such as human rights, can be used as strategies of change. Deliberation might allow a shift from rooted cultural ex-planations of exclusion; it might also allow the acknowledgement of the need for particular vocabularies as opposed to others to facilitate communication across borders. However, Lister rightly points out that such politics are not always possible; that 'there are some situ-ations in which conflicting interests are not reconcilable in this way and, by and large, political systems do not provide the time and space for such dialogue' (1998: 78).[9] Thus, it is important to recog-nize the boundedness of possibilities of deliberative democracy. First, it is probably more likely to succeed where conditions of gen-eralized scarcity are not present. Competition over resources, a ne-cessary part of democratic practice, can retain a deliberative element more readily where the resources over which competition takes

---

9   For a thoughtful delineation of the complexity and costs in making dialogue work across boundaries of conflict without significant support from the political system, see Cockburn (1998). She maps out the processes by which three sets of women in conflict zones have made networks of solidarity against all odds: the Women's Support Network in Belfast, Ireland; the Bat Shalom and the Jerusa-lem Link in Israel/Palestine; and the Medica Women's Association in Bosnia-Herzegovina – and concludes that the skills developed by these women can sustain cross-border contacts in different contexts. For an African perspective on women working across conflict/borders, see Tripp (2000).

place are relatively abundant. Insecurity hardens boundaries of interests, and reduces incentives for deliberation. Second, it is more likely to succeed where democratic practice has been consolidated than where violence is a feature of political life. Third, policy-making that addresses non-systemic issues rather than systemic change will have a greater chance of being deliberative.

The question of difference has thus been a central one for the women's movement, as have been attempts at bridging it (Fuss, 1989; Young, 1990; Mohanty, 1991; Phillips, 1993). The struggles for recognition within the women's movements have largely been those of cultural identity. However, as Lovell points out, '[c]ulture ... is a ravening concept. It swallows up and takes over the whole world of people, things, actions, practices.' She asks 'what the effect is, on social theory, of gathering ... everything that is subject to conceptu-alisation, ... into the single category of "culture"?' She concludes 'that the effect is not to dissolve the questions that were posed within Marxist and other materialisms, but to re-cast them' (2000: 23). This would not involve turning away from addressing differ-ences of identity to focusing on material deprivation based on class. It would, however, involve a more complex reformulation and stretching of boundaries of material and embodied marginalization. We have seen throughout this book that women as subjects have sought to forge alliances despite the power of these differences to dislocate and disrupt the attempts at bridge-building. Understand-ing the rooted nature of the shifting boundaries of difference has been important for feminist political practice.

Catherine Hoskyns and I have argued that '[f]or both strategic as well as practical reasons women have had to organize separately as women.... [However, the] feminist challenge is limited by a current lack of focus on the importance of redistributive policies that are rooted in the structural inequalities of capitalist production and ex-change' (1998: 362). In chapter 4 I posed the question: can gender recover class? Following Spivak, I would argue that a recognition of the importance of redistribution allows us '[b]oth in the economic area (capitalist) and in the political (world-historical agent) ... to con-struct models of a divided and dislocated subject whose parts are not continuous or coherent with each other' (Hoskyns and Rai, 1998: 276). And it is these dislocations and discontinuities that are the locus of agency for women seeking transformation within political economy as well as within the discursive circuits of power. This is particularly relevant now when SAPs and the retrenchment of wel-fare provision under globalization are creating tremendous pres-sures and inequalities across different social and spatial boundaries.

This increase in inequalities has also been accompanied by the decline of class-based movements, which have themselves suffered from a failure to recognize social exclusion based on issues other than class.

In conclusion I would urge that 'the next phase of women's struggles needs to take on board more centrally the issue of redistribution of resources if power relations in society are to be refashioned' (Hoskyns and Rai, 1998: 363). In this situation, alliances between women's and other social groups and solidarity among different emancipatory social movements, which expand the links between gender activism and other forms of transformative politics, become both more necessary and more possible.

Bibliography

Addison, Tony, 1998, *Underdevelopment, Transition and Reconstruction in Sub-Saharan Africa*, Helsinki: WIDER.

Adelman, Sammy, 1993, 'The International Labour Code and the Exploitation of Female Workers in Export-Processing Zones', in Sammy Adelman and Abdul Paliwala (eds), *Law and Crisis in the Third World*, London: Hans Zell Publishers.

Adelman, Sammy with Espiritu, Caesar, 1993, 'The Debt Crisis, Underdevelopment and Limits of the Law', in Sammy Adelman and Abdul Paliwala (eds), *Law and Crisis in the Third World*, London: Hans Zell Publishers.

Adelman, Sammy and Paliwala, Abdul (eds), 1993, *Law and Crisis in the Third World*, London: Hans Zell Publishers.

Afshar, Haleh and Dennis, Carolyne (eds), 1991, *Women and Adjustment Policies in the Third World*, London: Macmillan.

Agarwal, Bina, 1992, 'The Gender and Environment Debate: Lessons from India', *Feminist Studies*, vol. 18, no. 1 (Spring), pp. 119–58.

Agarwal, Bina, 1994, *A Field of My Own: Gender and Land Rights in South Asia*, Cambridge: Cambridge University Press.

Agarwal, Bina, 1995, 'Gender and Legal Rights in Agricultural Land in India', *Economic and Political Weekly*, 25 March.

Agarwal, Bina, 1997, 'Editorial: Re-sounding the Alert – Gender, Resources and Community Action', *World Development*, vol. 25, no. 9, pp. 1373–80.

Agnihotri, Indu and Mazumdar, Veena, 1995, 'Changing Terms of Political Discourse: Women's Movement in India, 1970–90', *Economic and Political Weekly*, 22 July.

Alavi, Hamza et al., 1982, *Capitalism and Colonial Production*, London: Croom Helm.

Albrow, Martin, 1996, *The Global Age*, Cambridge: Polity.

Ali, Shaheen Sardar, 2000, 'Law, Islam and the Women's Movement in Pakistan', in Shirin M. Rai (ed.), *International Perspectives on Gender and Democratization*, Basingstoke: Macmillan.

Allen, J., 1990, 'Does Feminism Need a Theory of the State?', in S. Watson (ed.), *Playing the State*, London: Verso.

All-India Democratic Women's Association, 1995, 'The UN "Platform for Action" Draft (May 1995): A Brief Critique from the All-India Democratic Women's Association', New Delhi.

Alvarez, Sonia, 1990, *Engendering Democracy in Brazil: Women's Movements in Transition Politics*, Princeton, NJ: Princeton University Press.

Amin, Samir, 1976, *Unequal Development: An Essay on the Social Formations of Peripheral Capitalism*, Hassocks: Harvester Press.

Amin, Samir, 1994, *Re-reading the Postwar Period: An Intellectual Itinerary*, New York: Monthly Review Press.

Amin, Samir, 1997, *Capitalism in the Age of Globalization: The Management of Contemporary Society*, London: Zed Books.

Amin, Samir, 1998, *Spectres of Capitalism: A Critique of Current Intellectual Fashion*, New York: Monthly Review Press.

Anand, Sudhir and Sen, Amartya, 1996, *Sustainable Human Development: Concepts and Priorities*, New York: United Nations Development Programme.

Anand, Sudhir and Sen, Amartya, 2000, 'Human Development and Economic Sustainability', *World Development*, vol. 28, no. 12, pp. 2029–49.

Anderson, Benedict, 1991, *Imagined Communities: Reflections on the Origin and Spread of Nationalism* (revised and extended), London: Verso.

Andriof, Jörg and MacIntosh, Malcolm (eds), 2001, *Perspectives on Corporate Citizenship*, Sheffield: Greenleaf.

Anthias, Floya and Yuval-Davis, Nira, 1989, *Woman–Nation–State*, London: Routledge.

Appadurai, Arjun, 1990, 'Disjuncture and Difference in the Global Cultural Economy', *Theory, Culture & Society*, vol. 7, pp. 295–310.

Arrellano-Lopez, Sonia and Petras, James F., 1994, 'NGOs and Poverty Alleviation in Bolivia', *Development and Change*, vol. 25, pp. 555–68.

Åseskog, Birgitta, 2002, 'National Machinery for Gender Equality in Sweden and Other Nordic Countries', in Shirin M. Rai (ed.), *National Machineries for Women: Mainstreaming Gender, Democratising the State?*, Manchester: University of Manchester Press.

Baden, Sally and Goetz, Anne-Marie, 1997, 'Who Needs [Sex] When You Can Have [Gender]? Conflicting Discourses of Gender at Beijing', *Feminist Review*, no. 56, Summer, pp. 3–25.

Bakker, Isabella, 1994a, 'Introduction: Engendering Macro-economic Policy Reform in the Era of Global Restructuring and Adjustment', in I. Bakker (ed.), *The Strategic Silence: Gender and Economic Policy*, London: Zed Books.

Bakker, Isabella (ed.), 1994b, *The Strategic Silence: Gender and Economic Policy*, London: Zed Books.

Bald, Suresht R., 1995, 'Coping with Marginality: South Asian Women Migrants in Britain', in Marianne Marchand and Jane L. Parpart (eds), *Feminism/Postmodernism/Development*, London: Routledge.

Barber, Benjamin, 1996, *Jihad vs. McWorld*, New York: Ballantine Books.

Bardhan, Pranas, 1983, 'Economic Growth, Poverty and Rural Labour Markets in India: A Survey of Research', Working Paper 54, Rural Employment Policy Research Programme, ILO.

Barlow, Tani (ed.), 1993, *Positions: East Asia Cultures Critique Volume 1: Part 2, Making Histories*, Durham, NC: Duke University Press.

Barrett, Jane, Dawber, Aneene, Klugman, Barbara, Obery, Ingrid, Shindler, Jennifer and Yawitch, Joanne, 1985, *South African Women on the Move*, London: Zed Books.

Barrett, Michele and Phillips, Anne (eds), 1992, *Destabilizing Theory*, Cambridge: Polity.

Barrientos, Stephanie, 2002, ' "Flexible" Female Employment and Ethical Trade in the Global Economy', in Peter Newell, Shirin M. Rai and Andrew Scott (eds), *Development and the Challenge of Globalisation*, London: IT Publishers.

Barrientos, Stephanie, McClenaghan, Sharon and Orton, Liz, 2000, 'Ethical Trade and South African Deciduous Fruit Exports: Addressing Gender Sensitivity', *European Journal of Development Research*, vol. 12, no. 1, pp. 140–58.

Bar-Tal, Daniel and Staub, Ervin (eds), 1997, *Patriotism in the Lives of Individuals and Nations*, Chicago: Nelson-Hall.

Barwa, Sharmishta and Rai, Shirin M., 2002, 'Gender Matters: Intellectual Property Rights Under Globalisation', in Peter Newell, Shirin M. Rai and Andrew Scott (eds), *Development and the Challenge of Globalisation*, London: IT Publishers.

Basu, Amrita with McGrory, C. Elizabeth (ed.), 1995, *The Challenge of Local Feminisms: Women's Movements in Global Perspective*, Boulder, CO: Westview.

Batliwala, Srilatha, 1993, 'The Meaning of Women's Empowerment: New Concepts from Action', in Gita Sen, A. Germain and L.C. Chen (eds), *Population Policies Reconsidered: Health, Empowerment and Rights*, Boston: Harvard University Press.

Baxi, Upendra, 1996, ' "Global Neighborhood" and the "Universal Otherhood": Notes on the Report of the Commission on Global Governance', *Alternatives*, no. 21, pp. 525–49.

Baxi, Upendra, 1997, 'Judicial Activism: Usurpation or Re-democratisation?', *Social Action*, vol. 47, October–December.

Baxi, Upendra, 2000, 'Human Rights: Suffering between Movements and Markets', in Robin Cohen and Shirin M. Rai (eds), *Global Social Movements*, London: Athlone Press.

Bayart, Jean-François, 1993, *The State in Africa: The Politics of the Belly*, London: Longman.

Beasley, Chris and Bacchi, Carol, 2000, 'Citizen Bodies: Embodying Citizens – a Feminist Analysis', *The International Feminist Journal of Politics*, vol. 2, no. 3, pp. 337–58.

Beck, Ulrich, 1992, *Risk Society: Towards a New Modernity*, London: Sage Publications.

Beck, Ulrich, 1997, *The Reinvention of Politics: Rethinking Modernity in the Global Social Order*, Cambridge: Polity.

Becker, Gary, 1981, *A Treatise on the Family*, Cambridge, MA: Harvard University Press.

Ben-Amos, Avner, 1997, 'The Uses of the Past: Patriotism Between History and Memory', in Daniel Bar-Tal and Ervin Staub (eds), *Patriotism in the Lives of Individuals and Nations*, Chicago: Nelson-Hall.

Beneria, Lourdes (ed.), 1985, *Women and Development: The Sexual Division of Labor in Rural Societies*, New York: Praeger.

Beneria, Lourdes, 1995, 'Toward a Greater Integration of Gender in Economics', *World Development*, vol. 23, no. 11, pp. 1839–50.

Beneria, Lourdes, 1999, 'The Enduring Debate over Unpaid Labour', *International Labour Review*, vol. 138, no. 3, pp. 287–309.

Beneria, Lourdes and Feldman, Shelley, 1992, *Unequal Burden: Economic Crises, Persistent Poverty, and Women's Work*, Boulder, CO: Westview.

Beneria, Lourdes and Sen, Gita, 1997, 'Accumulation, Reproduction and Women's Role in Economic Development: Boserup Revisited', in Nalini Visvanathan, Lynn Duggan, Laurie Nisonoff and Nan Wiegersma (eds), *The Women, Gender and Development Reader*, London: Zed Books.

Benhabib, Seyla, 1992, *Situating the Self: Gender, Community and Postmodernism in Contemporary Ethics*, Cambridge: Polity.

Benhabib, Seyla, 1999, 'Sexual Difference and Collective Identities: The New Global Constellation', *Signs: Journal of Women in Culture and Society*, vol. 24, no. 2, pp. 335–62.

Bereswill, Mechthild and Wagner, Leonie, 1998, 'Nationalism and the Women's Question: The Women's Movement and Nation', *The European Journal of Women's Studies*, vol. 5, pp. 233–47.

Berger, Peter L., 1976, *Pyramids of Sacrifice: Political Ethics and Social Change*, London: Allen Lane.

Bergere, M.C. and Chesneaux, J. (eds), 1977, *China from the Opium Wars to the 1911 Revolution*, Hassocks: Harvester Press.

Berry, W., 1991, 'Out of Your Car, Off Your Horse', *Atlantic Monthly*, February.

Bhaduri, Amit, 1986, 'Forced Commerce and Agrarian Growth', *World Development*, vol. 14, no. 2, pp. 267–72.

Bianco, Lucien, 1971, *Origins of the Chinese Revolution 1915–1949*, Stanford: Stanford University Press.

Blacklock, Cathy and MacDonald, Laura, 2000, 'Women and Citizenship in Mexico and Guatemala', in Shirin M. Rai (ed.), *International Perspectives on Gender and Democratisation*, Basingstoke: Macmillan.

Blair, Harry, 2000, 'Participation and Accountability at the Periphery: Democratic Local Governance in Six Countries', *World Development*, vol. 28, no. 1, pp. 21–39.

Block, Fred, 1990, *Postindustrial Possibilities: A Critique of Economic Discourse*, Berkeley, University of California Press.

Blom, Ida, Hagemann, Karen and Hall, Catherine (eds), 2000, *Gendered Nations: Nationalisms and Gender Order in the Nineteenth Century*, Oxford: Berg.

Blumberg, Rae Lesser, Rokowski, Cathy A., Tinker, Irene and Monteón, Michael (eds), 1995, *Engendering Wealth and Well-Being: Empowerment for Global Change*, Boulder, CO: Westview.

Boggs, Carl, 1995, 'Rethinking the Sixties Legacy: From New Left to New Social Movements', in Stanford M. Lyman (ed.), *Social Movements: Critiques, Concepts, Case-Studies*, Basingstoke: Macmillan.

Bohman, James and Rehg, William (eds), 1997, *Deliberative Democracy: Essays on Reason and Politics*, Cambridge, MA: MIT Press.

Boserup, Ester, 1989, *Woman's Role in Economic Development* (new edn), London: Earthscan.

Bouatta, Cherifa and Cherifati-Merabtine, Doria, 1994, 'The Social Representation of Women in Algeria's Islamist Movement', in Valentine M. Moghadam (ed.), *Identity Politics and Women: Cultural Reassertions and Feminisms in International Perspective*, Boulder, CO: Westview.

Braidotti, Rosi, Charkiewicz, Ewa, Hausler, Sabine and Wieringa, Saskia, 1994, *Women, the Environment and Sustainable Development: Towards a Theoretical Synthesis*, London: Zed Books in association with INSTRAW.

Braudel, Fernand, 1985, *Wheels of Commerce: Civilization and Capitalism, 15th–18th Century*, Vol. 2 (new edn), London: Fontana.

Brenner, Johanna, 1993, 'The Best of Times, the Worst of Times: US Feminism Today', *New Left Review*, no. 200, July/August, pp. 101–60.

Brenner, Robert, 1977, 'On Sweezy, Frank and Wallerstein', *New Left Review*, no. 104, July–August.

Brett, April, 1991, 'Introduction: Why Gender is a Development Issue', in Tina Wallace with Candida March (eds), *Changing Perceptions: Writings on Gender and Development*, Oxford: Oxfam.

Brodie, Janine, 1994, 'Shifting the Boundaries: Gender and the Politics of Restructuring', in Isabella Bakker (ed.), *The Strategic Silence: Gender and Economic Policy*, London: Zed Books.

Bromley, Simon, 1999, 'The Space of Flows and Timeless Time: Manuel Castells's *The Information Age*', *Radical Philosophy*, no. 97, September–October, pp. 6–17.

Brown, Wendy, 1992, 'Finding the Man in the State', *Feminist Studies*, vol. 18, no. 1, pp. 7–34.

Brundtland, Gro Harlem, 2000, 'Health and Population', Reith Lectures 2000, BBC <http://news.bbc.co.uk/hi/english/static/events/reith_2000/lecture4.stm>.

Burnell, Peter, 1997, *Foreign Aid in a Changing World*, Buckingham: Open University Press.

Burnham, Peter, 1999, 'The Politics of Economic Management in the 1990s', *New Political Economy*, vol. 4, no. 1, pp. 37–54.

Butalia, Urvashi, 1998, *The Other Side of Silence: Voices from the Partition of India*, New Delhi: Penguin Books India.

Butler, Judith and Scott, Joan W. (eds), 1992, *Feminists Theorize the Political*, London: Routledge.

Bystydzienski, Jill M., 1992, 'Introduction', in Jill M. Bystydzienski (ed.), *Women Transforming Politics: Worldwide Strategies for Empowerment*, Bloomington: Indiana University Press.

Bystydzienski, Jill M. and Sekhon, Joti (eds), 1999, *Democratization and Women's Grassroots Movements*, Bloomington: Indiana University Press.

Cable, Vincent, 1995, 'The Diminished Nation-State: A Study in the Loss of Economic Power', *Daedalus: Journal of the American Academy of Arts and Sciences*, Spring, pp. 23–54.

Çagatay, Nilufer, Elson, Diane and Grown, Caren, 1995, 'Introduction', *World Development*, vol. 23, no. 11, pp. 1827–36.

Cairncross, A.K., 1975, *Home and Foreign Investment*, New York: Harvester.

Campbell, B., 1989, 'Indebtedness in Africa: Consequence, Cause or Symptom of the Crisis?', in B. Onimode (ed.), *The IMF, the World Bank and the African Debt, Volume 2*, London: Zed Books.

Carr, Marilyn, 2002, 'Challenging Globalisation: The Response of Women Workers and Entrepreneurs to Trade and Investment Policies', in Peter Newell, Shirin M. Rai and Andrew Scott (eds), *Development and the Challenge of Globalisation*, London: IT Publishers.

Castells, Manuel, 1996, *The Information Age, Vol. 1: The Rise of the Network Society*, Cambridge, MA: Blackwell.

Cerny, Philip, 1990, *The Changing Architecture of Politics: Structure, Agency, and the Future of the State*, London: Sage.

Cerrutti, Marcela, 2000, 'Economic Reform, Structural Adjustment and Female Labour Force Participation in Buenos Aires, Argentina', *World Development*, vol. 28, no. 5, pp. 879–91.

Chakravarty, Uma, 1999, 'Rhetoric and Substance of Empowerment, Women, Development and the State' unpublished manuscript.

Chandhoke, Neera, 2001, 'The Civil and the Political in Civil Society', *Democratization*, vol. 8, no. 2, Summer, pp. 1–24.

Chang, Kimberly A. and Ling, L.H.M., 2000, 'Globalization and Its Intimate Other: Filipina Domestic Workers in Hong Kong', in Marianne Marchand and Anne Sissons Runyan (eds), *Gender and Global Restructuring*, London: Routledge.

Charlesworth, Hilary and Chinkin, Christine, 2000, *The Boundaries of International Law: A Feminist Analysis*, Manchester: Manchester University Press.

Charlesworth, Hilary, Chinkin, Christine and Wright, Shelly, 1991, 'Feminist Approaches to International Law', *American Journal of International Law*, vol. 85, October, pp. 613–45.

Charlton, Roger and Donald, David, 1992, 'Bringing the Economy Back In: Reconsidering the Autonomy of the Developmental State', paper presented at the Annual Conference of the Political Science Association (UK), Belfast, 7–9 April.

Chatterjee, Partha, 1993a, *The Nation and Its Fragments: Colonial and Postcolonial Histories*, New Delhi: Oxford University Press.

Chatterjee, Partha, 1993b, 'The Nationalist Resolution of the Women's Question', in Kumkum Sangari and Sudesh Vaid (eds), *Recasting Women: Essays in Colonial History*, New Delhi: Kali: for Women.

Chaudhuri, Maitrayee, 1996, 'Citizens, Workers and Emblems of Culture: An Analysis of the First Plan Document on Women', in Patricia Uberoi (ed.), *Social Reform, Sexuality and the State*, New Delhi: Sage.

Chazan, Naomi, 1990, 'Gender Perspectives on African States', in Jane L. Parpart and Kathleen Staudt (eds), *Women and the State in Africa* (2nd edn), Boulder, CO: Lynne Rienner.

Chinkin, Christine, 2000, 'Human Rights', in Hilary Charlesworth and Christine Chinkin (eds), *The Boundaries of International Law: A Feminist Analysis*, Manchester: Manchester University Press.

Chiriboga, Manuel, forthcoming, 'The International Finance Institutions and the Latin American NGOs: The Quest for a Regional Agenda', in Jan Aart Scholte and Albrecht Schnabel (eds), *Civil Society and Global Finance*, Tokyo: United Nations University Press.

Chossudovsky, Michel, 1998, *The Globalisation of Poverty: Impacts of IMF and World Bank Reforms*, London, Zed Books.

Chowdhry, Geeta, 1995, 'Engendering Development? Women in Development (WID) in International Development Regimes', in Marianne Marchand and Jane L. Parpart (eds), *Feminism/Postmodernism/Development*, London: Routledge.

Christiansen, Flemming and Rai, Shirin M., 1996, *Chinese Politics and Society: An Introduction*, Hemel Hempstead: Harvester Wheatsheaf.

CIDA (Canadian International Development Agency), 1999, *Gender Equality and Development*, Ottawa: CIDA.

Clark, John, forthcoming, 'Civil Society and Global Finance: Evolving Experience of the World Bank', in Jan Aart Scholte and Albrecht Schnabel (eds), *Civil Society and Global Finance*, Tokyo: United Nations University Press.

Cockburn, Cynthia, 1998, *The Space Between Us: Negotiating Gender and National Identities in Conflict*, London: Zed Books.

Cockburn, Cynthia, 2000, 'The Women's Movement: Boundary-Crossing on Terrains of Conflict', in Robin Cohen and Shirin M. Rai (eds), *Global Social Movements*, London: Athlone Press.

Cohen, Nick, 1999, 'U-Turns in the U-Bend', *The Observer*, 6 June.

Cohen, Robin and Rai, Shirin M. (eds), 2000a, *Global Social Movements*, London: Athlone Press.

Cohen, Robin and Rai, Shirin M., 2000b, 'Global Social Movements: Towards a Cosmopolitan Politics', in Robin Cohen and Shirin M. Rai (eds), *Global Social Movements*, London: Athlone Press.

Cohen, Sue, 2000, 'Social Solidarity in the Delors Period: Barriers to Participation', in Catherine Hoskyns and Michael Newman (eds), *Democratizing the European Union: Issues for the Twenty-first Century*, Manchester: Manchester University Press.

Commission on Global Governance, 1995, *Our Global Neighbourhood*, New York: Oxford University Press.

Connelly, Patricia M., Li, Tania Murray, MacDonald, Martha and Parpart, Jane L., 2000, 'Feminism and Development: Theoretical Perspectives', in Jane L. Parpart, Patricia M. Connelly and V. Eudine Barriteau (eds), *Theoretical Perspectives on Gender and Development*, Ottawa: IDRC.

Coole, Diana, 1997, 'Is Class a Difference That Makes a Difference?', *Radical Philosophy*, no. 77, May–June, pp. 17–25.

Corporate Watch, 1999, 'Facts from the Corporate Planet: Ecology and Politics in the Age of Globalization' <http://www.corpwatch.org/trac/feature/planet/fact_1.html>.

Cowen, M.P. and Shenton, R.W., 1995, *Doctrines of Development*, London: Routledge.

Cox, Robert with Sinclair, Timothy, 1996, *Approaches to World Order*, Cambridge: Cambridge University Press.

Crafts, Nicholas, 2000, 'Globalization and Growth in the Twentieth Century', IMF Working Paper, JEL Classification Numbers: N10, F43, O10.

Craske, Nick, 1998, 'Remasculinization and the Neoliberal State in Latin America', in Vicky Randall and Georgina Waylen (eds), *Gender, Politics and the State*, London: Routledge.

Crenshaw, Kimberley, 1993, 'Whose Story Is It, Anyway? Feminist and Antiracist Appropriations of Anita Hill', in Toni Morrison (ed.), *Race-ing Justice, En-gendering Power: Essays on Anita Hill, Clarence Thomas and the Construction of Social Reality*, London: Chatto and Windus.

CRIAW/ICREF (Canadian Research Institute for the Advancement of Women/Institut Canadien de Recherche sur les Femmes), 2000, 'Why are More Women Poor?' <http://www.criaw-icref.ca/Poverty_fact_sheet.htm>18/07/00.

Crocker, David, 1995, 'Functioning and Capability: The Foundations of Sen's and Nussbaum's Development Ethic', in Martha Nussbaum and Jonathan Glover (eds), *Women, Culture and Development*, Oxford: Clarendon Press.

Croll, Elizabeth, 1978, *Feminism and Socialism in China*, London: Routledge and Kegan Paul.

Crosby, Christina, 1992, 'Dealing with Differences', in Judith Butler and Joan W. Scott (eds), *Feminists Theorize the Political*, London: Routledge.

Crush, Jonathan (ed.), 1995, *The Power of Development*, London: Routledge.

Dahbour, Omar and Ishay, Micheline R. (eds), 1995, *The Nationalism Reader*, Atlantic Highlands, NJ: The Humanities Press International, Inc.

Davies, Miranda (compiled by), 1983, *Third World, Second Sex, Vols 1 and 2*, London: Zed Books.

Davin, Delia, 1992, 'Population Policy and Reform: The Soviet Union, Eastern Europe and China', in Shirin M. Rai, Hilary Pilkington and Annie Phizacklea (eds), *Women in the Face of Change: Eastern Europe, the Soviet Union and China*, London: Routledge.

DAW (Division for the Advancement of Women, UN), 1998, 'National Machineries for Gender Equality – A Global Perspective', background paper prepared by Division for the Advancement of Women for the Experts Group Meeting, 31 August–4 September.

DAW (Division for the Advancement of Women, UN), 1999, *World Survey on the Role of Women in Development*, New York: UN.

DAW (Division for the Advancement of Women, UN), 2000a, 'Commission on the Status of Women: Agreed Conclusions on the Critical Areas of Concern of the Beijing Platform for Action', New York: UN.

DAW (Division for the Advancement of Women, UN), 2000b, 'Women in Politics 2000: Situation in March 2000 as per official data', UN Map no. 4136.

DAWN (Development Alternatives with Women for a New Era), 1995, *Securing Our Gains and Moving Forward to the 21st Century*, paper produced for the UN Conference on Women, Beijing.

del Rosario, Virginia O., 1994, *Lifting the Smoke Screen: Dynamics of Mail-Order Bride Migration from the Philippines*, The Hague: Institute of Social Studies.

Dennis, Caroline, 1991, 'Constructing a "Career" under Conditions of Economic Crisis and Structural Adjustment: The Survival Strategies of Nigerian Women', in H. Afshar (ed.), *Women, Development and Survival in the Third World*, London: Longman.

Denny, Charlotte, 2000, 'Third World Debt May Soon Lose the Spotlight', *Guardian*, 4 October.

d'Entreves, Maurizio Passerin (ed.), 2002, *Democracy as Public Deliberation: New Perspectives*, Manchester: Manchester University Press.

Desai, A.R., 1989, *The Social Background of Indian Nationalism*, Bombay: Popular Prakashan.

Devetak, Richard and Higgott, Richard, 1999, 'Justice Unbound? Globalisation, States and the Transformation of the Social Bond', University of Warwick, CRGR Working Paper, 29/99.

DFID (Department for International Development), 1998, *World Poverty: A Challenge for the 21st Century*, White Paper on International Development <http://www.globalisation.gov.uk/>.

DFID (Department for International Development), 2000, *Eliminating World Poverty: Making Globalisation Work for the Poor*, <http://www.globalisation.gov.uk/>.

Diamond, Irene and Orenstein, Gloria (eds), 1990, *Reweaving the World: The Emergence of Ecofeminism*, San Francisco: Sierra Club.

Dietz, Mary, 1992, 'Context is All: Feminism and Theories of Citizenship', in Chantal Mouffe (ed.), *Dimensions of Radical Democracy*, London: Verso.

Drèze, Jean and Sen, Amartya, 1989, *Hunger and Public Action*, London: Clarendon Paperbacks.

Drèze, Jean and Sen, Amartya, 1990a, *The Political Economy of Hunger, Volume 1: Entitlement and Well-Being*, Oxford: Clarendon.

Drèze, Jean and Sen, Amartya (eds), 1990b, *The Political Economy of Hunger, Volume 2: Famine Prevention*, Oxford: Clarendon.

Dube, Shyama Charan, 1988, *Modernization and Development: The Search for Alternative Paradigms*, London: United Nations University; Zed Books.

Dworkin, Andrea, 2000a, *The Jews, Israel and Women's Liberation*, London: Virago.

Dworkin, Andrea, 2000b, 'What I Believe', *The Guardian Weekly*, 13 May.

Earle, Rebecca, 2001, 'Creole Patriotism and the Myth of the Loyal Indian', *Past and Present*, in press.

ECLAC (Economic Commission for Latin America and the Caribbean), 1998, 'The Institutionality of Gender Equity in the State: A Diagnosis for Latin America and the Caribbean', LC/R 1837.

Economic and Social Council, UN, 2000, *Review and Appraisal of the Implementation of the Beijing Platform for Action, Report of the Secretary General*, 19 January, New York: UN

Economist 1997, 'In Praise of the Davos Man', 2 January, p. 18.

Ehrenreich, Barbara and Piven, Frances Fox, 1983, 'Women and the Welfare State', in Irving Howe (ed.), *Alternatives: Proposals for America from the Democratic Left*, New York: Pantheon.

Einhorn, Barbara, 1992, *Cinderella Goes to the Market*, London: Verso.

Einhorn, Barbara, 2000, 'Gender and Citizenship in the Context of Democratisation and Economic Reform in East Central Europe' in Shirin M. Rai (ed.), *International Perspectives on Gender and Democratisation*, Basingstoke: Macmillan.

Eisenstein, Zillah (ed.), 1979, *Capitalist Patriarchy and the Case for Socialist Feminism*, New York: Monthly Review Press.

Eisenstein, Zillah, 1998, *Global Obscenities: Women of the World Unite*, New York: New York University Press.

Elson, Diane, 1989, 'How is Structural Adjustment Affecting Women?', *Development*, vol. 1, pp. 67–74.

Elson, Diane, 1994, 'Micro, Meso, Macro: Gender and Economic Analysis in the Context of Policy Reform', in Isabella Bakker (ed.), *The Strategic Silence: Gender and Economic Policy*, London: Zed Books.

Elson, Diane, 1995, 'Male Bias in Macro Economics: The Case of Structural Adjustment', in Diane Elson (ed.), *Male Bias in the Development Process*, Manchester: Manchester University Press.

Elson, Diane, 1998, 'Talking to the Boys: Gender and Economic Growth Models', in Cecile Jackson and Ruth Pearson (eds), *Feminist Visions of Development*, London: Routledge.

Elson, Diane, 1999, 'Labor Markets as Gendered Institutions: Equality, Efficiency and Empowerment Issues', *World Development*, vol. 23, no. 3, pp. 611–27.

Elson, Diane and Pearson, Ruth, 1997, 'The Subordination of Women and the Internationalization of Factory Production', in Nalini Visvanathan, Lynn Duggan, Laurie Nisonoff and Nan Wiegersma (eds), *The Women, Gender and Development Reader*, London: Zed Books.

Elster, Jon, 1997, 'The Market and the Forum: Three Varieties of Political Theory', in James Bohman and William Rehg (eds), *Deliberative Democracy: Essays on Reason and Politics*, Cambridge, MA: MIT Press.

Elster, Jon (ed.), 1998, *Deliberative Democracy*, Cambridge: Cambridge University Press.

Engels, Dagmar, 1989, 'The Limits of Gender Ideology: Bengali Women, the Colonial State, and the Private Sphere 1890–1930', *Women's Studies International Forum*, vol. 12, no. 4.

Enloe, Cynthia, 1989, *Bananas, Beaches and Bases: Making Feminist Sense of International Politics*, London: Pandora Press.

Escobar, Arturo, 1995a, *Encountering Development: The Making and Unmaking of the Third World*, Princeton, NJ: Princeton University Press.

Escobar, Arturo, 1995b, 'Imagining a Post-Development Era', in Jonathan Crush (ed.), *Power of Development*, London: Routledge.

Esteva, G., and Prakash, M.S., 1997, 'From Global Thinking to Local Thinking', in M. Rahnema with V. Bawtree (eds), *The Post-Development Reader*, London: Zed Books; Dhaka: University Press Ltd; Halifax, NS: Fernwood Publishing; and Cape Town: David Philip.

Evans, Alison, 1993, 'Contracted-out: Some Reflection on Gender, Power and Agrarian Institutions', *IDS Bulletin*, vol. 24, no. 3, July, pp. 21–30.

Evans, Harriet, 1997, *Women and Sexuality in China*, Cambridge: Polity.

Evans, Tony (ed.), 1998, *Human Rights Fifty Years On: A Reappraisal*, Manchester: Manchester University Press.

Evers, Barbara and Bernard Walters, 2000, 'Extra-Household Factors and Women Farmers' Supply Response in Sub-Saharan Africa', *World Development*, vol. 28, no. 7, pp. 1341–5.

Fanon, Frantz, 1990, *The Wretched of the Earth*, London: Penguin.

Ferber, Marianne A. and Nelson, Julie A. (eds), 1993, *Beyond Economic Man: Feminist Theory and Economics*, Chicago: University of Chicago Press.

Fernandez-Kelly, Maria Patricia, 1997, 'Maquiladoras: The View from the Inside', in Nalini Visvanathan, Lynn Duggan, Laurie Nisonoff and Nan Wiegersma (eds), *The Women, Gender and Development Reader*, London: Zed Books.

Figueroa, Adologo, 1996, 'The Distributive Issue in Latin America', *International Social Science Journal*, no. 148, June, pp. 231–44.

Fine, Robert and Shirin M. Rai, 1997, *Civil Society: Democratic Perspectives*, London: Frank Cass.

Folbre, Nancy, Bergmann, Barbara, Agarwal, Bina and Floro, Maria, 1992, *Issues in Contemporary Economy, Vol. 4: Women's Work in the World Economy*, Proceedings of the Ninth World Congress of the International Economics Association, Basingstoke: Macmillan in association with International Economics Association.

Frank, André Gunder, 1969, *Capitalism and Underdevelopment in Latin America: Historical Studies of Chile and Brazil*, New York: Monthly Review Press.

Fraser, Nancy, 1989, *Unruly Practices: Power, Discourse and Gender in Contemporary Social Theory*, Minneapolis: University of Minnesota Press; Cambridge: Polity.

Fraser, Nancy, 1997, 'From Redistribution to Recognition? Dilemmas of Justice in a "Poststructuralist" Age', *New Left Review*, no. 212, July–August.

Friedman, John, 1996, 'Rethinking Poverty: Empowerment and Citizen Rights', *International Social Science Journal*, no. 148, June, pp. 161–72.

Fukayama, Francis, 1991, *The End of History and the Last Man*, New York: Free Press.

Fuss, Diana, 1989, *Essentially Speaking: Feminism, Nature and Difference*, London: Routledge.

Gardiner-Barber, Pauline, 2002, 'Agency in Philippine Women's Migration and Provisional Diaspora', in Jane L. Parpart, Shirin M. Rai and Kathleen Staudt (eds), *Rethinking Empowerment in a Global/Local World*, London: Routledge.

Gedalof, Irene, 1999, *Against Purity*, London: Routledge.

Geiger, Susan, 1997, *TANU Women: Gender and Culture in the Making of Tanganyikan Nationalism, 1955–1965*, Oxford: James Currey.

Gellner, Ernest, 1983, *Nations and Nationalism: New Perspectives on the Past*, Oxford: Blackwell.

Gellner, Ernest, 1997, 'A Reply to My Critics', *New Left Review*, no. 221, Jan./Feb., pp. 81–118.

Giddens, Anthony, 1987, *Nation-State and Violence*, Cambridge: Polity.

Giddens, Anthony, 1990, *Consequences of Modernity*, Cambridge: Polity.

Giddens, Anthony, 1991, *Modernity and Self-identity: Self and Society in the Late Modern Age*, Cambridge: Polity.

Giddens, Anthony, 1999, *Runaway World: How Globalization is Reshaping Our Lives*, London: Profile.

Gilmartin, C.L. Rofel and Tyrene White, 1994, *Engendering China: Women, Culture and the State*, Cambridge, MA: Harvard University Press.

Goetz, Anne-Marie, 1991, 'Feminism and the Claim to Know: Contradictions in Feminist Approaches to Women in Development', in Rebecca Grant and Kathleen Newland (eds), *Gender and International Relations*, Bloomington: Indiana University Press.

Goetz, Anne-Marie, 1996, 'Dis/Organising Gender: Women Development Agents in State and NGO Poverty-Reduction Programmes in Bangladesh', in Shirin M. Rai and Geraldine Lievesley (eds), *Women and the State: International Perspectives*, London: Taylor and Francis.

Goetz, Anne-Marie (ed.), 1997, *Getting Institutions Right for Women*, London: Zed Books.

Goetz, Anne-Marie, 1998, 'Mainstreaming Gender Equity to National Development Planning', in Carol Miller and Shahra Razavi (eds), *Missionaries and Mandarins: Feminist Engagement with Development Institutions*, London: IT Publishers.

Goetz, Anne-Marie, 2002, 'National Women's Machinery: State-based Institutions to Advocate for Gender Equality', in Shirin M. Rai (ed.), *National Machineries for the Advancement of Women: Mainstreaming Gender, Democratising the State?*, Manchester: Manchester University Press.

Goetz, Anne-Marie and Gupta, Rina Sen, 1996, 'Who Takes the Credit? Gender, Power and Control over Loan Use in Rural Credit Programmes in Bangladesh', *World Development*, vol. 24, no. 1, January, pp. 45–64.

Gordon, Linda (ed.), 1990, *Woman's Body, Woman's Right: Birth Control in America*, New York: Penguin.

Grant, James P., 1977, 'Foreword' to International Labour Organization (ILO), *Employment, Growth and Basic Needs: A One-World Problem*, London: Praeger.

Grant, Rebecca and Newland, Kathleen (eds), 1991, *Gender and International Relations*, Bloomington: Indiana University Press.

Gray, John, 1995, *Enlightenment's Wake*, London: Routledge.

Gray, John, 1999, *False Dawn: The Delusions of Global Capitalism*, London: Granta Books.

Greer, Jed and Singh, Kavaljit, 2001, 'A Brief History of TNC's' <http://www.igc.org/trac/globalization/corp/history.html>.

Grieder, Jerome B., 1981, *Intellectuals and the State in Modern China: A Narrative History*, New York: Free Press.

Griesgraber, Jo Marie and Gunter, Bernhard G. (eds), 1995, *Promoting Development: Effective Global Institutions for the Twenty-First Century*, London: Pluto Press with Centre of Concern.

Griesgaber, Jo Marie and Gunter, Bernhard G. (eds), 1996, *Development: New Paradigms and Principles for the Twenty-First Century*, London: Pluto Press.

Griffin, Keith and McKinley, Terry, 1994, *Implementing a Human Development Strategy*, Basingstoke: Macmillan.

Group of Lisbon, 1995, *Limits to Competition*, Cambridge, MA: MIT Press.

Grown, Caren, Elson, Diane and Çagatay, Nilufer, 2000, 'Introduction', *World Development*, vol. 28, no. 7, pp. 1145–56.

Grusky, Sara, 2000, 'The World Bank and IMF Initiate a New Reform Package', *Participation*, <http://www.worldbank.org/participation/bread.htm>.

Guha, Ranajit (ed.), 1982, *Subaltern Studies: Writings on South Asian History and Society, Vol. 1*, Delhi and Oxford: Oxford University Press.

Guha, Ranajit (ed.), 1997, *A Subaltern Studies Reader 1986–1995*, Minneapolis and London: University of Minnesota Press.

Gunew, Sneja and Yeatman, Anna (eds), 1993, *Feminism and the Politics of Difference*, St Leonards, NSW: Allen and Unwin.

Haddad, L., Brown, L., Richter, A. and Smith, L., 1995, 'The Gender Dimensions of Economic Adjustment Policies: Potential Interactions and Evidence to Date', *World Development*, vol. 23, no. 6, pp. 881–96.

Hall, Catherine, 1992, *White, Male and Middle-Class: Explorations in Feminism and History*, Cambridge: Polity.

Halliday, Fred, 1999, 'The Pertinence of Imperialism', conference paper, Workshop on Historical Materialism and Globalisation, University of Warwick, 15–17 April.

Haq, Mahbub Ul, 1997, 'Employment in the 1970s: A New Perspective', *Development*, vol. 40, no. 1, pp. 57–62.

Harriss-White, Barbara, 1998, 'Female and Male Grain Marketing Systems: Analytical and Policy Issues for West Africa and India' in Cecile Jackson and Ruth Pearson (eds), *Feminist Visions of Development*, London: Routledge.

Harstock, Nancy, 1990, 'Foucault on Power: A Theory for Women?', in L.J. Nicholson (ed.), *Feminism/Postmodernism*, London: Routledge.

Hart, Gary, 1991, 'Engendering Everyday Resistance: Gender, Patronage and Production Politics in Rural Malaysia', *Journal of Peasant Studies*, vol. 19, no. 1, p. 93.

Hartmann, Betsy, 1997, 'Women, Population and the Environment: Whose Consensus, Whose Empowerment?', in Nalini Visvanathan, Lynn Duggan, Laurie Nisonoff and Nan Wiegersma (eds), *The Women, Gender and Development Reader*, London: Zed Books.

Harvey, David, 1993, 'Class Relations, Social Justice and the Politics of Difference', in Michael Keith and Steve Pile (eds), *Place and the Politics of Identity*, London: Routledge.

Held, David, McGrew, Anthony, Goldblatt, David and Perraton, Jonathan, 1999, *Global Transformations: Politics, Economics and Culture*, Cambridge: Polity.

Helie-Lucas, Marie, 1991, 'Women in the Algerian Liberation Struggle', in Tina Wallace with Candida March (eds), *Changing Perceptions: Writings on Gender and Development*, Oxford: Oxfam.

Hellum, Anne, 1993, 'Gender and Legal Change in Zimbabwe: Childless Women and Divorce from a Socio-cultural and Historical Perspective', in Sammy Adelman and Abdul Paliwala (eds), *Law and Crisis in the Third World*, London: Hans Zell Publishers.

Heng, Geraldine, 1997, 'A Great Way to Fly: Nationalism, the State and the Varieties of Third-World Feminism', in Jacqui M. Alexander and Chandra Talpade Mohanty (eds), *Genealogies, Colonial Legacies, Democratic Futures*, New York: Routledge.

Hernes, Helga Maria, 1987, *Welfare State and Women Power: Essays in State Feminism*, Oslo: Norwegian University Press.

Hewitt, Tom, Johnson, Hazel and Wield, David (eds), 1992, *Industrialization and Development*, Oxford: Oxford University Press in association with the Open University.

Hewson, Martin and Sinclair, Timothy J. (eds), 1999, *Approaches to Global Governance Theory*, New York: State University of New York Press.

Higgott, Richard, 1998, 'Reviewing "Globalisation"', report for the Economic and Social Research Council.

Higgott, Richard and Reich, Simon, 1997, 'Intellectual Order for the Global Order: Understanding Non-State Actors and Authority in the Global System', paper presented at the Inaugural Conference, Warwick University–ESRC Centre for the Study of Globalization and Regionalization, 31 October–1 November.

Hirst, Paul and Thompson, Graham, 1996, *Globalisation in Question: The International Economy and Possibilities*, Cambridge: Polity.

Hobsbawm, Eric, 1991, *Nations and Nationalism since 1780: Programme, Myth, Reality*, Cambridge: Cambridge University Press.

Hobsbawm, Eric and Ranger, Terence (eds), 1983, *The Invention of Tradition*, Cambridge: Cambridge University Press.

Hoffman, Paul, 1997, 'The Challenge of Economic Development', *Development*, vol. 40, no. 1, pp. 19–24.

Honig, Emily and Hershatter, Gail, 1988, *Personal Voices: Chinese Women in the 1980s*, Stanford, CA: Stanford University Press.

Hoogvelt, Ankie, 1997, *Globalisation and the Postcolonial World*, Basingstoke: Macmillan.

Hoogvelt, Ankie, 2001, 'Dependency Theory in the Age of Globalization: The Legacy', paper prepared for the Key Theme Panel of the 42nd Annual Convention of the International Studies Association at Chicago, 21–4 February.

hooks, bell, 1981, *Ain't I a Woman? Black Women and Feminism*, Boston: South End Press.

Hooper, Charlotte, 2000, 'Masculinities in Transition: The Case of Globalization', in Marianne H. Marchand and Anne Sissons Runyan (eds), *Gender and Global Restructuring*, London: Routledge.

Hopkins, Terence K. and Wallerstein, Immanuel (eds), 1980, *Processes of the World-System, Volume 3: Political Economy of the World-System Annuals*, London: Sage Publications.

Hoskyns, Catherine and Newman, Michael (eds), 2000, *Democratizing the European Union: Issues for the Twenty-first Century*, Manchester: Manchester University Press.

Hoskyns, Catherine and Rai, Shirin M., 1998, 'Gender, Class and Representation: India and the European Union', *European Journal of Women's Studies*, vol. 5, nos 3–4.

Hunt, Diana, 1989, *Economic Theories of Development: An Analysis of Competing Paradigms*, Hemel Hempstead: Harvester Wheatsheaf.

Huntington, Samuel P., 1968, *Political Order in Changing Societies*, New Haven, CT and London: Yale University Press.

Huntington, Samuel P., 1995, *The Clash of Civilizations and the Remaking of World Order*, New York: Simon and Schuster.

ILO (International Labour Organization), 1977, *Employment, Growth and Basic Needs: A One-World Problem*, London: Praeger.

ILO (International Labour Organization), 1979, *Report of the Director-General: Growth, Employment and Basic Needs in Latin America and the Caribbean*, Eleventh Conference of American States, Geneva, ILO.

IMF (International Monetary Fund), 1995, International Monetary Fund, Conference, 1994: 'Fifty Years after Bretton Woods: The Future of IMF and the World Bank', Washington, DC: International Monetary Fund.

IMF (International Monetary Fund), 2001, 'The IMF's Poverty Reduction and Growth Facility (PRGF), A Factsheet', March <http://www.imf.org/external/np/exr/facts/prgf.htm>.

Jacka, Tamara, 1996, 'Working from Within: Women and the State in the Development of the Courtyard Economy in Rural China', in Shirin M. Rai and Geraldine Lievesley (eds), *Women and the State: International Perspectives*, London: Taylor and Francis.

Jackson, Cecile, 1996, 'Rescuing Gender from the Poverty Trap', *World Development*, vol. 24, no. 3, pp. 489–504.

Jackson, Cecile and Pearson, Ruth (eds), 1998, *Feminist Visions of Development*, London: Routledge.

Jahan, Raunaq, 1995, *The Elusive Agenda: Mainstreaming Women in Development*, London: Zed Books.

Jain, Devaki, 1995, 'The United Nations Needs Structural Adjustment: Some Experiences in Working Together', in *Women, Gender and the United Nations: Views from NGOs and Activists*, report of the NGLS Panel held at the NGO Forum on Women, 1995, Huairou.

Jayawardena, Kumari, 1986, *Feminism and Nationalism in the Third World*, London: Zed Books.

Jeffrey, Patricia and Roger, 1998, 'Silver Bullet or Passing Fancy? Girls' Schooling and Population Policy', in Cecile Jackson and Ruth Pearson (eds), *Feminist Visions of Development*, London: Routledge.

Johnson, Carol, 1996, 'Does Capitalism Really Need Patriarchy?', *Women's Studies International Forum*, vol. 19, no. 3, pp. 193–202.

Johnson, Carol, 2000, 'The Fragility of Democratic Reform: New Challenges to Australian Women's Citizenship', in Shirin M. Rai (ed.), *International Perspectives on Gender and Democratisation*, Basingstoke: Macmillan.

Johnson, Kay Ann, 1983, *Women, the Family and Peasant Revolution in China*, Chicago: University of Chicago Press.

Jonasdottir, Anna, 1988, 'On the Concept of Interest: Women's Interests and the Limitations of Interest Theory', in Anna Jonasdottir and Kathleen Jones (eds), *The Political Interest of Gender: Developing Theory and Research with a Feminist Perspective*, London: Sage.

JustAct (Youth ACTion for Global JUSTice), 1998, Statement of the Third Women's Conference Against APEC, 8–9 November, Kuala Lumpur: 'Women Resist Globalisation! Assert Women's Rights'.

Kabeer, Naila, 1992, 'Triple Roles, Gender Roles, Social Relations: The Political Subtext of Gender Training', IDS Discussion Paper no. 313, Brighton: Institute of Development Studies, University of Sussex.

Kabeer, Naila, 1994, *Reversed Realities: Gender Hierarchies in Development Thought*, London: Verso.

Kabeer, Naila, 1995, 'Targeting Women or Transforming Institutions? Policy Lessons from NGO Anti-Poverty Efforts', *Development and Practice*, vol. 5, no. 2, pp. 108–16.

Kabeer, Naila, 1999, 'Resources, Agency, Achievements: Reflections on the Measurement of Women's Empowerment', *Development and Change*, vol. 30, pp. 435–64.

Kamal Pasha, M., 1996, 'Globalisation and Poverty in South Asia', *Millennium*, vol. 25, no. 3, Special Issue on 'Poverty in World Politics: Whose Global Era?', pp. 635–56.

Kandiyoti, Deriz, 1988, 'Bargaining with Patriarchy', *Gender and Society*, vol. 2, no. 3, pp. 274–90.

Kandiyoti, Deniz, 1991a, 'End of Empire: Islam, Nationalism and Women in Turkey', in Deniz Kandiyoti (ed.), *Women, Islam and the State*, Basingstoke: Macmillan.

Kandiyoti, Deniz (ed.), 1991b, *Women, Islam and the State*, Basingstoke: Macmillan.

Karam, Azza, 2000, 'Democrats without Democracy: Challenges to Women in Politics in the Arab World', in Shirin M. Rai (ed.), *International Perspectives on Gender and Democratisation*, Basingstoke: Macmillan.

Kardam, Nuket and Acuner, Salma, 2002, 'National Women's Machineries: Structures and Spaces', in Shirin M. Rai (ed.), *National Machineries for Women: Mainstreaming Gender, Democratising the State?*, Manchester: Manchester University Press.

Kaul, Inge, Grunberg, Isabelle and Stern, Marc A. (eds), 1999, *Global Public Goods: International Cooperation in the 21st Century*, Oxford: Oxford University Press.

Keduourie, Elie (ed.), 1970, *Nationalism in Asia and Africa*, London: Frank Cass.

Keith, Michael and Pile, Steve (eds), 1993, *Place and the Politics of Identity*, London: Routledge.

Kennedy, Mary, Lubelska, Cathy and Walsh, Val (eds), 1993, *Making Connections: Women's Studies, Women's Movements, Women's Lives*, London: Taylor and Francis.

Khor, Martin, 1996, 'The WTO and the Proposed Multilateral Investment Agreement: Implications for Developing Countries and Proposed Positions', Briefing Paper, Third World Network, Malaysia <http://www.cepr.net/globalization/bibl2.html>.

Kiss, Elizabeth, 1995, 'Alchemy or Fool's Gold? Assessing Feminist Doubts about Rights', in Mary Lyndon Shanley and Uma Narayan (eds), *Reconstructing Political Theory: Feminist Perspectives*, Cambridge: Polity.

Klein, Naomi, 2001, *No Logo*, London: Flamingo.

Kloppenburn, J., Jr, 1991, 'Social Theory and the De/reconstruction of Agricultural Sciences: Local Knowledge for an Alternative Agriculture', *Rural Sociology*, vol. 56, no. 4, pp. 519–48.

Knight, Jack and Johnson, James, 1997, 'What Sort of Political Equality Does Deliberative Democracy Require?', in James Bohman and William Rehg (eds), *Deliberative Democracy: Essays on Reason and Politics*, Cambridge, MA: MIT Press.

Koertge, Noretta (ed.), 1998, *A House Built on Sand: Exposing Postmodernist Myths about Science*, Oxford: Oxford University Press.

Kofman, Eleanor, 1998, 'Feminism, Gender Relations and Geopolitics: Problematic Closures and Opening Strategies', in Eleanor Kofman and Gillian Youngs (eds), *Globalization, Theory and Practice*, London: Pinter.

Kofman, Eleanor, 2000, 'Beyond a Reductionist Analysis of Female Migrants in Global European Cities: The Unskilled, Deskilled and Professional', in Marianne Marchand and Anne Sissons Runyan (eds), *Gender and Global Restructuring*, London: Routledge.

Korten, David C., 1990, *Getting to the 21st Century: Voluntary Action and the Global Agenda*, West Hartford, CT: Kumarian Press.

Kothari, Rajini, 1995, 'Under Globalization: Will the Nation State Hold?', *Economic and Political Weekly*, 1 July.

Kumar, Radha, 1989, 'Contemporary Indian Feminism', *Feminist Review*, no. 3, Autumn, pp. 20–9.

Kwesiga, Joy, 2002, 'The National Machinery for Gender Equality in Uganda: Institutionalised Gesture Politics?', in Shirin M. Rai (ed.), *National Machineries for the Advancement of Women: Mainstreaming Gender, Democratising the State?*, Manchester: Manchester University Press.

Kymlicka, Will, 1995, 'Introduction', in Will Kymlicka (ed.), *The Rights of Minority Cultures*, Oxford: Oxford University Press.

Laclau, Ernesto, 1971, 'Feudalism and Capitalism in Latin America', *New Left Review*, no. 67, May–June.

Laffey, Mark, 1992, 'Ideology and the Limits of Gramscian Theory in International Relations', paper presented at the International Studies Association annual meeting, Atlanta, Georgia, 1–4 April.

Laffey, Mark, 1999, 'Globalization and the Rule of Law: Reconstituting Property, Capital and the State', Workshop on Historical Materialism and Globalization, University of Warwick, 15–17 April.

Lairop-Fonderson, Josephine, 2002, 'The Disciplinary Power of Micro-Credit: Examples from Kenya and Cameroon', in Jane L. Parpart, Shirin M. Rai and Kathleen Staudt (eds), *Rethinking Empowerment in a Global/ Local World*, London: Routledge.

Lapidus, Gail, 1978, *Women in Soviet Society: Equality, Development and Social Change*, London: University of California Press.

Lasch, Christopher, 1995, *The Revolt of the Elites and the Betrayal of Democracy*, New York: W.W. Norton.

Lash, Scott and Urry, John, 1987, *The End of Organized Capitalism*, Cambridge: Polity.

Lehman, David, 1997, 'An Opportunity Lost: Escobar's Deconstruction of Development', *The Journal of Development Studies*, vol. 33, no. 4, April, pp. 568–78.

Lenin, V.I., *Imperialism: the Highest Stage of Capitalism*, Moscow: Progress Publishers.

Liddle, Joanna and Joshi, Rama, 1985, 'Gender and Imperialism in British India', *Economic and Political Weekly*, 26 October.

Liddle, Joanna and Joshi, Rama, 1986, *Daughters of Independence*, London: Zed Press.

Liddle, Joanna and Rai, Shirin M., 1993, 'Between Feminism and Orientalism', in Mary Kennedy, Cathy Lubelska and Val Walsh (eds), *Making Connections: Women's Studies, Women's Movements, Women's Lives*, London: Taylor and Francis.

Liddle, Joanna and Rai, Shirin M., 1998, 'Feminism, Imperialism and Orientalism: The Challenge of the "Indian Woman"', *Women's History Review*, vol. 7, no. 4, pp. 495–520.

Lim, L., 1990, 'Women's Work in Export Factories: The Politics of a Cause', in Irene Tinker (ed.), *Persistent Inequalities*, Oxford: Oxford University Press.

Ling, L.H.M., 1997, 'The Other Side of Globalization: Hypermasculine Developmentalism in East Asia', paper presented at the International Studies Association Meeting, Toronto, 18–22 March.

Ling, Lily, 2000, 'Hypermasculinity', in *Routledge Encyclopedia of Women's Studies*, New York: Routledge.

Lister, Ruth, 1997, *Citizenship: Feminist Perspectives*, Basingstoke: Macmillan.

Lister, Ruth, 1998, 'Citizenship and Difference: Towards a Differentiated Universalism', *European Journal of Social Theory*, vol. 1, no. 1, 1 July, pp. 71–90.

Lovejoy, Tom, 2000, 'Biodiversity', Reith Lectures 2000, BBC <http://news.bbc.co.uk/hi/english/static/events/reith_2000/lecture2.stm>.

Lovell, Terry, 2000, 'Feminisms Transformed? Poststructuralism and Post-modernism', in Bryan S. Turner (ed.), *The Blackwell Companion to Social Theory* (2nd edn), Oxford: Blackwell.

Lovett, Margot, 1990, 'Gender Relations, Class Formation, and the Colonial State in Africa', in Jane L. Parpart and Kathleen Staudt (eds), *Women and the State in Africa*, Boulder, CO: Lynne Rienner.

Lubeck, Paul, 2000, 'The Islamic Revival: Antinomies of Islamic movements under Globalization', in Robin Cohen and Shirin M. Rai (eds), *Global Social Movements*, London: Routledge.

Luckham, Robin and White, Gordon, 1996, *Democratization in the South: The Jagged Wave*, Manchester: Manchester University Press.

Lynch, Cecelia, 1998, 'Social Movements and the Problem of Globalization', *Alternatives: Social Transformation and Humane Governance*, vol. 23, no. 2, April–June, pp. 149–74.

Lyotard, Jean-François, 1984, *The Postmodern Condition: A Report on Knowledge*, Manchester: Manchester University Press.

McAfee, Anne, 1989, *Storm Signals: Structural Adjustment and Development Alternatives in the Caribbean*, London: Zed Books in association with Oxfam America.

McBride Stetson, Dorothy and Mazur, Amy G., 1995, *Comparative State Feminism*, London: Sage.

McClintock, Anne, 1993, 'Family Feuds: Gender, Nationalism, and the Family', *Feminist Review*, no. 44, Summer, pp. 61–80.

McGrew, Tony, 2000, 'Transnational Democracy: Theories and Prospects', paper circulated at the Centre for the Study of Globalization and Regionalization, University of Warwick.

Mackenzie, Fiona, 1995, 'Selective Silence: A Feminist Encounter with Environmental Discourse in Colonial Africa', in Jonathan Crush (ed.), *Power of Development*, London: Routledge.

McMichael, Philip, 2000, *Development and Social Change: A Global Perspective* (2nd edn), Thousand Oaks, CA: Pine Forge Press.

Magdoff, Harry, 1998, 'A Letter to a Contributor: The Same Old State', *Monthly Review*, vol. 49, no. 8, pp. 1–10.

Mainstream, 1995, 'Summary of Documents Adopted at Social Summit', March 25, pp. 31–5.

Mani, Lata, 1993, 'Contentious Traditions: The Debate on *Sati* in Colonial India', in Kumkum Sangari and Sudesh Vaid (eds), *Recasting Women: Essays in Indian Colonial History*, New Delhi: Kali for Women.

Mann, Michael, 1986, *The Sources of Social Power, Volume 1: A History of Power from the Beginning to A.D. 1760*, Cambridge: Cambridge University Press.

Mao Zedong, 1965, 'On Contradictions', in *Selected Works, Volume 2*, Beijing: People's Publishing House.

Marchand, Marianne, 1995, 'Latin American Women Speak on Development: Are We Listening Yet?', in Marianne Marchand and Jane L. Parpart (eds), *Feminism/Postmodernism/Development*, London: Routledge.

Marchand, Marianne and Parpart, Jane L. (eds), 1995, *Feminism/Postmodernism/Development*, London: Routledge.

Marchand, Marianne and Runyan, Anne Sissons (eds), 2000, *Gender and Global Restructuring*, London: Routledge.

Marshall, T.H., 1950, *Citizenship and Social Class, and Other Essays*, Cambridge: Cambridge University Press.

Marx, Karl, 1973, *English Selections, Marx's 'Grundrisse'*, St Albans: Paladin.

Marx, Karl, 1977, 'On the Jewish Question', in David McLellan (ed.), *Karl Marx: Selected Writings*, Oxford: Oxford University Press.

Massey, Doreen, 1984, *Spatial Divisions of Labour: Social Structures and the Geography of Product*, London: Macmillan.

Maunaguru, Malthi, 1995, 'Gendering Tamil Nationalism: The Construction of "Woman" in Projects of Protest and Control', in P. Jeganathan and Q. Ismail (eds), *Unmaking the Nation: The Politics of Identity and History in Modern Sri Lanka*, Colombo: Social Scientists' Association.

Mayoux, Linda, 1998, 'Gender Accountability and NGOs: Avoiding the Black Hole', in Carol Miller and Shahra Razavi (eds), *Missionaries and Mandarins: Feminist Engagement with Development Institutions*, London: IT Publishers.

Mba, Nina, 1990, 'Kaba and Khaki: Women and the Militarized State in Nigeria', in Jane L. Parpart and Kathleen Staudt (eds), *Women and the State in Africa*, Boulder, CO: Lynne Rienner.

Mehdid, Malika, 1996, 'En-Gendering the Nation-State: Women, Patriarchy and Politics in Algeria', in Shirin M. Rai and Geraldine Lievesley (eds), *Women and the State: International Perspectives*, London: Taylor and Francis.

Meinzen-Dick, Ruth S., Brown, Lynn R., Sims Feldstein, Hilary and Quisumbing, Agnes R., 1997, 'Gender, Property Rights and Natural Resources', *World Development*, vol. 25, no. 8, pp. 1303–15.

Merchant, Carol, 1980, *The Death of Nature: Women, Ecology and the Scientific Revolution*, New York: Harper and Row.

Metcalf, T.R., 1995, *Ideologies of the Raj*, Cambridge: Cambridge University Press.

Meyer, David S., 2000, 'Creating Communities of Change', in Robin L. Teske and Mary Ann Tétreault (eds), *Conscious Acts and the Politics of*

Social Change: Feminist Approaches to Social Movements, Community and Power, Volume 1, Columbia: University of South Carolina Press.

Meyer, Mary K. and Prügl, Elisabeth (eds), 1999a, *Gender Politics in Global Governance*, Lanham, MD: Rowman and Littlefield.

Meyer, Mary K. and Prügl, Elisabeth, 1999b, 'Introduction: Gender Politics in Global Governance', in Mary K. Meyer and Elisabeth Prügl (eds), *Gender Politics in Global Governance*, Lanham, MD: Rowman and Littlefield.

Mies, Maria, 1982, *Lace Makers of Narsapur: Indian Housewives Produce for the World Market*, London: Zed Books.

Mies, Maria, 1986, *Patriarchy and Accumulation on a World Scale: Women in the International Division of Labour*, London: Zed Books.

Mies, Maria and Shiva, Vandana, 1993, *Ecofeminism*, London: Zed.

Mies, Maria, Bennholdt-Thomsen, Veronika and von Werlhof, Claudia, 1988, *Women: The Last Colony*, London: Zed Books.

Miller, Carol, 1998, 'Gender Advocates and Multilateral Development Organizations: Promoting Change from Within', in Carol Miller and Shahra Razavi (eds), *Missionaries and Mandarins: Feminist Engagement with Development Institutions*, London: IT Publishers.

Miller, Carol and Razavi, Shahra, 1998, 'Introduction', in Carol Miller and Shahra Razavi (eds), *Missionaries and Mandarins: Feminist Engagement with Development Institutions*, London: IT Publishers.

Mitter, Swasti, 1999, 'Globalization, Technological Changes and the Search for a New Paradigm for Women's Work', *Gender Technology and Development*, vol. 3, no. 1, January–April, pp. 1–18.

Moghadam, Valentine M. (ed.), 1994a, *Gender and National Identity: Women and Politics in Muslim Societies*, London: Zed Books.

Moghadam, Valentine M. (ed.), 1994b, *Identity Politics and Women: Cultural Reassertions and Feminisms in International Perspective*, Boulder, CO: Westview.

Moghadam, Valentine M., 1995, 'Gender Dynamics of Restructuring in the Semiperiphery', in R.L. Blumberg, C.A. Rokowski, I. Tinker and M. Monteón (eds), *Engendering Wealth and Well-Being: Empowerment for Global Change*, Boulder, CO: Westview.

Moghadam, Valentine M. (ed.), 1996, *Patriarchy and Economic Development: Women's Positions at the End of the Twentieth Century*, Oxford: Clarendon Press.

Moghissi, Haideh, 1999, *Feminism and Islamic Fundamentalism: The Limits of Postmodern Analysis*, London: Zed Books.

Mohan, Giles, 1996, 'Globalization and Governance: The Paradoxes of Adjustment in Sub-Saharan Africa', in Eleanor Kofman and Gillian Youngs (eds), *Globalization: Theory and Practice*, London: Pinter.

Mohanty, Chandra Talpade, 1991, 'Under Western Eyes: Feminist Scholarship and Colonial Discourses', in Chandra Talpade Mohanty, Ann Russo and Lourdes Torres (eds), *Third World Women and the Politics of Feminism*, Bloomington: Indiana University Press.

Mohanty, Chandra Talpade, Russo, Ann and Torres, Lourdes (eds), 1991, *Third World Women and the Politics of Feminism*, Bloomington: Indiana University Press.

Molyneux, Maxine, 1979, 'Beyond the Domestic Labor Debate', *New Left Review*, no. 115, July–August.

Molyneux, Maxine, 1982, *State Policies and the Position of Women Workers in the People's Democratic Republic of Yemen, 1967–77*, Geneva: International Labour Organization.

Molyneux, Maxine, 1985, 'Mobilization without Emancipation? Women's Interests and the State in Nicaragua', *Feminist Studies*, vol. 11, no. 2, pp. 227–54.

Molyneux, Maxine, 1998, 'Analysing Women's Movements', *Development and Change*, vol. 29, pp. 219–45.

Monteón, M., 1995, 'Gender and Economic Crises in Latin America: Reflections on the Great Depression and the Debt Crisis', in Rae Lesser Blumberg, Cathy A. Rokowski, Irene Tinker and Michael Monteón (eds), *Engendering Wealth and Well-Being: Empowerment for Global Change*, Boulder, CO: Westview.

Morrison, Toni, 1993, *Race-ing Justice, En-gendering Power: Essays on Anita Hill, Clarence Thomas and the Construction of Social Reality*, London: Chatto and Windus.

Moser, Caroline O.N., 1989, 'The Impact of Recession and Structural Adjustment on Women: Ecuador', *Development*, vol. 1, pp. 75–83.

Moser, Caroline O.N., 1993, *Gender, Planning and Development: Theory, Practice and Training*, London: Routledge.

Mouffe, Chantal (ed.), 1992, *Dimensions of Radical Democracy*, London: Verso.

Munachonga, Monica L., 1990, 'Women and the State: Zambia's Development Policies and Their Impact on Women', in Jane L. Parpart and Kathleen Staudt (eds), *Women and the State in Africa* (2nd edn), Boulder, CO: Lynne Rienner.

Munck, Ronaldo, 2000, 'Labour in the Global: Challenges and Prospects', in Robin Cohen and Shirin M. Rai (eds), *Global Social Movements*, London: Athlone Press.

Munck, Ronaldo and O'Hearn, Denis (eds), 1999, *Critical Development Theory: Contributions to a New Paradigm*, London: Zed Books.

Myrdal, Gunnar, 1997, 'The Widening Income Gap', *Development*, vol. 40, no. 1, pp. 25–30.

Nairn, Tom, 1981, *The Break-up of Britain: Crisis and Neo-Nationalism* (2nd edn), London: Verso.

Nanda, Meera, 1998, 'The Epistemic Charity of the Social Constructivist Critics of Science and Why the Third World Should Refuse the Offer', in Noretta Koertge (ed.), *A House Built on Sand: Exposing Postmodernist Myths about Science*, Oxford: Oxford University Press.

Nanda, Meera, 1999, 'In Search of an Epistemology for Third World Peoples' Science Movements', *Rethinking Marxism*, June.

Nandy, Ashis, 1983, *The Intimate Enemy: Loss and Recovery of Self under Colonialism*, New Delhi: Oxford University Press.

Narayan, Uma, 1997, 'Towards a Feminist Vision of Citizenship: Rethinking the Implications of Dignity, Political Participation and Nationality', in Mary Lyndon Shanley and Uma Narayan (eds), *Reconstructing Political Theory: Feminist Perspectives*, Cambridge: Polity.

Nehru, J.L., 1990, *The Discovery of India*, Oxford: Oxford University Press.

Nelson, Barbara J. and Chowdhury, Najma, 1994, *Women and Politics Worldwide*, New Haven, CT: Yale University Press.

Nelson, Julie A., 1993, 'The Study of Choice or the Study of Provisioning? Gender and the Definition of Economics', in Marianne A. Ferber and Julie A. Nelson (eds), *Beyond Economic Man: Feminist Theory and Economics*, Chicago: University of Chicago Press.

Nelson, Julie A., 1996, *Feminism, Objectivity and Economics*, London: Routledge.

Nelson, Paul J., 1996, 'Internationalizing Economic and Environmental Politics: Transnational NGO Networks and the World Bank's Expanding Influence', *Millennium*, vol. 25, no. 3, pp. 605–35. Special Issue on 'Poverty in World Politics: Whose Global Era?'.

Newell, Peter, 2000, 'Environmental NGOs and Globalization: The Governance of TNCs', in Robin Cohen and Shirin M. Rai (eds), *Global Social Movements*, London: Athlone Press.

Newell, Peter, Rai, Shirin M. and Scott, Andrew (eds), 2002a, *Development and the Challenge of Globalisation*, London: IT Publishers.

Newell, Peter, Rai, Shirin M. and Scott, Andrew (eds), 2002b, 'Introduction: Development and the Challenge of Globalisation', in Peter Newell, Shirin M. Rai and Andrew Scott (eds), *Development and the Challenge of Globalisation*, London: IT Publishers.

Nijeholt, G.L., 1992, *Women and the Meaning of Development: Approaches and Consequences*, Institute of Development Studies Silver Jubilee Paper, Falmer, Sussex.

Nussbaum, Martha, 1995, *Sex and Social Justice*, Oxford: Oxford University Press.

Nussbaum, Martha, 1999, 'Women and Equality: The Capabilities Approach', *International Labour Review*, vol. 138, no. 3, pp. 227–45.

Nussabaum, Martha and Glover, Jonathan (eds), *Women, Culture and Development*, Oxford: Clarendon Press.

Nussbaum, Martha and Sen, Amartya (eds), 1993, *The Quality of Life: A Study Prepared for the World Institute for Development Economics Research (WIDER) of the United Nations University*, Oxford: Clarendon Press.

Nyerere, J.K., 1973, *Freedom and Development: A Selection from Writings and Speeches*, Dar Es Salaam: Oxford University Press.

Nzomo, Maria, 1995, 'Women and Democratization Struggles in Africa: What Relevance to Post-Modernist Discourse?', in Marianne Marchand and Jane L. Parpart (eds), *Feminism/Postmodernism/Development*, London: Routledge.

O'Brien, Robert, Goetz, Anne-Marie, Scholte, Jan Aart and Williams, Marc, 1997, *Complex Multilateralism: The Global Economic Institutions–Global Social*

Movements Nexus, report prepared for the UK Economic and Social Research Council, Global Economic Institutions Programme, University of Sussex.

O'Brien, Robert, Scholte, Jan Aart, Goetz, Anne-Marie and Williams, Marc, 2000, *Contesting Globalisation*, Cambridge: Cambridge University Press.

O'Hanlon, Rosalind and Washbrook, David, 1991, 'Histories in Transition: Approaches to the Study of Colonialism and Culture in India', *History Workshop Journal*, vol. 32, pp. 110–27.

O'Hearn, Denis, 1999, 'Tigers and Transnational Corporations: Pathways from the Periphery?', in Ronaldo Munck and Denis O'Hearn (eds), *Critical Development Theory: Contributions to a New Paradigm*, London: Zed Books.

O'Leary, Brendon, 1989, *The Asiatic Mode of Production: Oriental Despotism, Historical Materialism and Indian History*, Oxford: Basil Blackwell.

Ong, Aihwa, 1987, *Spirits of Resistance and Capitalist Discipline: Factory Women in Malaysia*, Albany: State University of New York Press.

Onimode, Bade (ed.), 1989, *The IMF, the World Bank and the African Debt, Volume 2*, London: Zed Books.

Owoh, Kenna, 1995, 'Gender and Health in Nigerian Structural Adjustment: Locating Room to Maneuver', in R.L. Blumberg, C.A. Rokowski, I. Tinker and M. Monteón (eds), *Engendering Wealth and Well-Being: Empowerment for Global Change*, Boulder, CO: Westview.

Oxaal, Zoë with Baden, Sally, 1997, 'Gender and Empowerment: Definitions, Approaches and Implications for Policy', *Bridge*, University of Sussex.

Palan, Ronen, 1999, 'Global Governance and Social Closure', in Martin Hewson and Timothy J. Sinclair (eds), *Approaches to Global Governance Theory*, New York: State University of New York Press.

Palmer, Ingrid, 1991, *Gender and Population in the Adjustment of African Economies: Planning for Change*, Geneva: International Labour Organization.

Papanek, Hannah, 1994, 'Ideal Woman and Ideal Society: Control and Autonomy in the Construction of Identity', in Valentine M. Moghadam (ed.), *Identity Politics and Women: Cultural Reassertions and Feminisms in International Perspective*, Boulder, CO: Westview.

Parpart, Jane L., 1999, 'Rethinking Participation, Empowerment and Development from a Gender Perspective', in J. Freedman (ed.), *Transforming Development*, Toronto: University of Toronto Press.

Parpart, Jane L. and Marchand, Marianne, H., 1995, 'Exploding the Canon: an Introduction/Conclusion', in Marianne H. Marchand and Jane L. Parpart (eds), *Feminism/Postmodernism/Development*, London: Routledge.

Parpart, Jane L. and Staudt, Kathleen, 1990a, *Women and the State in Africa* (2nd edn), Boulder, CO: Lynne Rienner.

Parpart, Jane L. and Staudt, Kathleen, 1990b, 'Women and the State in Africa', in Jane L. Parpart and Kathleen Staudt (eds), *Women and the State in Africa* (2nd edn), Boulder, CO: Lynne Rienner.

Parpart, Jane L., Connelly, Patricia M. and Barriteau, V. Eudine (eds), 2000, *Theoretical Perspectives on Gender and Development*, Ottawa: IDRC.

Parpart, Jane L., Rai, Shirin M. and Staudt, Kathleen (eds), 2002, *Rethinking Empowerment in a Global/Local World*, London: Routledge.

Patel, Reena, 1999, 'Labour and Land Rights of Women in Rural India, with particular reference to Western Orissa', unpublished PhD dissertation, University of Warwick.

Pateman, Carole, 1985, *The Sexual Contract*, Cambridge: Polity.

Pathak, Zakia and Sunder Rajan, Rajeswari, 1992, 'Shahbano', in Judith Butler and Joan W. Scott (eds), *Feminists Theorize the Political*, London: Routledge.

Pavri, Tinaz, 1997, 'The Enron Case and India's New Economic Policy: New Asian Tiger or Leopard With Old Spots?', paper presented at the International Studies Association Conference, Toronto, 18–22 March.

Payer, Cheryl, 1989, 'Causes of the Debt Crisis', in B. Onimode (ed.), *The IMF, the World Bank and the African Debt, Volume 2*, London: Zed Books.

Pearson, Ruth, 1998, ' "Nimble Fingers", Revisited: Reflections on Women and Third World Industrialization in the Late Twentieth Century', in Cecile Jackson and Ruth Pearson (eds), *Feminist Visions of Development*, London: Routledge.

Pearson, Ruth and Cecile Jackson, 1998, 'Introduction: Interrogating Development, Feminism, Gender and Policy', in Cecile Jackson and Ruth Pearson (eds), *Feminist Visions of Development*, London: Routledge.

Pearson, Ruth and Theobald, Sally, 1998, 'From Export Processing to Erogenous Zones: International Discourses on Women's Work in Thailand', *Millennium*, vol. 27, no. 4, pp. 983–93.

Pellerin, Helen, 1998, 'Global Restructuring and International Migration: Consequences for the Globalization of Politics', in Eleanor Kofman and Gillian Youngs (eds), *Globalization: Theory and Practice*, London: Pinter.

Peterson, V. Spike, forthcoming, 'Analytical Advances to Address New Dynamics', in Mary Ann Tétreault, Robert A. Denemark, Kurt Burch and Kenneth P. Thomas (eds), *New Odysseys in International Political Economy*, London: Routledge.

Peterson, V. Spike and Parisi, Laura, 1998, 'Are Women Human? It's Not an Academic Question', in Tony Evans (ed.), *Human Rights Fifty Years On: A Reappraisal*, Manchester: Manchester University Press.

Peterson, V. Spike and Runyan, Anne Sissons, 1999, *Global Gender Issues*, (2nd edn), Boulder, CO: Westview.

Pettman, J.J., 1996, *Worlding Women: A Feminist International Politics*, London: Routledge.

Phillips, Anne, 1993, *Democracy and Difference*, Cambridge: Polity.

Phillips, Anne, 1995, 'Democracy and Difference: Some Problems for Feminist Theory', in Will Kymlicka (ed.), *The Rights of Minority Cultures*, Oxford: Oxford University Press.

Phizacklea, Annie, 1999, 'Gender and Transnational Labour Migration', in Robert Barot, Harriet Bradley and Steve Fenton (eds), *Ethnicity, Gender and Social Change*, Basingstoke: Macmillan.

Phizacklea, Annie and Wolkowitz, Carol, 1995, *Homeworking Women: Gender, Racism and Class at Work*, London: Sage.

Picciotto, Sol, 1996, 'Fragmented States and International Rules of Law', Inaugural Lecture delivered at Lancaster University, 31 March.

Picciotto, Sol, 2000, 'Liberalization and Democratization: The Forum and the Hearth in the Era of Cosmopolitan Post-Industrial Capitalism', *Law and Contemporary Problems*, vol. 63, no. 4, Autumn.

Pieterse, Jan Nederveen, 1997, 'Going Global: Futures of Capitalism', *Development and Change*, vol. 28, pp. 367–82.

Pieterse, Jan Nederveen, 1998, 'My Paradigm or Yours? Alternative Development, Post-Development, Reflexive Development', *Development and Change*, vol. 29.

Pieterse, Jan Nederveen (ed.), 2000, *Global Futures: Shaping Globalization*, London: Zed Books.

Polanyi, K., 1944, *The Great Transformation: The Political and Economic Origins of Our Time*, Boston: Beacon Press.

Pollert, Anna, 1996, 'The Challenge for Trade Unionism: Sectoral Change, "Poor Work" and Organizing the Unorganized', in Leo Panitch (ed.), *The Socialist Register*, London: Merlin Press.

Prazniak, Roxann, 1997, 'Mao and the Woman Question in an Age of Green Politics: Some Critical Reflections', in Arif Dirlik, Paul Healy and Nick Knight (eds), *Critical Perspectives on Mao Zedong's Thought*, Atlantic Highlands, NJ: Humanities Press.

Prebisch, Raúl, 1963, *Towards a Dynamic Development Policy for Latin America*, New York: United Nations.

Pringle, Rosemary and Watson, Sophie, 1990, 'Fathers, Brothers, Mates: The Fraternal State in Australia', in Sophie Watson (ed.), *Playing the State: Australian Feminist Interventions*, London: Verso.

Pringle, Rosemary and Watson, Sophie, 1992, 'Women's Interests and the Poststructuralist State', in Michele Barrett and Anne Phillips (eds), *Destabilizing Theory*, Cambridge: Polity.

Prügl, Elisabeth and Meyer, Mary K., 1999, 'Gender Politics in Global Governance', in *Gender Politics in Global Governance*, Lanham, MD: Rowman and Littlefield.

Raghavan, K. Leena Sekhar, 1996, *Proceedings of the National Conference on Poverty and Employment: Analysis of the Present Situation and Strategies for the Future*, New Delhi: Institute of Applied Manpower Research/New Age International.

Rai, Satya M., 1996, 'Partition and Women', paper presented at the 28th Punjab History Conference, Punjabi University, Patiala, 12–14 March.

Rai, Shirin M., 1991, *Resistance and Reaction: University Politics in Post-Mao China*, Hemel Hempstead, Harvester Wheatsheaf.

Rai, Shirin M., 1995, 'Negotiating Boundaries: Women, State and Law in India', *Social and Legal Studies*, vol. 4, pp. 391–410.

Rai, Shirin M., 1996a, 'Gender and Democratization: Ambiguity and Opportunity', in Robin Luckham and Gordon White (eds), *Democratiza-

tion in the South: The Jagged Wave, Manchester: Manchester University Press.

Rai, Shirin M., 1996b, 'Women and the State: Issues for Debate', in Shirin M. Rai and Geraldine Lievesley (eds), *Women and the State: International Perspectives*, London: Taylor and Francis.

Rai, Shirin M., 1997, 'Gender and Representation: Women MPs in the Indian Parliament', in Anne-Marie Goetz (ed.), *Getting Institutions Right for Women*, London: Zed.

Rai, Shirin M., 1998a, 'Engendered Development in a Global Age', Centre for the Study of Globalization and Regionalization Working Paper no. 20/98, December.

Rai, Shirin M., 1998b, 'National Machineries for Women: The Indian Experience', paper presented at the UN Experts' Group Conference on National Machineries for the Advancement of Women, Santiago, Chile.

Rai, Shirin M., 1999, 'Developing Explanations for Difference(s): Gender and Village-Level Democracy in India and China', *New Political Economy*, vol. 4, no. 2, July, pp. 233–50.

Rai, Shirin M. (ed.), 2000a, *International Perspectives on Gender and Democratisation*, Basingstoke: Macmillan.

Rai, Shirin M., 2000b, 'Looking to the Future: Panchayats, Women's Representation and Deliberative Democracy', paper presented at the conference 'Women and the Panchayati Raj', New Delhi, 13 April.

Rai, Shirin M., 2002a, 'Institutional Mechanisms for the Advancement of Women: Mainstreaming Gender, Democratising the State', in Shirin M. Rai (ed.), *National Machineries for the Advancement of Women: Mainstreaming Gender, Democratising the State?*, Manchester: Manchester University Press.

Rai, Shirin M. (ed.), 2002b, *National Machineries for the Advancement of Women: Mainstreaming Gender, Democratising the State?*, Manchester: Manchester University Press.

Rai, Shirin M. and Sharma, Kumud, 2000, 'Democratising the Indian Parliament: The "Reservation for Women" Debate', in Shirin M. Rai (ed.), *International Perspectives on Gender and Democratisation*, Basingstoke: Macmillan.

Rai, Shirin M. and Zhang, Junzuo, 1994, 'Competing and Learning: Women and the State in Contemporary Rural Mainland China', *Issues and Studies*, vol. 30, no. 3, pp. 51–66.

Rai, Shirin M., Pilkington, Hilary and Phizacklea, Annie (eds), 1992, *Women in the Face of Change: Eastern Europe, the Soviet Union and China*, London: Routledge.

Ramusack, Barbara, 1990, 'Cultural Missionaries, Maternal Imperialists, Feminist Allies: British Women Activists in India 1865–1945', *Women's Studies International Forum*, vol. 13, pp. 309–23.

Ramusack, Barbara N. and Sievers, Sharon, 1999, *Women in Asia: Restoring Women to History*, Bloomington: Indiana University Press.

Randall, Vicky, 1998, 'Gender and Power: Women Engage the State', in Vicky Randall and Georgina Waylen (eds), *Gender, Politics and the State*, London: Routledge.

Razavi, Shahra, 1999, 'Gendered Poverty and Well-Being: Introduction', *Development and Change*, vol. 30, pp. 409–33.

Robertson, Roland, 1992, *Globalisation: Social Theory and Global Culture*, London: Sage.

Robinson, Mark and White, Gordon (eds), 1998, *The Democratic Developmental State: Politics and Institutional Design*, Oxford: Oxford University Press.

Rocheleau, Diane, Thomas-Slayter, Barbara and Wangari, Esther, 1996, 'Gender and Environment, A Feminist Political Ecology Perspective', in Dian Rocheleau, Barbara Thomas-Slayter and Esther Wangari (eds), *Feminist Political Ecology: Global Issues and Local Experiences*, London: Routledge.

Rogers, B., 1982, *The Domestication of Women*, London: Tavistock Publications.

Ronquillo-Nemenzo, Ana Maria, 1995, 'International Activism and National Activities', in *Women, Gender and the United Nations: Views from NGOs and Activists*, report of the NGLS Panel held at the NGO Forum on Women, Huairou.

Rosenau, James N., 1992, 'Citizenship in a Changing Global Order', in James N. Rosenau and Ernst-Otto Czempiel (eds), *Governance Without Government: Order and Change in World Politics*, Cambridge: Cambridge University Press.

Rostow, Walt Whitman, 1979, *Getting from Here to There*, London: Macmillan.

Rowlands, Jo, 1997, *Questioning Empowerment: Working with Women in Honduras*, Oxford: Oxfam.

Rubery, Jill, 1988a, 'Introduction', in Jill Rubery (ed.), *Women and Recession*, London: Routledge and Kegan Paul.

Rubery, Jill, 1988b, 'Women and Recession: A Comparative Perspective', in Jill Rubery (ed.), *Women and Recession*, London: Routledge and Kegan Paul.

Rueschemeyer, Marilyn, 1994, *Women in the Politics of Postcommunist Eastern Europe*, London: M.E. Sharpe, Inc.

Runyan, Anne Sissons, 1999, 'Women in the Neoliberal "Frame"', in Mary K. Meyer and Elisabeth Prügl (eds), *Gender Politics in Global Governance*, Lanham, MD: Rowman and Littlefield.

Ryan, Mary P., 1979, 'Femininity and Capitalism in Antebellum America', in Zillah Eisenstein (ed.), *Capitalist Patriarchy and the Case for Socialist Feminism*, New York: Monthly Review Press.

Sachdev, Radhika, 2000, 'Is China Threat Real?' <http://www.hindustantimes.com/nonfram/211100/HTH02.asp> 21 November.

Sachs, Wolfgang, 1997, 'The Need for the Home Perspective', in M. Rahnema with V. Bawtree (eds), *The Post-Development Reader*, London: Zed Books; Dhaka: University Press Ltd; Halifax, NS: Fernwood Publishing; and Cape Town: David Philip

Safa, Helen I., 1995, 'Gender Implications of Export-Led Industrialisation in the Caribbean Basin', in R.L. Blumberg, C.A. Rakowski, I. Tinker and M.

Monteón (eds), *Engendering Wealth and Well-Being: Empowerment for Global Change*, Boulder, CO: Westview.

Said, Edward, 1978, *Orientalism*, London: Routledge and Kegan Paul.

Sangari, Kumkum and Sudesh Vaid (eds), 1993, *Recasting Women: Essays in Indian Colonial History*, New Delhi: Kali for Women.

Sarkar, Sumit, 1983, *Modern India, 1885–1947*, Delhi: Macmillan India Ltd.

Sarkar, Tanika and Urvashi Butalia (eds), 1995, *Women and the Hindu Right: A Collection of Essays*, New Delhi: Kali for Women.

Sartre, Jean-Paul, 1990, 'Preface' to Frantz Fanon, *The Wretched of the Earth*, Harmondsworth: Penguin.

Sassen, Saskia, 1995, *Losing Control? Sovereignty in an Age of Globalization*, New York: Columbia University Press.

Sassen, Saskia, 1998, *Globalization and Its Discontents*, New York: New Press.

Sawer, Mariane, 1998, 'The Life and Times of Women's Policy Machinery in Australia', paper presented at the UN/DAW 'Experts' Group Meeting on National Machineries for Women', Santiago, Chile, 31 August–4 September.

Scholte, Jan Aart, 2000, *Globalisation: A Critical Introduction*, Basingstoke: Macmillan.

Scholte, Jan Aart and Albrecht Schnabel (eds), forthcoming, *Civil Society and Global Finance*, Tokyo: United Nations University Press.

Scholte, Jan Aart with O'Brien, Robert and Williams, Marc, 1998, 'The WTO and Civil Society', Centre for the Research of Globalization and Regionalization Working Paper no. 14/98.

Scott, Alan, 1990, *Ideology and the New Social Movements*, London: Routledge.

Scott, Joan W., 1992, 'Experience', in Judith Butler and Joan W. Scott (eds), *Feminists Theorize the Political*, London: Routledge.

Seager, Joni, 1997, *The State of Women in the World Atlas*, Harmondsworth: Penguin.

Seguino, Stephanie, 2000, 'Gender Inequality and Economic Growth: A Cross-Country Analysis', *World Development*, vol. 28, no. 7, pp. 1211–30.

Sen, Amartya, 1987a, 'Gender and Cooperative Conflicts', Working Paper no. 18, World Institute for Development Economics Research (WIDER).

Sen, Amartya, 1987b, *On Ethics and Economics*, Oxford: Basil Blackwell.

Sen, Amartya, 1990, 'Gender and Cooperative Conflicts', in Irene Tinker (ed.), *Persistent Inequalities*, Oxford: Oxford University Press.

Sen, Amartya, 1992, *Inequality Reexamined*, New York: Russell Sage Foundation; Oxford: Clarendon Press.

Sen, Amartya, 1995, 'Gender Inequality and Theories of Justice', in Martha Nussbaum and Jonathan Glover (eds), *Women, Culture and Development*, Oxford: Clarendon Press.

Sen, Amartya, 1999, *Development as Freedom*, Oxford: Oxford University Press.

Sen, Anupam, 1982, *The State, Industrialization and Class Formations in India: A Neo-Marxist Perspective*, London: Routledge and Kegan Paul.

Sen, Gita and Grown, Caren, 1985, *Development, Crises and Alternative Visions: Third World Women's Perspectives*, London: Earthscan.

Sen, Gita, Germain, Adrienne and Chen, Lincoln C. (eds), 1994, *Population Policies Reconsidered: Health, Empowerment and Rights*, Boston: Harvard Center for Population and Development Studies.

Senghor, Léopold Sédar, 1995, 'On African Socialism', in Omar Dahbour and Micheline R. Ishay (eds), *The Nationalism Reader*, Atlantic Highlands, NJ: The Humanities Press International, Inc.

Shadmi, Erella, 2000, 'Between Resistance and Compliance, Feminism and Nationalism: Women in Black in Israel', *Women's Studies International Forum*, vol. 23, no. 1, pp. 23–34.

Shanin, Teodor, 1983, *Late Marx and the Russian Road: Marx and the 'Peripheries of Capitalism'*, London: Routledge and Kegan Paul.

Shanley, Mary Lyndon and Narayan, Uma (eds), 1997, *Reconstructing Political Theory: Feminist Perspectives*, Cambridge: Polity.

Shiva, Vandana, 1989, *Staying Alive: Women, Ecology and Development*, London: Zed Books.

Shiva, Vandana, 2000, 'Poverty and Globalisation', Reith Lectures <http://news.bbc.co.uk/reith_2000>.

Shiva, Vandana and Holla-Bhar, Radha, 1996, 'Piracy by Patent: The Case of the Neem Tree', in Jerry Mander and Edward Goldsmith (eds), *The Case against Global Economy*, San Francisco: Sierra Club Books.

Shklar, Judith, 1991, *American Citizenship: The Quest for Inclusion*, Cambridge, MA: Harvard University Press.

Singh, Ajit and Zammit, Ann, 2000, 'International Capital Flows: Identifying the Gender Dimensions', *World Development*, vol. 28, no. 7, pp. 1249–68.

Smart, Carol, 1989, *Feminism and the Power of Law*, London: Routledge.

Smart, Carol, 1992, 'The Woman of Legal Discourse', *Social Legal Studies*, vol. 1, no. 1, pp. 29–44.

South Commission, 1990, *The Challenge to the South/The Report of the South Commission*, Oxford: Oxford University Press.

Spivak, Gayatri C., 1988, 'Can the Subaltern Speak?', in Cary Nelson and Lawrence Grossberg (eds), *Marxism and the Interpretation of Culture*, Basingstoke: Macmillan.

Squires, Judith, 2002, 'Deliberation and Decision-Making: Discontinuity in the Two-Track Model', in Maurizio Passerin d'Entreves (ed.), *Democracy as Public Deliberation: New Perspectives*, Manchester: Manchester University Press.

Stacey, Judith, 1983, *Socialism and Patriarchy in Communist China*, Princeton, NJ: Princeton University Press.

Staudt, Kathleen, 1991, *Managing Development: State, Society, and International Contexts*, London: Sage.

Staudt, Kathleen A., 1998a, *Free Trade? Informal Economies at the U.S.–Mexico Border*, Philadelphia, PA: Temple University Press.

Staudt, Kathleen, 1998b, *Policy, Politics and Gender: Women Gaining Ground*, Bloomfield, CT: Kumarian Press.

Staudt, Kathleen, 2002, 'The Uses and Abuses of Empowerment Discourse', in Jane L. Parpart, Shirin M. Rai and Kathleen Staudt (eds), *Rethinking Empowerment in a Global/Local World*, London: Routledge.

Stein, Howard, 1994, 'Theories of Institutions and Economic Reform in Africa', *World Development*, vol. 22, no. 2.

Stein, Howard, 1999, 'Globalisation, Adjustment and the Structural Transformation of African Economies? The Role of International Financial Institutions', Centre for the Study of Globalization and Regionalization Working Paper no. 32, May.

Stewart, Ann, 1993, 'The Dilemmas of Law in Women's Development' in Sammy Adelmann and Abdul Paliwala (eds), *Law and Crisis in the Third World*, London: Hans Zell Publishers.

Stewart, Frances, 1998, 'Adjustment and Poverty in Asia: Old Solutions and New Problems', Queen Elizabeth House Working Paper Series QEHWPS20, October.

Stichter, Sharon B. and Parpart, Jane L. (eds), 1988, *Patriarchy and Class: African Women in the Home and the Workforce*, Boulder, CO and London: Westview.

Stienstra, Deborah, 1994, *Women's Movements and International Organizations*, Basingstoke: Macmillan.

Stienstra, Deborah, 2000, 'Making Global Connections among Women, 1970–1999', in Robin Cohen and Shirin M. Rai (eds), *Global Social Movements*, London: Athlone Press.

Stiglitz, Joseph, 2000, 'Capital Market Liberalization, Economic Growth, and Instability', *World Development*, vol. 28, no. 6, pp. 1075–86.

Stokes, Susan, 1998, 'Pathologies of Deliberation', in Jon Elster (ed.), *Deliberative Democracy*, Cambridge: Cambridge University Press.

Stolcke, Verera, 1994, 'Invaded Women: Sex, Race and Class in the Formation of Colonial Society', *European Journal of Development Research*, vol. 6, no. 2, pp. 7–21, Special Issue on 'Ethnicity, Gender and the Subversion of Nationalism'.

Strange, Susan, 1995, 'The Defective State', *Daedalus: Journal of the American Academy of Arts and Sciences*, Spring, pp. 55–74.

Stromquist, Nelly, 2002, 'Education as a Means for Empowering Women', in Jane L. Parpart, Shirin M. Rai and Kathleen A. Staudt (eds), *Rethinking Empowerment in a Global/Local World*, London: Routledge.

Sylvester, Christine, 1999, ' "Progress" in Zimbabwe: Is "it" a Woman?', *International Feminist Journal of Politics*, vol. 1, no. 1, pp. 89–118.

Talwar, V.B., 1993, 'Feminist Consciousness in Women's Journals in Hindi: 1910–1920', in Kumkum Sangari and Sudesh Vaid (eds), *Recasting Women: Essays in Indian Colonial History*, New Delhi: Kali for Women.

Teske, Robin L. and Tétreault, Mary Ann (eds), 2000, *Conscious Acts and the Politics of Social Change: Feminist Approaches to Social Movements, Community and Power, Volume 1*, Columbia: University of South Carolina Press.

Tétreault, Mary Ann and Teske, Robin L., 2000, 'Introduction: Framing the Issues', in Robin L. Teske and Mary Ann Tétreault (eds), *Conscious Acts and the Politics of Social Change: Feminist Approaches to Social Movements, Community and Power, Volume. 1,* Columbia: University of South Carolina Press.

Thomas, Caroline, 1998, 'International Financial Institutions and Social and Economic Rights: An Exploration', in Tony Evans (ed.), *Human Rights Fifty Years On: A Reappraisal,* Manchester: Manchester University Press.

Thomas, Caroline and Wilkin, Peter (eds), 1997, *Globalization and the South,* Basingstoke: Macmillan.

Thomson, Bob, 1995, 'An Unauthorized History of Fair Trade Labels' <http://www.web.net/fairtrade/who/unauthor.htm>.

Tiessen, R., 1997, 'A Feminist Critique of Participatory Development Discourse: PRA and Gender Participation in Natural Resource Management', paper presented at the International Studies Association Conference, Toronto, 19 March.

Tinberger, Jan, 1976, *Reshaping the International Order: A Report to the Club of Rome,* New York: E.P. Dutton.

Tinker, Catherine, 2000, 'Parallel Centres of Power', in Robin L. Teske and Mary Ann Tétreault (eds), *Conscious Acts and the Politics of Social Change: Feminist Approaches to Social Movements, Community and Power, Volume 1,* Columbia: University of South Carolina Press.

Tinker, Irene, 1997, 'The Making of a Field: Advocates, Practitioners and Scholars', in Nalini Visvanathan, Lynn Duggan, Laurie Nisonoff and Nan Wiegersma (eds), *The Women, Gender and Development Reader,* London: Zed Books.

Tomlinson, John, 1999, *Globalization and Culture,* Chicago: University of Chicago Press.

Toth, James F., 1980, 'Class Development in Rural Egypt, 1945–1979', in Terence K. Hopkins and Immanuel Wallerstein (eds), *Processes of the World-System, Volume 3: Political Economy of the World-System Annuals,* London: Sage Publications.

Treiman, Donald J. and Hartmann, Heidi I. (eds), 1981, *Women, Work, and Wages: Equal Pay for Jobs of Equal Value,* Washington, DC: National Academy Press.

Tripp, Aili Mari, 2000, 'Rethinking Difference: Comparative Perspectives from Africa', *Signs: Journal of Women in Culture and Society,* vol. 25, no. 3, pp. 649–75.

True, Jacqui, 2000, 'Gendering Post-Socialist Transitions', in Marianne Marchand and Anne Sissons Runyan (eds), *Gender and Global Restructuring,* London: Routledge.

Truong, Thanh-Dam, 1990, *Sex, Money and Morality: Prostitution and Tourism in Southeast Asia,* London: Zed Books.

Truong, Thanh-Dam, 1999, 'The Underbelly of the Tiger: Gender and the Demystification of the Asian Miracle', Working Papers Series 269, Institute of Social Studies.

Turner, Bryan S. (ed.), 2000, *The Blackwell Companion to Social Theory* (2nd edn), Oxford: Blackwell.

Uberoi, Patricia (ed.), 1996, *Social Reform, Sexuality and the State*, New Delhi: Sage.

Udayagiri, Mridula, 1995, 'Challenging Modernization: Gender and Development, Postmodern Feminism and Activism', in Marianne Marchand and Jane L. Panpart (eds), *Feminism/Postmodernism/Development*, London: Routledge.

UN (United Nations), 1995, *Platform for Action*, New York: United Nations.

UN (United Nations), 1999, *World Survey on the Role of Women in Development: Globalization, Gender and Work*, New York: United Nations.

UNCTAD (United Nations Conference on Trade and Development), 2000, 'UNCTAD/World Bank Partnership' Last update: November <http:// www. unctad.org/en/subsites/dmfas/english/worldbank.htm>.

UNDP (United Nations Development Programme), 1994, *Human Development Report*, New York: Oxford University Press.

UNDP (United Nations Development Programme), 1998 'Social Impacts of the Asian Crisis: Policy Challenges and Lessons', Occasional Paper 33 <http:// www.undp.org/hdro/oc33d.htm>.

UNDP (United Nations Development Programme), 2000, *Overcoming Human Poverty* <http:// www. undp.org/povertyreport/chapters/ chapterindex.html>.

UNESCO, 2000, *World Culture Report* <http:// www. unesco.org/culture/ worldreport/>.

UNRISD (United Nations Research Institute for Social Development), 1995, *States of Disarray: The Social Effects of Globalization*, New York: UNRISD and Bonson.

Van Staveren, Irene, forthcoming, 'Global Finance and Gender', in Jan Aart Scholte and Albrecht Schnabel (eds), *Civil Society and Global Finance*, Tokyo: United Nations University Press.

Vargas, Virginia and Olea, Cecilia, 1999, 'The Tribulations of the Peruvian Feminist Movement', in Nira Yuval-Davis and Pnina Werbner (eds), *Women, Citizenship and Difference*, London: Zed Books.

Vega, Silvia, 2002, 'The Role of the Women's Movement in Institutionalizing a Gender Focus in Public Policy: The Ecuadorian Experience', in Shirin M. Rai (ed.), *National Machineries for Women: Mainstreaming Gender, Democratising the State?*, Manchester: Manchester University Press.

Vidal, John, 1999, 'The Seeds of Wrath', *The Guardian Weekend*, 19 June.

Visvanathan, Nalini, Duggan, Lynn, Nisonoff, Laurie and Wiegersma, Nan (eds), 1997, *The Women, Gender and Development Reader*, London: Zed Books.

Vos, Rob, 1994, *Debt and Adjustment in the World Economy: Structural Asymmetries in North–South Interactions*, New York: St Martin's Press in association with the Institute of Social Studies.

Walby, Sylvia, 1990, *Theorizing Patriarchy*, Oxford: Basil Blackwell.

Walby, Sylvia, 1997, *Gender Transformations*, London: Routledge.

Wallace, Tina with March, Candida (eds), 1991, *Changing Perceptions: Writings on Gender and Development*, Oxford: Oxfam.

Wallerstein, Immanuel, 1979, 'The Rise and Future Demise of the World Capitalist System', in Immanuel Wallerstein (ed.), *The Capitalist World Economy*, Cambridge: Cambridge University Press.

Warburton, Peter, 1999, *Debt and Delusion: Central Bank Follies That Threaten Economic Disaster*, London: Allen Lane/Penguin Press.

Ware, Vron, 1992, *Beyond the Pale: White Women, Racism and History*, London: Verso.

Waring, Marilyn, 1988, *If Women Counted: A New Feminist Economics*, San Francisco: Harper and Row.

Watson, Sophie (ed.), 1990, *Playing the State: Australian Feminist Interventions*, London: Verso.

Waylen, Georgina, 1997a, *Gender in Third World Politics*, Buckingham: Open University Press.

Waylen, Georgina, 1997b, 'Women's Movements, the State and Democratization in Chile: The Establishment of SERNAM', in Anne-Marie Goetz (ed.), *Getting Institutions Right for Women*, London: Zed Books.

WCED (World Commission on Economic Development), 1987, *Our Common Future*, New York: Oxford University Press.

Weber, Cynthia, 1995, *Simulating Sovereignty: Intervention, the State and Symbolic Exchange*, Cambridge: Cambridge University Press.

Weber, Heloise, 2002, *The Global Political Economy of Micro-Credit and Poverty Reduction*, Ph.D. dissertation.

WEDO (Women's Environment and Development Organization), 1998a, 'Global Survey Finds Progress on Women's Rights and Equality Compromised by Economic Globalization' <http://www.wedo.org/monitor/mapping.htm>.

WEDO (Women's Environment and Development Organization), 1998b, 'Key Findings', *Mapping Progress: A WEDO Report Assessing Implementation of the Beijing Platform* <http://www.wedo.org/monitor/findings.htm>.

Werbner, Pnina and Yuval-Davis, Nira, 1999, 'Women and the New Discourse of Citizenship', in Nira Yuval-Davis and Pnina Werbner (eds), *Women, Citizenship and Difference*, London: Zed Books.

White, Gordon, 1993, 'Towards a Political Analysis of Markets', *IDS Bulletin*, vol. 24, no. 3, July, pp. 4–11.

Whitehead, Ann and Lockwood, Matthew, 1999, 'Gendering Poverty: A Review of Six World Bank African Poverty Assessments', *Development and Change*, vol. 30, pp. 525–55.

Whyte, Robert Orr and Whyte, Pauline, 1982, *The Women of Rural Asia*, London: Westview.

Wieringa, Saskia (ed.), 1995, *Subversive Women: Historical Experiences of Gender and Resistance*, London: Zed Books.

Willetts, Peter (ed.), 1995, *The Conscience of the World: The Influence of Non-Governmental Organizations in the UN System*, London: C. Hurst.

Williams, Patricia, 1991, *The Alchemy of Race and Rights*, Cambridge, MA: Harvard University Press.

Wilson, John, 1973, *Introduction to Social Movements*, New York: Basic Books.

Wilson, William J., 1987, *The Truly Disadvantaged*, Chicago: University of Chicago Press.

Wolfe, Margery, 1985, *Revolution Postponed: Women in Contemporary China*, London: Methuen.

Women's Feature Service, 1993, *The Power to Change: Women in the Third World Redefine Their Environment*, London: Zed Books.

Women Working Worldwide, 2000a, 'A Preliminary Note Highlighting the Conceptual and Policy Links Between Gender and Trade' <http://www.poptel.org.uk/women-ww/gender_trade_and_the_wto.htm#Prelim>.

Women Working Worldwide, 2000b, 'World Trade is a Women's Issue!' <http://www.poptel.org.uk/women-ww/women_workers_and_social_clauses.htm>.

World Bank, 1990a, *Bangladesh: Strategies for Enhancing the Role of Women in Economic Development*, Washington, DC: World Bank.

World Bank, 1990b, *World Development Report*, Washington, DC: World Bank.

World Bank, 1991, *World Development Report*, Washington, DC: World Bank.

World Bank, 1994, *Good Governance*, Washington, DC: World Bank.

World Bank, 1999a, 'The Gender Dimension of Development', in *The World Bank Operational Manual: Operational Policies* <http://www.worldbank.org>.

World Bank, 1999b, *World Development Report: Entering the 21st Century*, Oxford: Oxford University Press.

World Bank, 2000, *World Development Report: Attacking Poverty*, Oxford: Oxford University Press.

WRPE (Women's Role in the Planned Economy), 1947 (The Sub-Committee on Women's Role in the Planned Economy), Bombay: Vora.

Yearly, Stephen and Forrester, John, 2000, 'Shell: A Sure Target for Global Environmental Campaigning?', in Robin Cohen and Shirin M. Rai (eds), *Global Social Movements*, London: Athlone Press.

Yeatman, Anna, 1993, 'Voice and Representation in the Politics of Difference', in Sneja Gunew and Anna Yeatman (eds), *Feminism and the Politics of Difference*, St Leonards, NSW: Allen and Unwin.

Young, Iris Marion, 1990, *Justice and the Politics of Difference*, Princeton, NJ: Princeton University Press.

Young, Iris Marion, 1995, 'Together in Difference: Transforming the Logic of Group Political Conflict', in Will Kymlicka (ed.), *The Rights of Minority Cultures*, Oxford: Oxford University Press.

Young, Iris Marion, 1997, 'Unruly Categories: A Critique of Nancy Fraser's Dual Systems Theory', *New Left Review*, no. 222, March–April, pp. 147–60.

Young, Kate, 1997, 'Gender and Development', in Nalini Visvanathan, Lynn Duggan, Laurie Nisonoff and Nan Wiegersma (eds), *The Women, Gender and Development Reader*, London: Zed Books.

Youngs, Gillian, 2002, 'Feminizing Cyberspace: Rethinking Technoagency', in Jane L. Parpart, Shirin M. Rai and Kathleen Staudt (eds), *Rethinking Empowerment in a Global/Local World*, London: Routledge.

Yuval-Davis, Nira, 1996, Background paper for the Conference on Women and Citizenship, Greenwich University, London, 16–18 July.

Yuval-Davis, Nira, 1997, 'Women, Citizenship and Difference', *Feminist Review*, vol. 57, Special Issue 'Citizenship: Pushing the Boundaries', pp. 4–27.

Yuval-Davis, Nira and Werbner, Pnina (eds), 1999, *Women, Citizenship and Difference*, London: Zed Books.

Zalewski, Marysia and Parpart, Jane L. (eds), 1997, *The 'Man' Question in International Relations*, Boulder, CO: Westview Press.

Zareska, Zuzana, 1998, 'Gender Awareness and National Machineries in Central and Eastern Europe: The Problems of Transitional Societies', paper presented at the UN/DAW 'Experts' Group Meeting on National Machineries for the Advancement of Women', Santiago, Chile.

Zirakzadeh, Cyrus Ernesto, 1997, *Social Movements in Politics: A Comparative Study*, London: Longman.

Zulu, Lindiwe, 2000, 'Institutionalising Changes: South African Women's Participation in the Transition to Democracy', in Shirin M. Rai (ed.), *International Perspectives on Gender and Democratisation*, Basingstoke: Macmillan.

Zwarteveen, M.Z., 1997, 'Water: From Basic Need to Commodity: A Discussion on Gender and Water Rights in the Context of Irrigation', *World Development*, vol. 25, no. 8, pp. 1335–49.

Index

91, 92, 93, 93 n, 99, 100 n, 115, 117,
119, 123, 124, 126, 128, 129, 134,
135, 136, 137, 138, 141, 144, 146,
155, 157, 158 n, 160, 176, 178, 181,
183, 200, 204, 209, 210
feminism, 35, 45, 81
Tilak, Bal Gangadhar, 29
trade, 47, 51, 60, 93, 93 n, 101, 101 n,
102, 102 n, 103, 126 n, 135, 136,
137, 161 n, 192, 205
ethical, 106 n
Trade Related Intellectual Property
Rights (TRIPs), 143
trade unions, 96, 98, 158
tradition, 11, 20, 26, 28, 29, 32, 37, 41,
56, 84, 106, 113, 190
transnational corporations, *see*
corporations
Truong, Than Dam, 97, 100 n, 123 n,
149
Turkey, 37, 38
Turkish Women's Federation, 38

underdevelopment, 50, 51, 52, 56, 60,
77, 78
United Kingdom, *see* Britain
United Nations (UN), 46, 49, 50, 51,
57, 69, 83, 107, 108, 118, 124, 159,
170, 176, 177, 178, 183, 189, 196
Beijing Conference/Platform for
Action, 83, 113, 172, 199
Commission on the Status of
Women, 60
Conference on Trade and
Development (UNCTAD), 49,
123 n, 125 n
Convention for the Elimination of
All Forms of Discrimination
Against Women (CEDAW), 57
Convention for the Equal
Remuneration for Men and
Women Workers for Work of
Equal Value, 51
Convention on the Political Rights
of Women, 51
Convention for the Suppression of
Traffic in Persons and the
Exploitation of Prostitution of
Others, 51
Decade of Development, 50, 51, 60
Decade of Women, 183

Development Programme (UNDP),
63, 64, 82, 102 n, 114, 115, 125 n,
138, 210
Division for the Advancement of
Women (DAW), 7, 8, 93, 94, 95,
98, 99, 100, 101, 122, 123 n, 178,
181
Economic and Social Council
(ECOSOC), 169, 173 n
Education, Scientific and Cultural
Organization (UNESCO), 113
Research Institute for Social
Development (UNRISD), 112
World Food Conference, 58, 64
United States of America, *see* America

Vaid, Sudesh, 2, 13, 20
vernacular, 13 n, 35
press, 30
violence, 16, 17, 26, 32, 37, 58, 79, 80,
101, 110, 111, 117, 144, 164, 188,
209, 215

Walby, Sylvia, 13, 15, 76
Wallerstein, Emmanuel, 78
Washington Consensus, 93
Watson, Sophie, 105
welfare, 51, 64, 81, 112, 117, 118, 125,
144, 150, 157, 164, 174, 177, 178,
180, 181, 196, 211, 215
welfare state, *see* state
well-being, 8, 102, 126, 133, 164
Western Europe, *see* Europe
White, Gordon, 96
Wolfensohn, James, 82, 124, 172, 174 n
Women in Development (WID), 45,
51, 59, 61, 62, 71, 72, 73, 74, 75, 82,
178
women, environment and
development (WED), 69
women, social status of, 60, 61, 61 n,
62
Women's Development Programme
(WDP, Rajasthan), 162, 183, 184,
185, 186, 209
Women's Environment and
Development Organization
(WEDO), 101, 110, 111
'Women's Eyes on the Bank', 118, 172,
174, 174 n, 176, 193
women's movements, *see* movements

work, 7, 9, 48, 53, 61, 64, 66, 81, 92, 94,
  95, 99, 101, 106, 122, 132, 133, 144,
  145, 149, 150, 152, 153, 154, 211
  flexibilization, 7, 106, 144
  part-time, 7, 101, 106
  triple burden of, 112
  waged, 71, 80, 88, 88 n, 144, 185,
    192 n
workers, 7, 53, 63, 147, 150, 152, 153,
  154, 186
  migrant, 7, 158 n
World Bank, 47, 55, 58, 70 n, 73 n, 82,
  82 n, 90, 93, 93 n, 103 n, 104 n,
  106 n, 107, 109, 116, 116 n, 118,
  124, 125, 125 n, 128, 129, 129 n,
  130, 136, 137, 138, 151, 158, 171,
  172, 173, 174, 174 n, 175, 208

  see also 'Women's Eyes on the
    Bank'
World Commission on Economic
  Development (WCED), 68
World Employment Programme, 62
World Summit for Social
  Development, 112, 113
world-system, 55, 58, 78, 79, 124
World Trade Organization (WTO), 94,
  107, 108, 116, 116 n, 136, 138, 141,
  143, 144, 170

Young, Iris Marion, 163, 190 n, 213
Yuval-Davis, Nira, 13, 27, 165, 190,
  191, 194, 213, 214

zamindar, 23

Printed in the United Kingdom by
Lightning Source UK Ltd., Milton Keynes
136677UK00001B/212/P